POLICING DELHI

POLICING DELHI

URBANIZATION, CRIME, AND LAW ENFORCEMENT

O.P. MISHRA

OXFORD
UNIVERSITY PRESS

OXFORD
UNIVERSITY PRESS

Oxford University Press is a department of the University of Oxford.
It furthers the University's objective of excellence in research, scholarship,
and education by publishing worldwide. Oxford is a registered trademark of
Oxford University Press in the UK and in certain other countries

Published in India
by Oxford University Press
YMCA Library Building, 1 Jai Singh Road, New Delhi 110 001, India

© Oxford University Press 2011

The moral rights of the author have been asserted

First Edition published in 2011

ISBN-13: 978-0-19-807595-0
ISBN-10: 0-19-807595-2

Typeset in Wilke LT STD 9.75/14.5
by Sai Graphic Design, New Delhi 110 055
Printed in India at G.H. Prints Pvt. Ltd., New Delhi 110 020

To

Abhishek, Abhishank, and Arti

POLICEMAN

The Policeman is denounced by the public, criticised by the preacher, ridiculed by the movies, berated by prosecuting officers and judges.

He is shunnd by the respectables, he is exposed to countless temptation and dangers, condemned while he enforces the law and dismissed when he does not.

He is supposed to posses the qualifications of soldier, doctor, lawyer, diplomat and educator. With remuneration less than of a daily labourer.

August Volimore

CONTENTS

FOREWORD

Policing Delhi: Urbanization, Crime, and Law Enforcement by O.P.
Mishra is an outstanding contribution to the study and analysis of
the nature of crime, its control, and administration in the backdrop
of its history, social structure, culture and political economy of
urbanization, and growth. It highlights the imperatives of continual
policy innovations for policing Delhi metropolis, which has had
a unique past and is evolving through a dynamic present. The
contemporary nature of its urbanization poses ever new challenges.
The most significant ones being rapid expansion and its impact
upon ecology, continual influx of migrant population due to the
uneven nature of urban growth in India, and the cities' pull factor—
economic and social attractions. Delhi is also unique as it is the
national capital, which adds to a variety of additional policing
responsibilities, maintenance of security, law, and order, in addition
to control of crime. Embedded as the metropolis is into a millennia
of old history, diversities of cultures, communities, ecology, and
historical memories, its social dynamics has a potential to ignite
numerous forms of social contradictions and social deviance.

O.P. Mishra's book offers the readers a comprehensive and
systematic analysis of these problems from a holistic sociological
perspective. The work is rich in the uses of history and historical
records, statistical and case study data, empirical surveys, and

personal observations. The author's own more-than-a-decade-old personal experience of policing in Delhi as a senior police officer adds clarity and perspective to the exposition of complex issues in policing the metropolis. The themes of analysis have a comprehensive coverage. These deal with the nature of crime, its distribution or patterns, its typology, and its trends in the process of the growth of the metropolis. The crimes against women and juveniles and other sensitive social categories have been examined from an extended sociological perspective. The problem of terrorism and its control also receives a fuller treatment owing to the book's holistic nature. The book not only indicates a variety of infrastructural limitations or constraints in policing and management of crime but also offers a systematic strategy for crime control and its efficient administration by anticipating the future growth and urban dynamics of Delhi metropolis.

The book is written in a simple and lucid style. It is rich in presentation of facts and systematic sociological explorations. I am sure it will be widely read and will be of immense utility to those engaged in police administration and policy planning, as well as for readers in general, since it is bound to enhance public awareness on issues of policing, urbanization, and crime.

YOGENDRA SINGH
Professor Emeritus
Jawaharlal Nehru University

ACKNOWLEDGEMENTS

This book is primarily based on the Ph.D thesis submitted at Jawaharlal Nehru University, New Delhi in 2009. I am grateful to Professor Yogendra Singh, Professor Emeritus in Sociology at JNU for accepting me as a student after twenty-five years of my leaving the university. It is a matter of great honour that he agreed to write a Foreword for the book.

I would like to thank the many whose encouragement or active help got me to the end of this challenging project. I had an extensive discussion with Professor Satish Chandra and I am privileged to have his comments and suggestions to finalize the manuscript. I am also grateful to Professor Romila Thapar for providing me several resources including her own writings on Delhi.

I would like to thank assistance staff of Nehru Memorial Museum Library, India International Centre Library, and office of the Registrar General and Census of India at various stages for collecting materials and data sheet for the book. I have relied on crime figures and statistics at various places in the book. These facts and figures have been taken out from *Annual Review* booklets released every year during annual press conference by Police Headquarters and data compiled by research cell Crime Branch. I especially thank Rajan Bhagat, Additional DCP, and Public Relations Officer for making available the required facts; and Inspector Rajendra Kalkal, in charge of Delhi Police Museum for helping me gain access to the archival facilities.

In 2005–6, I had edited two books on basic principles of VIP security. By the recommendation of Bureau of Police Research and Development, the books were used as a resource book for training purposes in all Police Training Institutes in the country. The compilation of the above books was done under the guidance of the present Commissioner of Police, B.K. Gupta when was holding charge of Special Commissioner of Police. It gives me immense pleasure that the present book is getting published under his tenure. I would like to thank him for his constant encouragement, recognition and professional motivation.

I have dedicated this book to my sons, Abhishek and Abhishank, and wife Arti in recognition of the sacrifice and love I have received. Without their patience, cooperation, and understanding of my two lovely school-going children, this project would not have been possible.

The manuscript of the book has undergone scrutiny and editing at various levels under expert hands at Oxford University Press (OUP). Their suggestions and inputs have enriched the quality of the book immensely. I would specially like to thank Nitasha Devasar and Dr Preeti Singh for their meaningful inputs in finalizing the manuscript. I would like to place on record my gratitude to the editorial team at OUP who have been involved in publication of the book.

I would like to conclude by saying that the views expressed in the book are my own and not the official view point of Delhi Police.

O.P. MISHRA

INTRODUCTION

After attending a public meeting at Town Hall grounds in old Delhi on 2 October 1950, Jawaharlal Nehru, the first Prime Minister of India, expressed his displeasure regarding the excessive deployment of policemen at the meeting venue. In a note written to then principal private secretary, he observed:

> I should like you to inform the Home Ministry that I am becoming very doubtful about the competence of police authorities of Delhi. Their idea of dealing with any situation is to have masses of policemen about, even though the place might be wilderness. I went to the Town Hall grounds in the city today for the public meeting. All along the route from my house to the place of meeting, which must be about six miles or more from here, the police were lined on either side. Even the wide and empty expanse of the central vista had these policemen on either side. Approaching the station, their numbers grew. It was hardly possible for anyone to walk about without pushing a policeman. At the meeting itself, there was a regular army of them. In fact, I had an impression that Delhi was a beleaguered city.[1]

These feelings of the first Prime Minister of India regarding security deployment at a particular place of public function needs to be seen in the backdrop of the overall security environment prevalent in Delhi immediately after Independence as well as the expectations of the then head of government from the police.

In the same locality today, at the Red Fort Grounds, on 15 August every year, a multilayered security arrangement, which also includes cordoning the entire route from the prime minister's residence to the venue of the function, is a regular and normal affair. When the prime minister travels to the venue, traffic on the right carriageway is stopped to facilitate the free movement of the motorcade. There is a heavy deployment of policemen on both sides of the road, including quick-reaction teams to prevent any collision with the VVIP motorcade. Over the years, the scale of these deployments has seen a lot of changes.

The changes in police deployment at similar public functions attended by the prime minister over a period of time reflect both the changing dimensions of the public function as well as the methodology used by the police to deal with them. The nature and form of policing, and the patterns of deployment from the law and order point of view, have been changing with the overall growth of the city as well as the pattern of changes in the various dimensions of society. Policing is not static in nature. It is dynamic and keeps changing in size, shape, and priorities as per the needs of the society. The success of any police organization depends on how it has adjusted and attuned its style of day-to-day functioning with the growing needs of the society. Theoretically speaking, various processes of social change shape the nature and pattern of policing. While inaugurating the annual conference of director generals of police (DGPs) on 26 August 2010, the present Prime Minister of India, Manmohan Singh, said, 'Policing in our country has become increasingly complex over the years. Social tensions, religious disputes, growing economic disparities, and regional, linguistic, and ethnic differences have long been major challenges to effective policing in India.'[2]

Urbanization acts as a very important catalyst for multidimensional changes in society. Before we discuss its implications from the policing point of view, it is necessary to briefly understand the process itself. Urbanization basically refers to the process whereby an increasing proportion of the population of a society becomes congregated in towns and cities. The United Nations (UN) has defined the process of urbanization as the movement of people from rural areas to urban areas, with population growth equating to urban migration. The process of urbanization is, thus, logically linked with other important social processes like modernization, westernization, globalization, and industrialization. Therefore, it is an important instrument of social change.

Societies all over the world have undergone tremendous transformation due to the process of urbanization. Urbanization rates vary from country to country and city to city. Urbanization has affected the working of several socio-economic and political institutions in society. Sociologically speaking, the process of urbanization has redefined the concept of space and culture, and introduced new culture and value patterns in the existing society. It has influenced interpersonal relations, the conduct, and the response and behaviour pattern of human beings in a big way. Since crime is a reflection of human behaviour not in conformity with the established norms and laws of the land, urbanization has affected the form and nature of crime and policing everywhere. The very process itself has produced criminal activities in the city which are essentially urban in nature. Recognizing the nature of typical urban crimes and crimogenic factors, the seventh report on National Police Commission (NPC) has observed:

> ... the existence of a large floating population, the presence of gullible rural migrants, give rise to crimes involving cheating, confidence tricks, etc. Large populations and heavy densities increase anonymity, and the flow of large cash in the handling of business through banks, cinema houses, and major retail outlets increase the temptation as well as the opportunity for crime.[3]

Unlike other cities and metropolitan centres in India, Delhi has witnessed a much faster rate of urbanization. It has grown in shape and size beyond one's imagination. With 93 per cent urban population today, Delhi has reached the peak of urban growth. It has gradually swallowed up all its villages, bringing the number of urbanized villages up to 160. The remaining villages are already so urbanized in nature that it only requires them to fulfil certain mandatory criteria laid out by the government to fall into the category of a town. The urban expansion of the city has virtually stopped further horizontal expansion, compelling it to expand vertically to accommodate the growing numbers. To accommodate the growing housing needs of the people, the city's architecture is also changing. It has become a city of sky liners. Several colonies of Delhi that once had only independent single-storey houses have been converted into multi-storey apartment complexes. Moreover, since the entire population could not be accommodated within the formal and planned housing sector, they have occupied space for living by squatting on land wherever it is available. As a result, the city has seen the parallel growth of unauthorized jhugi/jhompri (JJ) clusters, slums, and illegal structures.

Today, Delhi is the most populated city in India, with a population density of 9224 per sq mt, compared to an all-India average of 324 per sq mt. According to the *Delhi Human Development Report 2006*, almost 65 per cent of the population in the city lives today in unplanned colonies such as slums (19.1 per cent), JJ clusters (14.8 per cent), JJ resettlement colonies (12.7 per cent), regularized unauthorized colonies (12.7 per cent), and unauthorized colonies (5 per cent). A very distinctive characteristic of the living habitat of Delhi is the close proximity of affluent colonies to unauthorized clusters occupied by the underprivileged sections of the society. These living establishments reflect extreme disparities and economic inequalities. Within the same locality, there is a wide gap in access to basic civic amenities like water, electricity, and other resources necessary for good living. A combination of all these factors in the city has promoted criminal activities.

Ideally, the process of urbanization requires concomitant and simultaneous increase and widening of the resource base of the city for a harmonious balance between the individual and his habitat. Cities which have undergone unplanned, erratic, and unstructured urban expansion (like Delhi) have witnessed more problems, and infrastructure and resource-based challenges than those cities where proper pro-active planning has been done to take care of the issues emerging out of urbanization.

The over-urbanization of the city has posed serious structural constraints in various service delivery institutions. They have not been able to cope with the pressure of an increasing population. Urbanization has also posed several challenges before the Delhi Police in day-to-day policing. Some of the broad challenges faced by the Delhi Police from the policing point of view are categorized below:

1. **General Increase in Crime with New Dimensions**: As far as general crime in the city is concerned, it has registered an increasing trend over the years. This is a normal trend, in tune with the increasing population of the city and correlated crimogenic factors. The city has also seen typical crimes which have emerged due to economic liberalization, modernization, and technological advancement. Cheating and financial frauds, real estate property disputes, cyber crime, drugs smuggling, lottery frauds, etc. need to be seen in this context. Affluence in a certain section of the city's population has prompted criminals to target wealthy people by abducting them for ransom.

2. **Traffic**: The city has seen an unprecedented increase in the number of vehicles on the road over the years. In the year 1996–7, the total number of vehicles on the road used to be 28.48 lakh, which increased to 52.32 lakh in 2006–7. The maximum increase of 91.13 per cent was registered in the category of privately-owned vehicles. According to the Society of India Automobile Manufacturers (SIAM), in Delhi there are 85 private cars per 1000 people as compared to the national average of eight cars per 1000. This number is more than ten times the national average. This unprecedented and ever increasing number of vehicles on the road has posed a major challenge before the Delhi Traffic Police (DTP). As there is no place for people to park their vehicles inside their houses, they park the vehicles on the side

roads and lanes in their locality. This has led to an increase in the theft of vehicles. It has also increased the number of road accidents. We will see how Delhi Traffic Police, with a strength of 5000 traffic officers, is trying to meet the challenge of enforcement and regulation in a city of 12 million people.

3. Law and Order Arrangements: In its Fifth Report on Public Order, the Second Administrative Reforms Commission has observed:

> The perception of an average citizen is that the police is essentially a crime prevention and investigating agency. Unearthing evidence in a crime, identifying the culprit, establishing the means, motive and opportunity, presenting evidence in a court of law through the prosecution and securing conviction are all critical functions of the police.[4]

However, these core functions of the police have come under serious threat due to increasing responsibilities on the law and order front. Unlike other metropolitan cities, this has become the core aspect of day-to-day policing for the Delhi police force. No other police force in the country has to handle such a large number of law and order arrangements of different varieties on a regular basis as the Delhi Police does.

Being the seat of national government and power, Delhi attracts a lot of social, cultural, and political rallies from different states. It has become the battle ground for various political parties and protesting groups to show their strength on different issues. In 2010, Delhi Police had to handle as many as 1124 demonstrations, 224 processions, 1208 *dharnas*, 294 meetings, 91 strikes, and 152 rallies in different parts of the city till 15 December. Most of these rallies and processions are very sensitive in nature and require heavy police *bandobast*. Manpower for these arrangements is made out of the existing strength of the police station. In several cases, the deployment is made by diverting policemen from other duties like crime prevention and investigation. This has emerged as a major challenge before Delhi Police.

4. VIP Security Duties: All important political executives such as the president, vice-president, prime minister, and other cabinet ministers live in Delhi. All the members of the Lok Sabha and Rajya Sabha also stay in Delhi at different locations. All these important persons are provided security cover on the basis of their position and threat perceptions by the Delhi Police on a round-the-clock basis. Heavy police deployment is made at various places of visits and routes during the movement of several VVIPs. In 2010, Delhi Police handled as many as 99 functions of the President of India, 150 functions of the Vice-President of India, 187 functions of the Prime Minister of India, 107 functions of the United Progressive Alliance (UPA) chairperson, 288 functions of foreign heads of state/ government, and 380 functions of distinguished foreigners till 15 December. Providing foolproof security cover to such persons in the context of increasing terrorist incidents across the globe has emerged as a daunting challenge before the Delhi Police, which has created a separate unit to meet the requirements and challenges of VIP security.

5. Terrorism: The international dimension of terrorism has affected normal policing duties of law enforcing agencies across the globe. This has emerged as a major challenge before the police today. By convention, the police force is not trained in handling terrorist-related incidents. However, as a capital city, Delhi is very vulnerable to terrorist incidents. Several incidents have taken place in different parts of the city since 1990. Anti-terror policing now occupies centre stage in the day-to-day policing activities of Delhi Police. In fact, Delhi Police has taken up the challenge of terrorism in a professional manner and a separate wing has been created to handle such cases. Over the years, Delhi Police has evolved into a force specializing in terror-cracking, with notable detections and apprehensions to its credit despite several infrastructural and resource constraints.

The present book is an attempt to understand both the nature of crime in Delhi and the challenges faced in the policing of the city and the National Capital Region (NCR), in the context of its urbanization and growth. It will focus on how all these have brought about changes in the overall pattern of policing over a period of time. The book will also evaluate the successes (and failures) in the overall response patterns of the Delhi Police in handling the multifaceted challenges posed by the megacity.

1

THE SEVEN CITIES OF DELHI AND THE PATTERNS OF POLICING

In order to understand the present day Delhi and the current pattern of policing, it will be proper to go through the historical background of the city. Delhi is one of the most ancient and historic cities of India and has often been called the 'city of cities'. It has been the capital of mighty empires and kingdoms and as such no political ruler can ignore the city's socio-political importance. Many different cities have come into existence at different periods of time within the boundaries of present-day Delhi. Many of these cities were subsequently ravaged and destroyed as per prevailing political circumstances. Most of these cities were named after their respective rulers and each ruler constructed and designed the city according to his own desire, administrative needs, and prevailing political conditions. If we go by the rulers who have ruled Delhi chronologically, one could talk of eighteen or nineteen Delhis. For a meaningful understanding of the urban growth of the city, one can refer to the classification of Delhi into 'Seven Cities' in a chronological order, till the arrival of British, done by Hearn Gordon. However, as Delhi grew, each one of the cities discussed by Gordon has undergone tremendous changes. Gordon says that Delhi can be described as the Indian Rome. It has been the imperial city of India for over 700 years and the 'Seven Hills of Rome' are represented by the seven cities of Delhi.[1] Further, Gordon also says that in modern Rome the hills are difficult to distinguish, because of many newer buildings that covered the older sites. Similarly, the old historical sites of Delhi have witnessed rapid urbanization.

THE SEVEN CITIES OF DELHI

First City: Indraprastha

Indraprastha is usually considered to be the first Delhi. It was built in the Vedic period, probably in the tenth century BC. According to the great Indian epic Mahabharata, Indraprastha was built by Yudhisthira during the great conflict between the Pandavas and the Kauravas. The city was founded on the western banks of the river Yamuna. Around the first century AD, before the Macedonian invasion, Raja Dillu founded a new city few miles north of Indraprastha near Qutub Minar. The earliest mention of Delhi as a city of that name occurs in the songs of the Hindu bards. There is a story in one of these plays of the site having been abandoned for 792 years before it was inhabited. This city was named Dillu. It is generally agreed that Delhi derived its name from this word and was first occupied sometime around AD 300.[2] The city was abandoned afterwards for some time for causes not clearly known and was not inhabited until 1052, after the final retreat of Mahmud of Ghazni. However, Delhi was considered the most important Hindu city in this part of India during this period, and as many as twenty-seven temples were built within its limits. Later, Delhi was retained as their principal city by various victorious Muslim kings.

Second City: Siri Fort

A century later, the confined area of Old Delhi was not able to accommodate the growing population and suburbs stretched out into the plains to the north-east. This is the period when great hordes of Mughals invaded India and indulged in the plundering of the suburban areas which lacked proper, safe boundaries. These developments forced Alauddin Khilji in 1303 to entrench his army at Siri to cover them, and after the Mughals retreated, Khilji constructed the second of Delhi's cities, Siri. According to the memoirs of Timur there were seven gates in the city, of which three opened towards Jahanpanah, although the only gate mentioned in history is the Baghdad Gate.[3] In this city there was a palace of thousand pillars which is not in existence today.

The city, once surrounded by walls and gates during the Khilji period, has undergone tremendous changes due to urbanization and expansion. The same Siri Fort today has a sports complex and many important institutional buildings have also come up around the complex. The land next to the historical ruins was developed into a beautiful games village for the Asian Games in 1982. The single and duplex houses, first occupied by reputed players during the games, were sold to public sector undertakings (PSUs) and government institutions to house the offices and residences of their officers. Next to the old monuments of the historical fort is an urbanized village called Shahpur Jat. The village could not escape the process of urbanization. In due course of time, primarily due to acquisition of land meant for agricultural purposes, the villagers were forced to build multi-storey houses for the purpose of renting them out and this became an alternate source of income for them. The urbanization of villages around the historical city of Siri has led to the emergence of several colonies over a period of time. Some of the prominent colonies in existence today are Panchshila Park, Mayfair Garden (primarily occupied by Sindhis), Soami Nagar, Sarvapriya Vihar, and Sadhna Enclave.

Third City: Tughlaqabad

In 1320, Tughlaq Shah came to the throne. The prospect of war and the nature of his enemies forced him to build a city beyond the limits of Old Delhi and Siri. He was very apprehensive of the low walls of Old Delhi from a security point of view. All these factors forced him to build a city five miles to the east, around a rocky hill which provided him with isolation. The rocky hills had their own limitations in terms of availability of water. As a result, most of the inhabitants of the city were forced to settle down in the plains during his reign. Tughlaqabad is generally considered to be the third city after Old Delhi and Siri. It is very difficult to build up the real history of Tughlaqabad. However, it is generally believed that much of the city was built over a period of two years during the short tenure of Ghiyas-ud-Din Tughlaq. Some very well-known stories are attached to the building of Tughlaqabad. According to one story, Ghiyas-ud-Din Tughlaq proposed to his master Mubarak Shah Khilji that he should build a fort on this easily defendable outcrop. Mubarak Shah laughed at him and told him to build the city when he himself became sultan. His words turned out to be prophetic.

Another interesting story is related to the strained relationship between Ghiyas-ud-Din and the Sufi saint, Nizamudin Aulia. While Tughlaqabad was being built, Nizamudin Aulia was engaged in constructing his *baoli* (stepwell) and he was utilizing the same labourers used for the construction of Tughlaqabad. Ghiyas-ud-Din prevented the labourers from working for Nizamudin Aulia. Despite his instructions, the labourers worked for the saint during the night. This enraged the ruler and he prohibited the sale of oil to Nizamudin. This did not make any difference to the saint and water from his baoli miraculously gave sufficient light for the workers to carry out work during the night. However, Saint Nizamudin was hurt and cursed Tughlaqabad. He pronounced that it would either be inhabited by the Gujjars or it would remain barren. The historic curse actually became true and the area was inhabited by the nomadic, denotified Gujjar community. Even today a sizeable proportion of the population in Tughlaqabad is that of the Gujjars. The historical city, on the border of Haryana and very close to Suraj Kund, has witnessed massive urbanization. Apart from certain institutional establishments, the area has seen the emergence of many unauthorized colonies which accommodate the migrant population, which came years ago in search of jobs and gradually settled down in the city. Sangam Vihar, one of the largest colonies in Asia, has come up in the hilly tracts adjoining Tughlaqabad extending up to the borders of Haryana. The area also accommodates various institutional buildings around the fort.

Fourth City: Jahanpanah

The large population which resided between the hills of Siri and Old Delhi on the plains was in a very insecure position. Mohd Tughlaq, the second ruler of the Tughlaq Dynasty, found it proper to construct walls on either side to join up the two cities. This helped lay the foundations for the emergence of the fourth city, Jahanpanah, around 1328. There were six gates in the western wall and seven in the eastern, but the name of only one gate survives—Maidan Gate on the west near an Old Idgah.[4] Ibn Batuta who lived in Delhi during 1333–41, gives a vivid description of Jahanpanah. He clearly mentions the demarcation of earlier cities like Lal Kot (also described by him as Delhi), Siri, and Jahanpanah and he also talks of Tughlaqabad. Batuta considered Lal Kot as a city with exceptionally wide walls. He also talks of Jahanpanah as an area enclosed within the new walls, apparently meant to be the residence of the sultan. Although the sultan had plans to include Tughlaqabad as part of the royal palace, the idea had to be dropped because it was very expensive. It is generally considered that Lal Kot was within the main urban area, Siri was the military zone, and the remaining area was reserved for the royal palace.[5] Although Jahanpanah was originally conceived to be the royal palace, it was later joined by several tombs, mainly of saints and holy men. The existence of several extremely large mosques in Jahanpanah, built not very long after the walls, suggest a rapid increase in population.

Jahanpanah, as it exists today, has seen the emergence of posh localities like Greater Kailash, Nehru Place, and Alaknanda around it due to urbanization. The area has spacious private bungalows occupied by the affluent sections of the society. Several multi-storey housing complexes were also developed by Delhi Development Authority (DDA). The adjoining multiplexes, sprawling bungalows, and busy commercial centres have blurred the existence of this historical city. The surrounding areas also have urbanized villages like Chiragh Delhi and Devli, which have now been converted into busy commercial centres. The Jahanpanah City Forest, situated in the heart of south Delhi, has been declared a reserve forest and its preservation is being monitored by the Supreme Court.

Fifth City: Firozabad

When Firoz Shah finally acquired the throne after Mohd Tughlaq, he also constructed a city, Firozabad, five miles to the north-east of Siri in 1354. The exact extent of this city is not quite clear but it covered a portion of the modern city and perhaps extended up to (and even around) the ridge to the north.[6] When Firoz Shah came to the throne in 1351, Delhi consisted of three contiguous walled enclosures: Lal Kot containing the main mosque and other ceremonial buildings, Siri, and the area enclosed by Jahanpanah walls that contained Muhammad Shah's palace. Historically speaking, it is very difficult to get an actual idea of Firoz Shah's Delhi. The limits of the city of Firozabad cannot be traced because the city of Shahjahanabad was built at a short distance from it. Roughly speaking, the city extended over a semicircle with a radius of a mile and a half from the centre of the Kotila on the riverbank. Starting from this point, the edge of the houses went up to Darya Ganj and then across to the end of Chandni Chowk.[7] Unlike earlier cities, it is generally believed that Firozabad was not a walled city. Hearn Gordon believes that on the river side of the Kotila, there was no necessity for walls. On the southern side, the great ravine structurally made it difficult to build a wall. The subsequent construction of walls by Sher Shah also negates the exact fortification of city of Firozabad.[8]

Sixth City: Dinpanah

After the coming of the Mughals, Humayun built the Purana Qila in 1534. After he was turned out, Sher Shah's son Islam built the walls of a sixth city which occupied only a part of Firozabad. Only a few hundred feet of the walls of this city remain and even that short length is considered by some historians not to have belonged to the outer walls at all.[9] The city was expanded and extended up to Ferozshah Kotla.

Seventh City: Shahjahanabad

The seventh and the last city was built in 1648 by Shahjahan, the fifth great Mughal emperor. He actually pulled down what was left of Firozabad as well as the walls of Sher Shah's city to build the walls of his own city, Shahjahanabad.

Of all the old cities of Delhi, the most important city from social, political, and economic growth is Shahjahanabad. It is also known as one of the oriental cities of the medieval period. The site was built as the capital city by Shahjahan and was named after the king himself. The site for Shahjahanabad had been chosen primarily for two reasons: first, the availability of a high canal on the banks of River Yamuna, and second, the natural fortification provided by the two arms of Aravali Range and the Yamuna, forming three sides of the triangular site.[10] As compared to previous cities, the construction of Shahjahanabad was more systematic. The Persian engineer, Ali Muradan Khan, supervised the construction work of the city. An immaculate and novel arrangement for supplying water to the city was made by the architect. A canal system was laid linking River Yamuna to fulfil the water needs. It was secured and enclosed by a ten kilometre wall. Ten gates surrounded the city and connected it with the other parts of the region. Lahore Gate was the main entrance to the Red Fort, besides Delhi Gate. The Kashmere Gate, Calcutta Gate, Mori Gate, Kabul Gate, Ferozshah Gate, Ajmeri Gate, and the Turqman Gate were the other major links of the city with the highways to other regions.[11] Despite the massive urbanization of the city and although they are surrounded by clusters of houses, one is able to locate these gates even today in the central district of Delhi.

The city was actually covered with a network of landmarks, focal points, local markets, and a spatial subdivision. Red Fort and Royal Palace were the climaxes of the whole plan. The city was located on the western banks of the Yamuna, which provided it with a prominent landscape. The accommodations on the northern and eastern sides were provided to the rich and the nobility. The proximity of the house to the palace determined the social status of the person. Bernier,[12] who lived in the city immediately after it was built, was impressed by the social, economic, and political life, and its linkages with the monarch, court and *umera*. There were numerous *karkhanas* for craftsmen under the patronage of the aristocracy. While he noticed great opulence and abundance of provisions, the city also had great squalor. It had some stone and some brick palaces, but was dominated by mud and thatch houses. The merchants worked in and lived in the second storey of the buildings and arcades along the two boulevards radiating from the palace. Faiz Bazar and Chandni Chowk, the two other wards, were asymmetrical. Bernier explained that this may be because they were built by different individuals at different times. However, the more likely reason was that it was built deliberately to make ingress more difficult for invading troops. *Katras* developed around the nuclei derived their names from provincial groups communities (Kashmiri Katra, Katranil) and *muhallas* and *kuchas* were named after the commodities sold there, or after prominent persons living there (Muhalla Imli Kucha Nawab Wazir).[13]

As a matter of fact, there were no suburbs in the sense of people moving out of the crowded city to the open spaces beyond. This was true till the nineteenth century. However, Bernier used the word 'suburb' not in the modern sense but to describe the ruins of old cities near Shahjahanabad and pockets of habitation around wholesale markets. They were akin to *faubourgs* of Paris and were separated by large royal or aristocratic pleasure/preserve gardens or hunting lodges, particularly Jahanuma in the north-west and Shalimar Bagh in the north.[14] Delhi was fed from the Doab, and from the grain emporia east of the river in Shahdara, Ghaziabad, and Patparganj. These were linked to the intramural markets near the Fatehpuri Mosque. Vegetables and fruits came from the northwest and were sold in the wholesale markets of Subzi Mandi in Mughalpura, outside the city wall on the G.T. Road to Lahore.[15]

POLICING DURING THIS PERIOD

Ancient Period

Historical references indicate the existence of a very rudimentary and informal system of village policing during ancient India. Since the society was simple, the overall security and safety of the residents was organized by the villagers themselves. Gradually, as situations changed with the establishment of new kingdoms in ancient India, the method of policing also changed. The emergence of new issues in the society had to be addressed by the respective rulers through a more complex system of policing. Mauryan rulers have significantly contributed in this new system of policing. Kautilya talks of external policing as well as internal policing. He advised the kings that the borders of the kingdom should be protected by responsible officials appointed by the king. All persons entering the kingdom should be thoroughly checked and their credentials verified. They should be disarmed and allowed to enter only on the basis of some kind of passport. These were the basic tenants of external policing.

Inside the kingdom, policemen were deployed at prominent places for the overall safety and security of citizens. Kautilya also suggested that there should be *sthaniya* for 800 villages, a *dronamukha* for 400 villages, a *kharvata* for 200 villages, and a *sangrahana* for 10 villages to effectively manage the affairs of policing. He also made a distinction between city policing and village policing. The responsibility for city policing was to be with the *Nagarika*, while *Gramadhyaksa* should manage the policing responsibilities in the village. Kautilya also suggested recruitment of spies to collect information on behalf of the state. One also finds tips given by Kautilya for investigation of sudden deaths. However, the system of policing underwent changes in the reign of subsequent rulers in the Gupta period.

Medieval Period

The emergence of a more systematic and well organized policing system is seen during the medieval period. The operational dimensions of policing during this period revolved around an officer called the *kotwal*. The kotwal was appointed by the king and was entrusted with enormous responsibilities. One finds a description regarding a kotwal in the famous book written by Abul Fazal, *Ain-e-Akbari*. The duties and responsibilities of the kotwal in the town are aptly summarized in the following words:

> The appropriate person for this office should be vigorous, experienced, active, deliberate, patient, astute and humane. Through his watchfulness and night patrolling, the citizen should enjoy the repose of security and

the evil disposed lie in the slough of non existence. He should keep a register of houses and frequented roads and engage the citizens in a pledge of reciprocal assistance and bind them to a common participation to a weal and woe. He should form a quarter for the union of a certain number of inhabitance and name one of his intelligent subordinates for its superintendence and receive a daily report under his seal of those who enter or leave it and of whatever events therein occur. And he should appoint one spy, one among the obscure residents with whom the other should have no acquaintance, and keeping their reports in writing employ needful scrutiny. He should establish a separate *Serai* (Inn) and cause unknown arrivals to alight therein and by the aid of detectives take account of them. He should minutely observe income and expenditure of various classes of men and by a refined address make his vigilance reflect on his administration. When night is a little advanced he should prohibit people from entering or leaving the city. He should settle the idle to some handicrafts. He should remove formal grievances and forbid any one from forcibly entering the house of another. He should discover thieves and goods they have stolen and be responsible for the loss. He should use his discretion in the reduction of prices and not allow purchases to be made outside the city. The rich shall not take beyond what is necessary for their consumption.[16]

The policing duties of the kotwal outlined in the *Ain-e-Akbari* were in tune with the existing problems and needs of the society.

During medieval times, Delhi was divided into various wards (*muhallas/kuchas*) and the kotwal of the city was assisted by their respective wardens (*mir mohalla*), in the overall maintenance of law and order, and control of crime. The *Kotwali* or the headquarters of the city police was generally located near the seat of power, the king's palace. In Delhi, the headquarters or the Kotwali, has been shifting with the change of rulers. In the early Sultanate period, the Kotwali was in Qila Rai Pithora (Mehrauli). During the period of the Tughlaqs, the Kotwali moved to Tughlaqabad and later to Feroz Shah Kotla. During the Mughal period, when Shahjahan shifted the capital to Shahjahanabad, the Kotwali was shifted to Chandni Chowk, near present day Sisganj Gurudwara. The system of policing headed by the kotwal remained in existence throughout the medieval period.

ARRIVAL OF THE BRITISH AND
EXPANSION OF THE CITY

The British acquired the city of Delhi through the East India Company (EIC) from the Marathas in 1803, through the treaty of Surji Arjungaon. During that time, the territory comprised the Delhi and Hisar Divisions, which were sub-divided in 1819 into the districts of Haryana, Rohtak, Panipat, Gurgaon, and Delhi.[17]

The British built two cities when they came here as colonial rulers. The centre was built north of Shahjahanabad. There were two primary reasons for this. First, the distrust towards the city and second, they wanted to maintain a distance between the ruler and the ruled. This was known as Civil Lines, built along the lines of other district towns built elsewhere with huge bungalows and compounds. As soon as the population increased, further expansion of the city took place with the development of Sadar Bazar, Kingsway Camp, and Deputy Ganj.

The city underwent further changes after the revolt of 1857. This saw the reversal of pre-1857 military and civilian positions. Due to their bitter experiences in the revolt, the British decided to introduce a lot of changes in the existing structure of Shahjahanabad. From a security point of view, the government decided to demolish some of the grandest buildings, like Kucha Bulaga Begum, Haveli Nawab Wazir, Akbarabadi Maszid, the palaces of *nawabs* of Jhajur, Ballabhgari, Faruck Nagar, and Bahadurgarh.[18] The people who lost their houses in this clearance migrated and settled outside the walled city. This is the time when the city started growing beyond the walled city and into the rural hinterland.

Eighth City: Lutyens' Delhi

The capital city built by the British, the gracious imperial city of New Delhi, was situated to the south-west of Shahjahanabad. The first offices of the new capital functioned from a building, known today as the Old Secretariat, in the year 1912. As a matter of fact, ever since the capital was shifted from Calcutta to Delhi, the hunt for the new imperial capital had started. The idea of the new imperial capital originated from a very strong British conviction that traditional Indian cities were dirty, unhealthy, and inherently lawless. Through the construction of a new city, the British wanted to reflect the superiority of Western science, art, and civilization. Before Raisina Hill was considered for the construction of the new capital, the cantonment in the Ridge area and Civil Lines in the north-west area also competed as sites for the new capital. While Civil Lines was rejected on the ground of being far away from the mainstream, Delhi Cantonment was ruled out partly because the area was thought to be malarial and partly because it was feared that even if the government houses were constructed right at the ridge, it would still not be sufficiently visible from all parts of the new capital.[19]

However, very soon the limitations of the other two sites were realized and thus considered unsuitable. After the deliberations of a Town Planning Committee consisting of G.S.C. Swinton, Edwin Lutynes, and J.A. Brodie, the location of the new capital was changed from north to extreme south, in and around Raisina Hill.

The British conceptualized the construction of a new city on the pattern of the Grand Manor. According to the urban historian, Spiro Kostov, Grand Manor reflects an urban grandeur beyond utility and pragmatic consideration, whether it is ancient Babylon or Nazi Berlin. Its instruments are heroic scale, visual fluency, and the luxury of building materials.[20] The new capital was to reflect the political supremacy of the British over other earlier rulers of the past in every manner. It was laid out on the garden city pattern to accommodate a population of 65,000.[21] The new city, although close to Shahjahanabad, was separated by an open space. It was accessible from the walled city only through two underpasses, the Minto and Lady Hardinge bridges.

Beyond this new city were to be Connaught Place, Government Complex, and India Gate in a geometric pattern formed over the triangular base of these three structures. The centrepiece of the plan was the Central Vista. The senior-most gazetted officers were accommodated in sprawling, single-storey bungalows, slightly to the south. The joint secretaries moved further southwards, while lower-ranking administrators like deputy secretaries, under secretaries, registrars and superintendents were placed west of Janpath, between the railway station and the secretariat, followed by the higher ranks of European clerks. North of Rajpath in Allenby Road (present day Bishambhar Das Road), near Gole Dak Khana, for example, were officials from the post and telegraph department. The residential areas in the north accommodated the lower- and middle-income employees. Connaught Place, the famous shopping centre, came up near New Delhi Railway Station. Affluent Indians, including smaller princes, were allotted plots along the roads leading away from Connaught Place, on Curzon Road (present day Kasturba Gandhi Marg).

Similarly, preferential and influential Indians were also encouraged to buy plots on what was then the outskirts of the city, like Lodi Colony. Delhi's first apartment complex, Sujan Singh Park, was built by the famous builder Sir Sobha Singh, father of noted writer Khushwant Singh. (Khushwant Singh lives in and writes out of one of these flats.) As a matter of fact, the construction of the new capital by the British and spatial allotments of plots and residential houses as per the status of the individual clearly reflect a pattern of stratification based on ethnic and racial characteristics. However, such a stratification of cities is nothing new. It follows the usual trend of construction of colonial cities by colonial powers in other parts of the world. One finds similar hierarchies expressed in spatial terms in Hanoi built by the French, Manila built by the Americans, and Lusaka built by the British.[22]

Thus, allocations though gradations emerge to be a very significant characteristic of all colonial cities. Delhi was not an exception to this global colonial trend. However, one finds manifestations of race, rank, and status in the case of New Delhi in its extreme form due to past and immediate political upheavals and developments. The allocation, location, and construction of houses in New Delhi clearly reflected the professional status, size of the house and garden, width of the road, racial profile of the occupant, and his proximity to the seat of power. The main feature of New Delhi's street pattern is a broad processional avenue,[23] which was earlier known as King's Way, now known as Rajpath. Complementing this are the old Viceroy House, now known as the Rashtrapati Bhawan, and the secretariat buildings, now housing the offices of the Indian government.

In contrast to a compact and congested walled city, the basic philosophy behind designing the new city was to project an extrovert area with low density pattern with a maximum density of 25 persons per sq km. The city was designed to be a colony of elites and influential sections of the society.

The initial plan proposed large plots of one to six acres for residential development. The city actually remained deserted and barren for decades. With a view to populate the new city, housing allowance was given to government employees working in New Delhi. Businessmen were given options to open shops in Connaught Place. A city on which 115 million rupees were spent was finally completed in 1931, when the population of Delhi was 6,36,000—a growth of 1,50,000 persons in a decade.[24]

Ninth City

Till now, we have been talking about the cities of Delhi, which were actually built by erstwhile rulers and the British in the pre-Independence period. Town planners and urban architects talked about a Delhi which was to emerge after Independence. The foundation for New Delhi under the Master Plan scheme envisaged by Jawaharlal Nehru was called 'Ninth Delhi'. According to Jag Mohan, the setting up of Ninth Delhi was fraught with formidable problems. It had to deal with some of the unhealthiest features of the earlier cities, as already discussed. It had to reckon with the structural legacies of the seventh and eighth cities. The city had to face the problems of sprawling rehabilitation colonies, which were hastily planned and developed in the wake of the flux of displaced persons from Pakistan.[25] It is almost in this similar sense that the famous urban architect, Patwant Singh, talks of Ninth Delhi. According to Patwant Singh, Ninth Delhi, unlike its predecessors, is not a clearly defined entity. It is the national capital trying to consolidate all the Nine Delhis and fuse them into a greater Delhi by building new infrastructure, through infilling, by densification, and by such measures as can make the metropolis meet, with some measure of confidence, the challenging demands of the twentieth century.[26]

The basic foundation for the emergence of Ninth Delhi actually rests on the concept of the Master Plan. A very significant feature of Ninth Delhi was to treat the squatter as an integral part of the community and provide him not only living space on secure tenure and environmental facilities, but also development-oriented avenues of employment as well as the opportunity of acquiring a stable family life.[27] The emergence and expansion of the city limits in the Ninth Delhi has been beyond imagination. Before 1962, the total developed and semi-developed areas of urban Delhi were about 40,000 acres. The developmental effort of Ninth Delhi covered an area more than 40,000 acres. In other words, the development of Delhi during the last 10–15 years is almost equivalent to the entire Delhi developed over the centuries (Seventh and Eighth combined, plus the rehabilitation colonies and other settlements constructed after 1947).

Let us see the changing dimensions of policing in various phases of the development of the city over a period of time.

Policing during 1803–1911

The British entered Delhi on 11 September 1803. The British took some time to establish a new administrative set-up in the city.

Delhi became part of the Bengal Presidency, and the city and the surrounding villages that came under its overall administrative control, were called the Delhi Territory. This territory was placed under a British Resident who functioned under the direction of the governor-general.

Under the new system, the Resident performed his duties as chief administrator of the territory. He was assisted by several civil officers called assistants. One of the assistants was in-charge of the policing responsibilities. This officer was also known as the superintendent of police. A police force was raised under him, though the overall command remained with the Resident.

The city continued to be divided into wards, with each ward under the charge of a junior officer. The officer was responsible for keeping watch and the maintenance of law and order in his area. Unlike the practice in the Regulation Provinces, where the police were entrusted with the responsibility of enquiring into the crimes whether reported or not, Delhi Police only investigated those cases which were reported to the police under the new system.

The headquarters of the city police was located at the Residency at Kashmere Gate. The police stations and police posts kept on shifting from one part of the city to another as per the requirements of the law and order situation and increase in population. The policeman, *sipahi* (or sepoy as the British called them), was given a distinct identity through a special uniform, which no other citizen was allowed to don. The sipahi wore khaki shirts and shorts, boots, *pugree*, and *patti* on the legs. While on duty, he carried with him a lathi (a stick, which served as a symbol of authority).

Policing in the villages and maintenance of law and order was done by the villagers. The safety and security of the village was maintained through an indigenous system of patrolling called *Thikri-Pahra*. Under this system, all the able-bodied men in the village were enrolled in the *Patwaris* book and their names were written on small potsherds called *theecur*. These were thrown together into a large pot kept in a village hall or *chaupal* with a second empty pot beside it. Everyday it was the Patwaris job to visit the chaupal and draw at random from the filled pot the required number of names for the purpose of patrolling. He inscribed the names in his book. The system continued till all the names were taken out from the pot. The system of Thikri Pehra reflected community policing and participation of citizens in prevention and detection of crime in their area. The system is still in practice in several outlying villages of Delhi in a different form.

In the year 1833, the Bengal Presidency was divided by the British into two provinces—Bengal and North Western Province, through the Charter Act of 1833. Delhi came under North Western Province. A new division called 'Delhi Division', with headquarters at Agra, was created. Under the new set-up, the divisional commissioner was made the head of the police department. William Fraser, the first divisional commissioner in the system, was the head of Delhi Police. However within a year of his assuming charge, Fraser was murdered. As a result, another act was passed by government in 1837. This act brought some new changes in the system of policing and administration. The policing responsibilities were entrusted to an officer of the rank of Superintendent of Police (SP). He was under the close control of the Inspector General of Police (IGP). This system of policing continued till 1857. Thus, policing in the new system got closer and exclusive supervision under a newly-created officer of the rank of IGP.

The 1857 revolt, also known as First War of Independence, was a major jolt to the British and led to several administrative changes. The overall administration of India passed from the EIC to the Crown. The British government was forced to adopt more effective methods of policing and other administrative controls in the aftermath of mass massacre of their own officers during the Revolt in various parts of the country. Delhi was brought under Punjab in February 1858. The British realized that both the police and the army let them down during the Revolt. Separate commissions were set up with a view to reorganize both the army and the police. The recommendations of the Police Commission led to the enactment of Police Act of 1861.

The Police Act of 1861   The basic philosophy of the act was to reorganize the police to make it a more efficient instrument for the prevention and detection of crime (the Preamble) to cope with the changing dimensions of the city and emergence of problems like increase in population, law and order, and other aspects of policing. The following are some of the important features of the Act:

1. Constitution of the force (Section 2): The entire police establishment under a state government shall be deemed to be one police force.

2. The administration of the police throughout a general police district shall be vested in an officer to be styled the inspector general of police and in such deputy inspector general and assistant inspector general as the state government may deem fit.

3. Under Section 4, the police was not only put under the control of their immediate superior officers in the hierarchy but also under the executive. This was done primarily by the British to maintain its effective control in the districts.

4. The Act tried to involve the members of the society for assistance to the police in times of grave crisis like riots or disturbances through an institution called Special Police officers (Section 17). This provision also figured in Delhi Police Act 1978 where Special Police officers are appointed on the recommendation of Station House Officers (SHO) by the area district DCP.

5. The Act also mentioned specific duties like execution of all orders and warrants issued to him by any competent authority, collection and communication of intelligence affecting the public peace, to prevent commission of offences and public nuisances, detect and bring offences to justice and to apprehend all persons whom he is legally authorized to apprehend and for whose

apprehension sufficient grounds exist. Furthermore, it was to be lawful for every police officer for any of the purposes mentioned in this section, without warrant to enter and inspect any drinking shop, gaming house or other places of resort of loose and disorderly characters (Section 23). However, over a period of time the duties and responsibilities of the police have increased beyond what was enshrined in Section 23 of IPA, 1861.

6. The act also tried to regulate public assemblies and various processions through issuance of prior permission by the competent authority.

7. The Act also addressed its concern towards unclaimed properties, nuisance of music in the streets, cruelty towards animals in various sections of the Act.

The perusal of the various sections of the Act reflects the profound wisdom and far-sightedness of the lawmakers in showing their concern towards a broad range of issues having implications for law and order and overall security and safety of the society. It also empowered the law enforcing agencies to tackle the menace of various kinds of nuisance prevailing in the society at that time. The Act is still used as resource book with slight modifications by police forces across the country.

Under the provisions of the Act of 1861, the IGP Punjab was made the overall in charge of the police. The Punjab province was divided into four police ranges: Ambala, Lahore, Rawalpindi, and Multan. Delhi came under the administrative control of Ambala range. The policing responsibilities in Delhi was carried out by an SP with the assistance of an Assistant SP, a DSP, 2 inspectors, 27 sub-inspectors, 110 head constables, 985 foot constables, and 27 mounted constables, under the overall supervision of IGP Punjab.

In the year 1889, the Punjab government appointed a committee under the leadership of C.L. Tupper, Commissioner, Rawalpindi Division to suggest measures to improve the working of the police. The committee suggested several measures including reorganization of police stations, improvement in pay and allowances of policemen and increase in expenditure on the police as a whole. The committee also suggested the fingerprint method for identification of criminals. In pursuance of the recommendations of the Tupper Committee, the police stations were further reorganized in the city of Delhi as well as its outer periphery. The policing in Delhi city zone was carried out through three police stations: Kotwali, Subzi Mandi, and Paharganj. The policing in outer Delhi was carried out through the police stations of Alipur, Nangloi, and Nazafgarh. The area of Mehrauli came under the Ballabhgarh zone. Each police station was headed by a sub-inspector and had 2 head constables and 10 foot constables.

During the Delhi Durbar of 1911 in which King George V and Queen Mary participated, the king announced the transfer of the imperial capital to Delhi. Delhi's status as capital saw further administrative changes including changes in the overall system of policing.

Policing during 1912–47   Changes in the dimensions of policing during this period needs to be seen in the context of overall political events taking place during the period. Lord Hardinge, the Governor-General and Viceroy of India, made his first entry in the new capital on 28 December 1912. Hardinge who was at the head of a majestic procession on an elephant in Chandni Chowk, was attacked with a bomb by Indian revolutionaries in which the mahout riding the Hardinge's elephant died. Hardinge also received serious wounds and collapsed. This was a very serious incident which shook the entire British administration, forcing them to take further new and effective measures regarding police administration in the capital.

In the year 1912, Delhi was detached from Punjab and came under a separate administrative unit under the overall charge of a chief commissioner. The chief commissioner was also notified as ex-officio IGP.

As per Gazette of India Extra Ordinary Notification Number 1406, 1912 it is mentioned:

> In exercise of powers conferred by section 2 Sub-section (1) and (2), of the Police Act of 1888 as in force in British India or as locally applied, the Governor General of Council is pleased:
>
> 1. To create a general police district embracing all the lands situated within the Punjab, the Province of Delhi, the North West Frontier Province and Native States referred to in the list appended.
> 2. To order the enrolment under the police Act of 1861 of a general Police Force for the service therein[28].

The Chief Commissioner was also vested with the powers and functions of the Inspector General of Police.[29]

At serial number 8 of the same notification it is mentioned that 'The Chief Commissioner is pleased to direct that the Province of Delhi shall form a general Police District as defined in Section 1 of the police Act 1861.'[30] Serial number 9 of the same notification further mentioned that 'In exercise of the power conferred by Section 3 of the Police Act 1861, the Chief Commissioner is pleased to appoint himself to be Inspector General of Police for the Province of Delhi.'[31]

The perusal of correspondence files of the home department during 1912–22 shows the growing concern of chief commissioners and SP's towards improving the overall pattern of policing with increase in crime and population in the capital city. The importance of Delhi as capital of the country was recognized and the logistics and other infrastructure of Delhi Police also accordingly improved. Officers rationalized the increase in number of police stations and the force as a whole in the backdrop of increasing crime and increase of population. Policing in Delhi was reorganized at three levels: City Police, Suburban Police, and Rural Police. Different areas of Delhi territory came under these categories as per their physical and geographical location in the city.

The historical description of the various cities of Delhi helps us in drawing following important conclusions regarding expansion, urbanization, and policing during that period.

First, historically the boundaries of the city have been shifting from north to south due to political compulsions and individual likes and dislikes of the ruler of that period. A very typical characteristic of the city has been its aristocratic nature. The prime concern of the ruler was to secure his territory through the construction of walls. Around these fortified cities various monuments were made by different rulers.

Second, in the pre-British period, Delhi was only a political and cultural centre with the king as its head. The population of Delhi at that time consisted primarily of the courtiers, the nobles, and the king's army. When the king left Delhi for a long period, all of these people followed along with their families and servants. Even the merchants had to accompany them, as in their absence there would not be much trade left.

Later, with the establishment of the British rule in upper India, Delhi emerged as a thriving commercial centre. With the improvement of unsettled conditions and introduction of better civic amenities, stable growth of the city's population started. The city came under British in 1803. The population of the city at that time was estimated to be about 1,50,000 inhabitants.[32] The next forty years saw a very slow growth in its population. In 1847, the city's population along with its suburbs was 1,60,279, showing an increase of about 6.5 per cent.[33] In an enumeration in 1868, the population of Delhi stood at 1,54,417, a decrease of about 3.7 per cent. This was primarily because of the 1857 revolt, after which many people were expelled from the city and many killed.

Policing in Delhi also evolved from more general to specific in actual coverage of the area. Till 1912, since Delhi was a part of other larger provinces, policing had been at par with the prevailing system in the area. The focus of policing has been broad based in nature, with issues having general ramifications for the combined provinces as a whole. More specific and city-based issues of policing in Delhi did not get priority. Gradually, Delhi was bifurcated from the larger province and the need for city-specific policing was realized by the rulers. As the city started growing in size, more and more areas were brought under the ambit of policing, leading to creation of more and more police stations and police posts. However, the central focus of policing was to provide effective and efficient cover to the British ruling establishment, which was trying to reconsolidate its position in the wake of various national and local level uprisings seeking the independence of the country. In other words, policing was ruler-oriented and the concerns of the ruling establishment got priority over the needs of the general people.

2

DELHI

Acropolis to Metropolis and the
Nature of Policing

TREND OF URBANIZATION

The real signs of expansion and urbanization of Delhi could be seen after the 1857 Revolt when the population from the walled city and Red Fort started moving towards the villages. The population of the city started increasing. In 1881, the first regular, simultaneous census in different provinces of the country was carried out. Since then more than twelve censuses were carried out up to 2001. However, one difficulty in obtaining comparable figures for all the nine censuses up to 1971 arises due to administrative changes. For the first four censuses of 1891 to 1911, the census operations in this area were carried out as a part of Punjab. Till then, it was included in the so called 'Delhi District' which consisted the *tehsils* of Delhi, Sonipat, and Ballabgarh with a total area of 1,276 stone miles.[1] In 1912, a separate Delhi province was formed, which included Delhi Tehsil and a small portion of Ballabgarh Tehsil. In 1915, an area of 46 square miles on the eastern banks of Yamuna was transferred to Delhi from Ghaziabad Tehsil of the United Provinces.[2] Thereafter, there has not been any change except marginal modifications made on the basis

TABLE 2.1   Area of Delhi

Year	Area (Sq Mtrs)
1931	1536
1941	1484
1951	1497
1961	1466.88
1971	1485
1981	1483
1991	1483
2001	1483

of physical surveys of India. With these marginal modifications, the area of Delhi changed as shown in Table 2.1.

The perusal of Table 2.1 reflects that there has been increase in the overall area of Delhi since 1931 which continued till 1981. After 1981, the area has almost remained constant till 2001.

The real growth of city of Delhi actually began only after 1921. By this time, some kind of stability was visible in the administrative set-up. This is the period which also witnessed visible improvements in commercial conditions and industrial facilities in the city. A large number of labourers, artisans, imperial government officials, and their families came to settle down in Delhi. The process of migration started in the city with the interplay of push and pull factors.

The decade between 1931 and 1943 also shows an increasing trend in population growth of the city. This period also shows gradual movement of population towards Karol Bagh in the west and beyond Subzi Mandi in the northwest[3]. Similarly, Shahdara village located on the east across river Yamuna developed into a township of 8000 persons who were actually dependent on the city for employment. The gradual increase of population by 1941 was 44 per cent.

Table 2.2 reflects the increasing trend of population growth in the city since 1921. It has been increasing in every decade. The phenomenal growth of the city immediately after 1947 can be considered as a landmark in the overall growth of Delhi. The

TABLE 2.2 Variation in Population

Year	Persons	Decade	Decade
1921	4,88,452	+74,601	+18.03
1931	6,36,246	+1,47,794	+30.26
1941	9,17,939	+2,81,693	+44.30
1961	26,58,612	+9,14,540	+52.44
1971	40,65,698	+14,07,086	+52.92
1981	62,20,406		+53 per cent
1991	94,20,644		51.45
2001	1,38,50,507		47.2

Source: *Delhi Statistical Handbook*, 2007.

partition of country in 1947 brought a huge influx of refugees into Delhi. In fact, this movement of population into Delhi outnumbered those immigrants who had come from individual provinces. As it is evident from the figures, the census of 1951 actually demonstrates an increase of 90 per cent. This phenomenal growth of the city after 1947 has very important implications in the overall socio-economic and political growth of the city as a whole.

The exclusion of Lahore from the country after Partition forced a redistribution of commerce and wholesale trade patterns in northern India. Trade and commerce gravitated towards Delhi and Old Delhi was already congested and under strain.[4] The national capital, Delhi, also attracted an influx of administrative and bureaucratic establishments, foreign missions, as well as institutional bodies, and served as the infrastructural and logistical base of state.

By the year 1950, nearly twelve colonies covering about 3000 acres were opened up officially accommodating about two lakh refugees—930 acres were developed in the west, 241 in the north, and 2.6 in the east. The largest acreage developed—encompassing Nizamuddin, Jangpura, Lajpat Nagar, Kalkaji, and Malviya Nagar—was in the south. In 1920, north Darya Ganj was developed for residential plots, while south Darya Ganj was allocated to schools and charities.

Following core areas also emerged in the city:

1. In the south this was formed by Lajpat Nagar, Kalkaji, Nizamuddin, and Malviya Nagar.

2. In the west, two Rajender Nagars, three Patel Nagars, Moti Nagar, Ramesh Nagar, and Tilak Nagar.

3. In the north, Kingsway, spreading up to Timarpur, Roop Nagar, Kamla Nagar, Jawahar Nagar, and Shakti Nagar.

4. In the east, Gandhi Nagar and Shahdara.

5. In Old Delhi, Chandni Chowk, Hindu Rao, Subzi Mandi, Sadar Bazar, Sarai Rohilla, Jhandewalan, Pahar Ganj, Shakur Basti, and Old Rohtak Road.

These areas provided a totally new and different look to the southern limits of the existing city.[5]

Simultaneously, the barren and wild lands in the western and north-western parts of Delhi (earlier establishments of Gujjars and other tribal communities) were deployed by Delhi Improvement Trust in the shape of one- or two-storied buildings meant for the middle classes. These extensions covered roughly 2800 acres of land in the western boundaries of the city.

As a matter of fact, Delhi has registered a very slow pace of population growth up to 1931. The year 1941 onwards, the city has shown an upward trend which still continues. Delhi has outpaced all other million plus cities in the country.

According to the Census of 2001, Delhi has emerged as the third most populated city in India. Amongst the four metropolitan cities, Mumbai Urban Agglomeration occupies the first position with highest population of 16.37 million. The second and third positions have been occupied by Kolkata and Delhi with a total population of 13.22 million and 12.79 million, respectively. The distribution of population in various states, and union territories of the country as per the Census of 2001 may be seen in Appendix 2.1.

The gradual urbanization and horizontal expansion of the city has swallowed up several villages. This is very evident from the decreasing figures of villages in various censuses:

TABLE **2.3** Villages in Delhi

1961	1971	1981	1991	2001
300	258	231	209	165

The density of rural and urban population has also been increasing throughout. The year 1951 shows phenomenal increase in the density of population in rural as well as urban areas due to influx of refugees after Partition. As a matter of fact, the rural population of the state did not indicate marked changes up to 1931. It began to rise sharply after 1931. In the decade 1941–51, the rural population of Delhi territory jumped by almost 40 per cent. This increase was partly due to an increase in natural growth and partly due to immigration of refugees from West Pakistan. It may be pointed out that according to the Census of 1951, the displaced persons settled in rural areas numbered 25,005 as against 4,70,386 in the urban areas out of a total of 4,95,391.[6]

The population of the whole of Delhi is essentially urban in nature. Only 7 per cent of the population is rural. The way villages have been declining since Independence, the day is not far when the so called distinction between rural and urban in Delhi will disappear, making the states comprise only the urban population. Out of nine districts, Central and New Delhi districts are truly urban where the rural population is zero. The only district which has comparatively more rural population is the South-West District.

The trend of urbanization in Delhi as a whole reflects the fact that urban areas have increased from 326.54 sq km in 1961 to 591.90 sq km in 1981, 700.23 sq km in 1991, and 924.68 sq km in 2001.

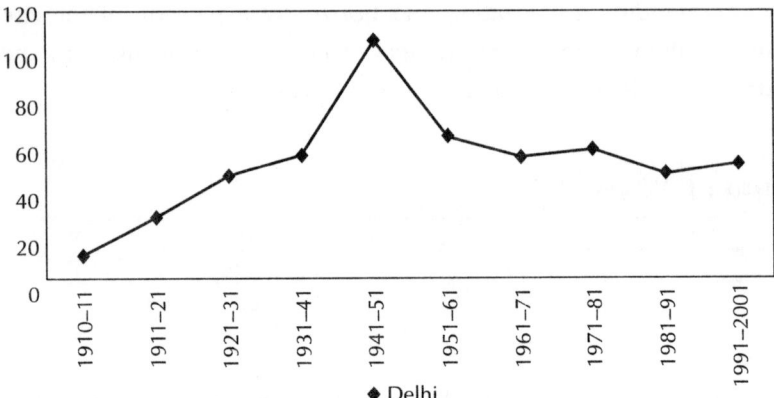

FIGURE 2.1 NCT of Delhi Decennial Growth in Urban Population, 1901–11 to 1991–2001

Source: Economic Survey, 2007–8.

This urban area was 22 per cent in 1961, 40 per cent in 1981, 47 per cent in 1991, and 62 per cent in 2001 of the total area. Similarly, the urban population of Delhi which was 14.37 lakh in 1951, increased to 23.59 lakh in 1961, 84.71 lakh in 1991, and 129.05 lakh in 2001. The total urban population was 88.72 per cent in 1961, 92.73 per cent in 1981, 89.94 per cent in 1991, and 93.81 per cent in 2001 of the total population of Delhi. The overall pattern of urbanization in Delhi over a period of time as shown in Figure 2.1.

Figure 2.1 reflects the pattern of urbanization in the city since 1901 on a decadal basis. The pace of urbanization has been increasing in every decade. The decade *c.* 1941–51 shows the maximum urban growth of the city.

Figure 2.2 reflects the pattern of urbanization in Delhi with the trend of urbanization at all-India level in every consecutive census since 1901. The overall trend of urbanization in Delhi has been faster as compared to the national trend.

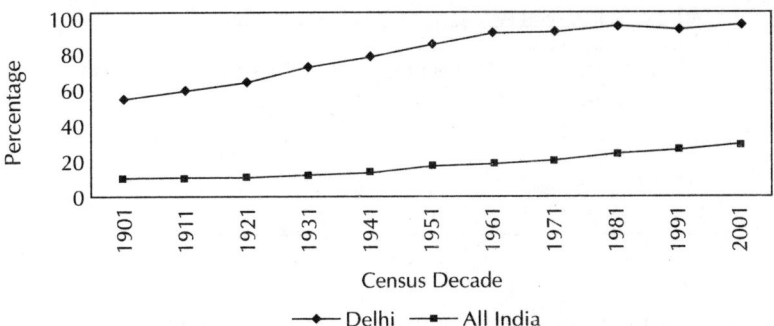

FIGURE 2.2   Trend of Urbanization, India and NCT of Delhi, 1901–2001

Source: Economic Survey, 2007–8.

MIGRATION

Migration has contributed substantially in the overall population growth of the city. However, the process of migration in Delhi has some peculiar features not very common to the growth of other urban centres in the country. The process of migration can be briefly classified into following categories.

Forced Migration

The initial migration in the city particularly after Independence was different from the normal trend of migration. Post-Partition movement of people into the city can be characterized as forced migration. It was a movement of people in which the individuals had no role. They had no option but to leave a particular place. This is different from the movement of people in the city where decisions were taken by individuals after calculating the advantages and disadvantages of movement at the point of origin and at the point of destination. The extent of mass migration during Partition as enumerated in the Census of 1951 was 4,95,391. The heaviest arrivals of the displaced

TABLE 2.4   Displaced Persons in Delhi Due to Partition

Month	Number of Displaced Persons Arrival in Delhi
August 1947	1,26,668
September 1947	1,13,215
October 1947	85,437
Total	3,25,320

persons in Delhi from August 1947 to October 1947 are shown in Table 2.4.

During the decade 1941–51, Delhi had a net gain by internal migration of about 78 million people or about 54 per cent of the average population of the decade.[7] However, the extent of non-refugee immigrants to Delhi during the same period is also very important. The index of non-refugees immigrants into Delhi from 1940–56 is shown in Table 2.5.

From Table 2.5, it is clear that from 1942 to 1946 the pace of migration was slow. The job opportunities in urban Delhi during this period were not very high and it was just above normal. Due to war efforts, the primary incentive to move to Delhi was not very high. As soon as Delhi assumed the status of capital after Independence in 1947, the overall pace of migration accelerated. The opportunities offered by Delhi as the primary city of the region suddenly widened. This led to subsequent increase in the figures in 1951–2. The same trend continued till 1956.

Normal Migration

The normal migration in the city increased after Independence due to overall importance of the capital. The primary reason for increasing trend of migration was due to increase in construction and developmental activities in the city as visualized under five-year plan. The enhanced opportunities of jobs in Delhi acted as pull factors at

TABLE **2.5** Non-refugee Immigrants in Delhi

Year	Non-refugee Immigrants
1940	6,036
1941	7,373
1942	13,243
1943	10,568
1944	13,992
1945	13,710
1946	15,614
1947	21,403
1948	20,798
1949	15,139
1950	25,434
1951	16,684
1952	2,23,635
1953	24,847
1954	31,059
1955	37,468
1956	28,753

the point of destination, while relative unavailability of employment opportunities and over all underdevelopment in rural areas acted as push factors at the point of origin. The interplay of both these pushes and pulls factors led to large number of people migrating to Delhi for better fortunes. The process did not stop and continued unabated for a long time.

With the increasing developmental activities in Delhi, mass scale conversion of transport system in Delhi, increasing network of Metro Rail, the pace of migration increased manifold. The migration data released by Registrar General of India (RGI) for the Census of 2001 indicates that Delhi's total population of 138.50 lakh consists of 82.04 lakh from within Delhi, while the remaining 53.18 lakh constitutes migrant population from various states. The percentage of migration from various states for the period 1981 to 1991 and 1991 to 2006 are shown in Tables 2.6 (a) and (b).

TABLE 2.6 (a)   State-wise Migration (1981–91)

State	Percentage
Uttar Pradesh	49.91
Haryana	11.82
Bihar	10.99
Rajasthan	6.17
Punjab	5.43
West Bengal	2.79
Madhya Pradesh	2.71
Kerla	1.61
Tamil Nadu	1.56
Maharashtra	1.48
Himachal Pradesh	1.45
Others	4.08

TABLE 2.6 (b)   State-wise Migration (1991–2006)

State	Percentage
Uttar Pradesh	43.56
Haryana	10.26
Bihar	13.87
Rajasthan	5.16
Punjab	4.72
West Bengal	3.18
Madhya Pradesh	1.85
Others	17.39

A perusal of Tables 2.6 (a) and (b) show that the largest share of migration in Delhi is from UP, Haryana, and Bihar. The most important reasons for migration continued to be ample job opportunities in the city and comparatively higher wages. The migration during 1981–91 was due to various reasons. It included factors like maintaining older family ties (a process, essentially the product of chain migration), employment, education, and other miscellaneous reasons.

The major reasons for migration to Delhi are shown in Table 2.7.

Table 2.7 reflects that employment continues to be the main reason for migration.

Migration in the city has been in the form of individual as well as group migration. The individual migration of people from rural areas to the urban areas has been through an initial contact or a relative or a friend with whom the person shares an intimate relationship. Logically speaking, individual migration has been essentially a chain migration where one person at one point of time has facilitated the movement of some persons, who in turn have facilitated the

TABLE 2.7 Migrants Classified by Reasons for Migration

Reasons	Per cent of Migrants 1981–1991	Per cent of Migrants 1991–2001
Employment	31.29	37.6
Business	4.07	0.5
Education	2.28	2.7
Family moved	41.45	36.8
Marriage	15.62	30.8
Natural calamities	0.13	Nil
Others	5.16	8.6

movement of other persons who came in contact. This is what Richard D. Lambert calls 'family centered associational migration'.[8]

On the other hand, group migration has been facilitated through professional agents and labour contractors. These agents and contractors have organized group movement of people from villages through their organized networks. Rural areas have always acted as reservoir for the agents and contractors.

Migrants to the city can be grouped into following broad categories:

1. Those migrants who came to the city a long time back and have settled down, acquired properties and become permanent residents in the long run. Such people have very distinct contact with their original home.

2. Those people who have migrated to the city by virtue of their professional assignments. Their stay in the city is not permanent. After staying for a few years, they move on. They are able to maintain their links with their native state and keep visiting at regular intervals. This group has also made Delhi an alternate home.

3. Those migrants who are utilizing the opportunities in the city to improve their standard of living and earn more money. Such people still maintain their ancestral links in their native villages. They

occasionally visit their hometown/village. Construction workers who are involved in various projects in the city fall under this category.

The increasing pace of urbanization and migration has led to emergence of several resettlement colonies, JJ clusters, regularized unauthorized colonies, unauthorized colonies, and slum clusters. These unplanned housing and dwelling premises all over the city gave a new profile to the metropolis and posed an additional dimension for the overall policing in the city. In Delhi, almost 65 per cent of the population live in unplanned colonies (slums—19.1 per cent; JJ clusters—14.8 per cent; JJ resettlement colonies—12.7 per cent; regularized unauthorized colonies—12.7 per cent; and unauthorized colonies—5.3 per cent). Delhi's housing stock comprises units which range from single-room units (38 per cent) to two-room units (27 per cent) and extends to over six rooms which has a share of 4.1 per cent.[9] However, this developmental dimension of the city is nothing new and is not special to Delhi only. Almost all the growing cities all over the world including India have faced this at one point of time or another. Throughout the world today, a majority of housing is built outside of any legislative or regulatory framework, either because it does not correspond to the planning permission granted or has been delivered without authorization or, as is most often the case, because housing has been built on somebody else's property, often on public land. Between 40 to 80 per cent of the urban population in India lives in housing that has no formal status, a situation shared by 30 to 40 per cent of the urban dwellers in Latin America.[10]

This peculiar dimension of urbanization has tremendous implications for the overall growth of the city and its habitat as a whole. It also led to emergence of different kinds of problems and challenges before policymakers and service delivery institutions including serious bearing on the interpersonal human relations in the city. We are going to touch some of these issues in the book.[11]

The emergence of unplanned structures in different parts of the city has led to the emergence of a different social set-up and subculture within the city, separate from the mainstream culture. This new social set-up within the city has promoted social imbalance for the inhabitants, promoting a culture of violence and deviance in day-to-day living.

DELHI METROPOLITAN AREA (CENTRAL NATIONAL CAPITAL REGION)

Delhi today has reached a stage where further horizontal expansion of the city is not possible. This has resulted in changes in the building architecture of the city, with multi-storey buildings and high-rises coming up at a very fast pace. Over-urbanization and stress on the existing structure and resource base of the city led to the concept of Delhi Metropolitan Area (DMA). The basic philosophy of the plan is to decongest overgrowing Delhi by spreading the population to nearby NCR towns. The concept of DMA was first conceptualized in the first Master Plan of Delhi (MPD) in the year 1962. According to MPD 1962, an area of 800 sq km comprising the entire area of Union Territory of Delhi and the ring towns of Loni and Ghaziabad in UP, Faridabad, Ballabhgarh, and Gurgaon of erstwhile Punjab, and Narela in Delhi constitute DMA. The basic objective behind this concept was to rationalize the growth of Delhi. The MPD also realized that the overall development of Delhi is closely linked with the development of these ring towns. The overall emphasis was also to distribute the urban population in an integrated manner in all the adjoining towns with a view to decongest the city and reduce the pressure and strain on Delhi.

The First NCR Plan (NCR 2001) defined DMA as an area comprising of controlled areas of contiguous towns of Ghaziabad and Noida in UP, Faridabad–Ballabhgarh complex, Gurgaon, Bahadurgarh, Kundli, and the extension of Delhi Ridge in Haryana. The NCR Plan 2001 recognized the long-term economic prospects of these adjoining towns with saturation in Delhi. The NCR Plan

2021, notified recently, aims to promote growth and balanced development of the NCR. The plan has used a different nomenclature for DMA. It is now called 'Central National Capital Region' (CNCR) which comprises of the notified controlled/development/regulated areas of the contiguous towns of Ghaziabad, Loni, Noida, Gurgaon, Manesar, Faridabad, Ballabhgarh, Bahadurgarh, Sonepat, Kundli, and the extension ridge in Haryana.

The interaction between Delhi and the adjoining towns within DMA has become more and more intensive and has also projected interdependence in various aspects. This concept has also been able to shift the focus of socio-economic activities from Delhi to other DMA towns due to extensive urbanization, globalization, and liberalization.

The concept of integrated development plan and strategy of ring towns around an expanding metropolitan city with a view to decongest and decentralize the economic activities from the core town is practiced in other parts of the world as well. There are a lot of examples in the world wherein sincere plans were visualized to develop settlements outside the metropolitan cities precisely due to factors like congestion of city centre/downtown areas, traffic and transportation problems, high rental values, prevalence of urban blight, etc. The concept of Garden city evolved in 1944 just after World War II in London under the guidance of Professor Patrick Abercrombie and F.J. Foreshaw was essentially to rebuild London after the War and relieve the over-increasing and intolerable overcrowding and congestion. Similar initiatives were also taken up in China and USA to redistribute the strain on core cities due to over-urbanization and liberalization of economic activities.

Every city has its own operational limitations in physically accommodating people within its jurisdictional limits. Every new entrant to the city needs two basic facilities: a place to live and means to survive. Historically, we have seen that 1962 onwards Delhi started experiencing the negative dimensions of urbanization in relation to basic infrastructural facilities. Thus, the basic purpose

TABLE 2.8   Number of Years Spent in DMA Towns Post-migration (in per cent)

Sl No	Name of the City/Town	0–5	6–10	11–15	16–20	21 and Above	Non-migrants	Total
1	Ghaziabad	20	30	34	12	2	2	100
2	Noida	8	32	22	28	4	6	100
3	Faridabad	4	10	22	24	14	26	100
4	Gurgaon	8	28	4	6	8	46	100
5	Bahadurgarh	12	16	10	18	12	32	100

of DMA towns and the concept of NCR Vision had twin objectives: first, to reduce the burden on the overgrowing city of Delhi and, second, to plan an integrated and harmonious development of the entire NCR.

The overall developmental strategy for the NCR towns in the logical process will arrest in-migration towards Delhi and simultaneously increase the pace of development in the satellite towns. The NCR Plan and integrated development of DMA towns has been able to ease pressure on Delhi and, in the process, has also accelerated the pace of growth and development in the DMA towns. This is evident from the pattern of migration and population growth in these towns.

A recent evaluation study of DMA towns by the Ministry of Urban Development (MUD) has revealed that the localities in DMA towns have seen a majority of respondents migrating during the period 1990–2000. In fact, in all the surveyed localities, a majority of the respondents in the cities of UP are migrants, while the cities of Haryana have less migrants as compared to Ghaziabad and Noida. The pattern of migration in these towns are shown in Table 2.8.

Table 2.8 reflects that about 46 per cent respondents in Gurgaon and 32 per cent respondents in Bahadurgarh are non-migrants. Ghaziabad and Noida are growing at a faster pace than their counterparts in Haryana. Table 2.8 clearly reflects that in Ghaziabad and Noida, 50 per cent and 40 per cent of the migrants respectively have settled down during the last ten years. On the other hand, in

TABLE **2.9**   Migration Pattern to DMA Towns from Other States (in per cent)

Sl No	Name of City/Town	Delhi	UP	Haryana	West Bengal	Uttarakhand	Punjab	Non-migrant	Other States	Total
1	Ghaziabad	48	34	0	0	0	6	0	10	100
2	Noida	66	18	0	0	2	4	6	4	100
3	Faridabad	6	26	12	4	2	12	26	12	100
4	Gurgaon	18	8	12	0	6	2	46	8	100
5	Bahadurgarh	22	8	32	0	0	2	32	4	100

Faridabad, Gurgaon, and Bahadurgarh, 14 per cent, 36 per cent, and 28 per cent of the migrants respectively have settled down during the same period. Out of these three towns, Gurgaon shows a better trend.

In conclusion, one can say that Gurgaon, Ghaziabad, and Noida have witnessed an unprecedented addition in terms of residential development, mostly in the form of group housing societies built by private developers, which in a way has helped in easing the pressure on housing in Delhi and that too at better, negotiable, and affordable prices as compared to NCT Delhi. A very significant feature of migration pattern of DMA towns reveals that the majority of migrants are from NCT Delhi (see Table 2.9).

From Table 2.9, the following conclusions can be drawn:

1. The maximum number of migrants from Delhi is in Noida (66 per cent). Noida is supposed to be the closest from the district boundaries of Delhi.

2. Among all the selected DMA towns, the minimum migration from Delhi is to Faridabad (6 per cent).

3. The migration pattern also shows the movement of people to DMA towns from adjoining states as well as the same state itself. Ghaziabad, Noida, and Faridabad have 34 per cent, 18 per cent, and 26 per cent migrants respectively hailing from Uttar Pradesh,

while Gurgaon and Bahadurgarh have 12 per cent and 32 per cent of respondents hailing from Haryana.

4. UP DMA towns have attracted more migrants as compared to Haryana.

5. The obvious reasons for migration to these DMA towns are:

    a. Availability of housing facilities at low prices.

    b. Proximity to NCT, Delhi.

    c. Strategic location of Noida and Ghaziabad.

    d. New work-related options and employment opportunities.

As a matter of fact, the over-urbanization and strain on the existing physical and infrastructural base of Delhi has proved to be a boon for the nearby DMA towns. The concept of planned development of the NCR has increased the social-economic and political importance of some of these DMA towns globally. A *Newsweek* report listed Ghaziabad among the ten most dynamic cities in the world. By virtue of becoming part of NCR, Ghaziabad, a small industrial town of Uttar Pradesh emerged as an upcoming industrial base, full of resources at relatively reasonable rates. Similarly, Gurgaon, a little known town of Guru Dronacharya, the teacher of the Pandavas and Kauravas, has earned the status of cyber city. Gurgaon has been able to attract foreign capital from various multinational companies and is home to the corporate offices of leading national and multinational companies like Maruti Udyog Limited (MUL), Hero Honda, Alcatel, IBM (International Business Machines), Siemens, and Bharti Telecom, among others. The city is developing at a faster pace than ever before. In a similar manner, the UP DMA towns of Noida and Greater Noida are also developing at an unprecedented scale. Out of all the DMA towns, Ghaziabad, Gurgaon, and Noida are actually competing with each other to woo the maximum number of national and international customers for investments in their respective areas. The latest to join the fray is Faridabad in Haryana. Like Delhi, these DMA towns are witnessing the possibilities of further expansion in both vertical and horizontal directions.

URBANIZATION AND CHANGING
DIMENSIONS OF POLICING

The growth of Delhi in the post-independence period added new dimensions to the working of the police, which were not included in the essential duties of police as discussed in Section 23 of IPA 1861. Apart from the normal prevention and detection of crime; maintenance of law and order, crime investigation, security of VIPs, and traffic control assumed importance in day-to-day policing activities. Urbanization of a city required simultaneous increase in other infrastructures like availability of housing, electricity, water, sanitation, as well as the creation of many more civic facilities for better living. The process also required an increase in the delivery mechanism and base of various formal institutions. The overall safety and security of citizens in the society became an important responsibility of the police. Delhi Police has been trying to cope with the increasing pace of urbanization in the city through expansion of the force and introduction of several specialized units. There has been an attempt to bring the expanding areas of an ever-growing Delhi under the ambit of regular policing through creation of more and more police stations and police districts. The limitations of policing and its operational constraints in meeting the requirements of an increasing city at a fast pace has been realized by the authorities from time to time. Special commissions and committees were constituted to understand these constraints and suggest measures regarding reorganization of the force so that it could meet the emerging challenges of policing like increase in crime, law and order, traffic, security of not only the ordinary citizens but also vital government installations and VIPs occupying different positions in the ruling hierarchy. The G.D. Khosla Commission Report and Srivastava Committee Report have done in-depth analysis of Delhi Police in the wake of urbanization and increasing challenges and constraints of policing. Apart from suggesting several immediate measures to improve the working of the police in the capital, they also identified certain concrete yardsticks for the future expansion of the force.

Let us understand these changes chronologically.

After Independence, Delhi territory was divided into Old Delhi, New Delhi, and rural Delhi, each under the in charge of an SP. However, Delhi was considered one district for the overall purpose of administration under the command of a single district magistrate (DM) for the whole territory, in tune with provisions of Section 10 of Code of Criminal Procedure. There were 18 police stations in Delhi in December 1951, which rose to 38 in November 1962. In the year 1965, there were three police districts—south, north, and central—for whole of Delhi. The actual breakup of different police stations in the three districts is given in Table 2.10. This table will give us a broad overview of the jurisdictional responsibilities of the various areas in Delhi and the way they have changed to different districts with overall expansion of the force over a period of time.

The perusal of Table 2.10 shows that initially many parts of present east district like Gandhi Nagar and Shahdara were under the administrative control of north district, and these areas gradually became part of the new east district. Similarly, areas like Tilak Nagar, Punjabi Bagh, Moti Nagar, Najafgarh, Nangloi, Narela, and Alipur, which were part of central district originally, got shifted to other districts with bifurcation.

In 1965, a commission was constituted under the chairmanship of Justice G.D. Khosla to undertake the reorganization of Delhi Police in the backdrop of growing population, crime, and other concerns of policing and agitational activities of Delhi policemen on issues related to housing, pay, and other working conditions. After a detailed interaction with various sections of the society to understand the prevailing situation, the commission suggested various measures for the improvement of policing in Delhi. The recommendations of the commission can be categorized into the following important heads:

TABLE **2.10**   Police District-wise Distribution of Police Stations in Delhi, 1965

North District	Central District	South District
	Darya Ganj	Parliament Street
Kotwali	Paharganj	Tughlak Road
Lahori Gate	Hauz Qazi	Chanakyapuri
Kashmere Gate	Kamla Market	Tilak Marg
Sadar Bazar	Jama Masjid	Mandir Marg
Roshanara	Karol Bagh	Rajinder Nagar
Sarai Rohilla	Original Road	Delhi Cantt
Civil Lines	Patel Nagar	Vinay Nagar
Subzimandi	Moti Nagar	Lodhi Colony
Kingsway Camp	Tilak Nagar	Hauz Khas
Shahdara	Punjabi Bagh	R.K. Puram
Gandhi Nagar	Najafgarh	Mehrauli
	Nangloi	Lajpat Nagar
	Narela	Nizamuddiun
	Alipur	Kotla Mubarakpur
		Kalkaji
		Shrinivas Puri

1. Change of policing from magistrate system to commissioner system.

2. Overall expansion of the police force—suggested creation of more districts.

3. Specialization in professional working—suggested creation of specialized units.

4. Increase in pay and allowances, housing, training, prosecution, recruitment, etc.

In pursuance of acceptance of several recommendations of the commission, another district was carved out from the south district and New Delhi was created. While recommending the expansion and reorganization of the districts, the commission took into account factors like area, population, crime, nature of population, nature of the area, nature of the police work and its special problems, as well as the staff under the Deputy Commissioner of Police (DCP) required to properly police an area. These factors have acted as the guiding principles for subsequent expansion of the force from time to time. The subsequent increase in the number of police stations from 1971 onwards are shown in Table 2.11.

The total number of police stations in Delhi today is 185. Apart from territorial police stations (166); Railway (5), Metro (8), and Airport (2), 4 specialized units of Delhi Police—Special Cell, Economic Offences Wing, Special Police Unit for Women and Children (SPUWC), and Crime Branch—have also got police stations.

For a better understanding, it is important to mention that each range is headed by an officer of the rank of Joint Commissioner of Police (JCP), and includes at least three districts under it. A district is headed by an officer of the rank of DCP, and each district is further divided into various subdivisions under the charge of an ACP-level officer who exercises control over 2–3 police stations. A police station is further divided into various beats for day-to-day policing, which is carried out by the head constables and constables.

TABLE 2.11   Year-wise Increase in the Number of Police Stations in Delhi

Year	Number of Police Stations
1971	45
1985	63
1985–7	75
1988–97	100
1998	115
1999–2006	116
2007	121
2008	133
2009	155
2010	166

The increasing urbanization of the city not only required effective police cover in the expanding settlements and colonies in various parts of the city, it also required special concern towards new dimensions of crime and criminal activities. This led to the creation of specialized units dealing with specific dimensions of the problem. Some of the important specialized units created over a period of time are as given below.

Crime Branch

The perusal of correspondence files of the home department during 1912–33 shows that the need for this agency was realized as far back as 1933. This is evident from the following remarks of the then Senior Superintendent of Police (SSP) in 1933:

> The necessity for creation of Central Investigating Agency is briefly that a small body of capable investigators is required for the investigation of cases with ramifications outside the district or province of cases committed by gangs operating in several jurisdictions and of complicated and lengthy cases for the investigation of which the ordinary Police Station staff has no time or the knowledge of conditions outside its own jurisdiction. Experience has shown that local knowledge and vigilance are not sufficient for dealing with the modern criminals who operate inter-provincially. The barriers of jurisdiction have to be broken down and information collected, coordinated and applied. This is essentially the function of a central Investigating Agency, which would not only investigate cases of the nature described above but would also maintain a modus operandi system of records of well known criminals, habitual offenders and criminal tribesmen.[12]

The crime branch further expanded in subsequent years, with separate sections for dealing with specialized crimes. For example, it has a homicide section dealing only with cases of murder. The unit has addressed itself to the changing nature of criminal activities in the city and created special cells to deal with them. The basic philosophy behind creation of this unit was to achieve excellence in investigation and concentrate on detection and apprehension of notorious criminal gangs. Since the unit is not preoccupied in dealing with mundane and routine law and order and other dimensions of active policing, it can devote more time to investigation and detection. This unit also coordinates issues related to other states on behalf of the force as a whole.

Economic Offences Wing

The rate of white collar crime started increasing after Independence. The economic liberalization and globalization of economic activities produced a sophisticated, suave, and intelligent category of offenders who specialized in economic frauds through different means. The developmental activities in Delhi and escalating land prices increased such activities in the capital. To deal with this kind of a sophisticated crime and criminals, the economic offences wing was carved out from the old crime branch in 1996. The economic offences wing of Delhi Police deals with all kinds of cheating and forgery-related crimes.

The workload of this unit has increased due to incidence of several cases related to cheating and forgery. The wing today has dedicated investigating teams under the supervision of ace investigators concentrating on various dimensions of new crimes. It has a dedicated wing to deal with cases related to intellectual property rights. All cyber-related cases are handled by this cell today. The unit has got functional autonomy in registration of cases and investigation through establishment of a separate police station. Earlier, the cases used to be registered by the officers in the respective jurisdictional police station where the offence is reported to have been committed. With its own police station the cell can register cases related to any area of Delhi and can investigate them. The unit is headed today by an officer of the rank of additional commissioner of police assisted by a DCP and several ACPs and inspectors.

Special Police Unit for Women and Child

This unit was started in 1984 initially as a special cell dealing with cases related to dowry deaths only. With increasing cases of marital disputes in the metropolis, the nomenclature of the cell was changed to Crime against Women Cell in 1995. Subsequent increase in juvenile delinquency in the city and implementation of various guidelines related to juveniles, increased the role of the police. As a result, the unit was reconstituted with a new nomenclature and became the nodal agency to different police stations for ensuring the implementation of various guidelines related to women and children. The unit has been organizing several self-defence camps in various schools and colleges for women and children to fight the menace of eve-teasing.

Delhi is predominantly characterized by nuclear families. The unit also acts as a mediation centre for such families. Various dowry-related harassment cases are handled by the officers of this unit on a daily basis. In many cases, they have successfully counselled and prevented marriages from breaking up. The unit has been making women and young girls self-sufficient and confident in handling day-to-day eve-teasing incidents at public places through self-defence camps organized in various girls' schools and colleges during the vacations.

Provisioning and Logistics Unit

An ever-increasing number of policemen and police stations needs additional logistics and other necessary infrastructural facilities at the workplace. To centralize the procurement of all such needs of the police stations and the force as a whole, a separate unit was created in 1971. This unit acts as warehouse for the whole force. This unit has been awarded ISO certification for its procurement.

Special Branch

Intelligence has been considered as an integral part of policing since time immemorial. This is a proactive method through which important pieces of information are collected by the field officers through their interaction with different stakeholders in the society. These inputs are collated and passed on to law enforcing agencies for proper action. Delhi Police has an elaborate set up with specialized wings devoted to different aspects having ramifications for law and order. The unit has a vast database regarding antecedents of persons with dubious backgrounds. All passport-related verifications are carried out by this unit. Officers detailed in this unit coordinate the movement of various political and religious processions taking place in the city on a day-to-day basis.

Special Cell

Originally, this cell was part of the special branch. The unit was created in 1989 and the basic responsibility of this cell is to coordinate all efforts related to anti-terrorism. The unit collates, interprets, and executes all information related to terrorism across the city through various proactive and reactive methods.

Narcotics and Crime Prevention Cell

In order to comply with the guidelines of United Nations Drug Control Programme (UNDCP) and to effectively tackle the menace of drug trafficking, a separate narcotics and crime prevention cell was created in 1994. In order to provide autonomy to the unit, a separate police station was notified under the branch to register cases directly.

Police Control Room

Delhi Police is commonly identified today with the telephone number 100. This is a phone number that is used by the rich and poor of the city in times of distress and crisis. The day-to-day monitoring of these calls is done by a unit known as police control room (PCR). This unit initially started as a flying squad in 1956. The unit has grown in number over a period of time. More than 666 PCR vans, stationed all across the city, rush to the scene of crime as soon as the call is made to 100. Apart from these mobile PCR vans, 10 vans are stationed at important tourist places. These mobile vans have been doing excellent work in the overall detection and prevention of crime in various parts of the city. The PCR received 17,99,250 calls in 2009 as compared to 14,59,277 calls in 2008. The number of calls has been increasing every year. These mobile vans also act as a common man's ambulance. In 2009, a total number of 50,765 injured persons were transported to hospitals by PCR vans. Out of these, 18,094 were road accident victims and the remaining 32,671 were victims of other incidents. Delhi is city which attracts a lot of national as well as international tourists. For the facilitation of tourists, separate vans are earmarked as tourist police vans and they are stationed at prominent tourist places, including the airport and railway stations. The unit has dedicated helplines for vulnerable sections of society like women, children, and students. In 2009, 2057 calls from students, 7646 calls from women, and 2708 calls were received by these helplines. Apart from initiating action on various calls received from the affected groups, these vans have also apprehended criminals during their day-and-night patrols. A total number of 1022 criminals, including dacoits, robbers, snatchers, and burglars were arrested by these vans stationed across the city. These vans provide a solid back up for the local police in their area and re-strengthen the existing resources detailed for prevention and detection of crime. The deployment of these vans is being done on the basis of analysis of crime in the area and their overall vulnerability. In the long run, these vans try to cover the existing gaps in the police population ratio. With the introduction of latest technology in different spheres of police work, the central police control room has been upgraded. A new automatic call distribution system, map projection, and liquid crystal display (LCD) panel with global positioning system (GPS) location and a GPS-based automatic vehicle tracking system has been introduced.

VIP Security Unit

The growing number of VIP-category people in the city over a period of time led to the creation of a separate unit dealing with the arrangements for these persons only. At present, the overall security unit has to deal with security bandobast of following categories of people:

1. Prime minister, ex-Prime Ministers, and other Special Protection Group (SPG) Protectees: Although the close proximate security of the PM and his family members in office and residence is looked after by an elite SPG created after the assassination of the Indira Gandhi, security at other public functions are handled by a special sub-unit created within the VIP security unit itself. The security at vice-president house and Rashtrapati Bhavan is managed by the personnel of Delhi Police on a 24x7 basis.

2. President, Vice-President of India: The overall responsibility for the security of the head of the state in this country lies with the Delhi Police. All public functions of both these protectees are coordinated and executed on ground throughout the city by a sub-unit of the VIP security unit.

3. Visiting Foreign Head of States (HOSs) and heads of governments (HOGs): Delhi, being the capital of the country, attracts a large number of HOGs and HOSs ever year in connection with bilateral negotiations with the Indian government. The entire

security arrangement from airport arrival, departure to places of their stay, etc. is handled by the members of this unit.

4. Cabinet Ministers, Members of Parliament, and Top Bureaucrats: The security of these protectees is provided on the basis of threat perceptions and positional requirements as per the security protocol outlined in various statute books meant for their security. It includes deployment of plainclothes security officers, armed guards at their residences, and deployment of pilot and escort vehicles. The number of persons falling in these category varies between 300–400.

5. Security of High Court and Supreme Court and other District Courts: Terrorist incidents in two courts in Varanasi forced the law enforcing agencies to review the existing state of security and enhance its scale. In the wake of these incidents and general vulnerability of various courts due to trials of sensitive nature of cases including terrorist related cases, their security was enhanced and the responsibility for management of High Court and Supreme Court was handed over to security wing of Delhi Police.

While plainclothes inner cordon security is provided by the members of this specialized unit, the outer cordon deployment on the route and around places of function is done by the local civil uniform police. The concern towards VIP security has increased manifold and has emerged as a challenging and daunting task for Delhi Police after the 9/11 terrorist attacks and the volatile situation in neighbouring countries. Constant preoccupation with security duties for some police stations in Delhi on a regular basis has affected other normal duties related to prevention and detection of crime.

Diplomatic Security Force

There are approximately 137 diplomatic establishments in Delhi. These establishments are concentrated mainly in New Delhi and south Delhi areas. As per the Vienna Convention on diplomatic relations signed in 1961, the responsibility of security of diplomatic missions and diplomats lies with the host country. In pursuance to this, the diplomatic security force was created in 1973 and was later on modified in 1975.

Traffic Police

Historically speaking, the management of traffic has been done by the available policemen in police stations. During the British era the traffic police duties were discharged by the regular watch and ward staff of the police station only. However this arrangement affected the overall police deployment meant for prevention and detection of crime in the city. The gradual increase in the volume of traffic forced the police authorities to go for a separate wing, the traffic police. The perusal of correspondence files of home department during 1912–33 shows that a separate traffic unit was created way back in the year 1925.

Like the growth in population, the number of vehicles has been increasing over a period of time in Delhi. Everyday, about 550 new vehicles are added to Delhi roads (or about 2800 each week). Out of total number of cars in the five mega cities, Delhi has almost half, to the tune of 46 per cent followed by Mumbai with 17 per cent. The increase in number of vehicles has led to several problems including road accidents, pollution, and congestion on the roads. In Delhi today, one traffic policeman is available for every 1105 vehicles. With the increasing pressure of traffic in the city, Delhi Police has been trying to diversify and specialize in its day-to-day area of operations. The traffic wing of the city is headed by an officer of the rank of Special Commissioner of Police (SCP). The entire traffic of the city is managed through creation of new traffic districts under the charge of a DCP-level officer.

Under the commissioner system, the day-to-day policing was also governed by a specially passed Delhi Police Act of 1978. The

Act empowered an average field police officer in Delhi to take care of day-to-day challenges of policing through relevant sections and provisions, otherwise not covered in other standard statute books. Several provisions of the Act were in tune with the challenges of policing in the wake of urbanization. Since Delhi has been historically part of Punjab Police, the field policing is also governed by Punjab Police Rules. Delhi has under gone tremendous changes since 1978 and has posed several new challenges before the police. These challenges required proper legal and institutional back up for effective handling. Keeping in tune with the changing times, the Delhi Police Act of 1978 required amendment, incorporating new provisions in the light of new challenges and problems of policing in the city. Accordingly, the Delhi Police Act has been amended. The final draft of Delhi Police Act, which has also undergone public debate, is likely to be passed by the Parliament soon. The new Act incorporates provisions and recommendations of various police commissions set from time to time. The Ministry of Home Affairs (MHA), Government of India, intends to make it a model police act so that it works as a reference point for other state police forces.

Through the discussion above, it is clear that Delhi Police has been increasing in numbers from time to time. The expansion of the force has not only been in the lower ranks but in the higher supervisory level officers as well. In 1951, the strength of Delhi Police was 8000 personnel—1 IGP, 8 SPs, 1 police radio officer, 1 ASP, 21 DSPs, 54 inspectors, 228 sub-inspectors, 1132 head constables, and 6202 constables—across three police districts (New Delhi, central, and south).[13] Two more police districts, namely east and west, were soon created. Subsequently, three more police districts, namely north-east, north-west, and south-west were created in 1998. Two more districts, outer and south-east, were created in September 2007 and October 2008, respectively, taking the number to 11 districts. The sanctioned strength of the force has gone up to 83,740.[14] Today, Delhi Police is the largest metropolitan police force in the world, larger than the police of London, New York, Tokyo, and Paris. We have also seen the creation of specialized units in the police to address emerging problems of policing, due to the rapid pace of urbanization and industrialization of the city, adequately and in a focused and systematic manner. The specialization and diversification of police working underwent fundamental changes with the introduction of two more inspectors in each city police station with specific responsibilities—inspector (investigations) and inspector (anti-terrorist operations) other than the SHO. The basic objective of the former is to achieve excellence in investigation of cases and secure conviction. The latter aims to focus on emerging dimensions of policing in the wake of terrorism. It will not be out of place to mention that both these changes are also in tune with the new challenges of policing and recommendations of various police commissions and committees.

3

DELHI

A Unique Metropolis

The geographical location of Delhi and its political importance has given the metropolis some unique and peculiar characteristics not to be found in other metros of the country. The uniqueness of Delhi is reflected not only in the socio-economic features of the city, but also in the unique dimensions of the law enforcement agencies and administration. The functioning of Delhi Police needs to be understood in the context of the unique and peculiar features of administration and social profile, as well as the way it has oriented and re-oriented itself in the day-to-day policing of the city. The peculiarities and unique characteristics of Delhi as a city have been recognized by various commissions associated with the reorganization of the administration and policing. The uniqueness of policing in Delhi was recognized by the Srivastava Committee constituted by Bureau of Police Research and Development (BPR&D) for reorganization of Delhi Police immediately after the assassination of Indira Gandhi in 1984. The committee observed: 'The environment within which the Delhi Police functions and the constraints to which it is subjected are unlike those in any other metropolitan city in India.'[1]

The unique character of the city emerges out of its historical growth over a period of time. While depicting the typical character of Delhi, the Khosla Commission observed:

Unfortunately, though Delhi is one of the oldest cities in India, unlike other cities like Bombay, Calcutta and Madras, it has no well defined personality. There was an old walled city of the Muslim emperors with villages around it. Then after mutiny, a new city grew up in the civil lines consisting mostly of the new administrators and those who flourished under the new administration. For the most part they were British or had come from Punjab. Then came New Delhi which became the new capital of the country with new multiple administrative complexes. Then came refugees, not only from West Pakistan but migrants from all parts of the country.[2]

Galbraith[3] classified cities into five main categories: the political household, the merchant city, the industrial city, the camp, and the polyglot metropolis. If we closely look at the historical growth of Delhi over the centuries, it is perhaps one of the few cities in the world which combines the characteristics of all the five categories of cities which Galbraith talks about. Its rich historicity with presence of magnificent monuments and its colonial past is manifested in boulevards, and the stately buildings of New Delhi reflect its rich political heritage. The typical katras and bazaars of Shahjahanabad reflect the characteristics of a merchant city. The existence of industrial features could be found right amidst the residential complexes and flow of toxic wastes and sewage in Najafgarh drain and Yamuna river. The existence of sprawling farmhouses in Mehrauli, Kapashera, Najafgarh, and Nangloi depict the camp characteristics of the city. The emergence and existence of multiplexes, shopping malls, and reflection of typical Western style of life represent the characteristics of a polyglot metropolis. The uniqueness of Delhi can be understood at three levels: social structure, administration, and policing.

THE URBAN PECULIARITIES OF DELHI

Urban sociologists have tried to understand the urban social fabric as different from other social formations on the basis of some peculiar urban characteristics specific to these societies. The most celebrated depiction of city life has been done by an American sociologist, Louis

Wirth. His classic article 'Urbanism as a way of life' first appeared in 1938 in the *American Journal of Sociology*. Wirth considered three concepts: size, density, and heterogeneity as key features of any city. It is on the basis of these three features that he differentiated between city life and others. Louis Wirth considered that the forms of social action and organization that often emerged in cities could be logically attributed to its unusual size, density, and heterogeneity. On the basis of these three features, Louis Wirth formulated the following propositions regarding city life:[4]

1. Growth and diversity are associated in the city with relatively weak bonds among co-residents. This is due to the fact that city dwellers have not lived together for generations under a common tradition like country dwellers.

2. As a town or a city grows, it becomes less likely that any resident will know all the others personally. This characteristic particularly refers to the nature and character of social relationships that exist in cities. The majority of a person's social contact in the city is likely to be impersonal, superficial, transitory, and segmental.

3. A highly developed division of labour is associated with the emphasis on the treatment of social relationship as means to ones' ends.

4. The elaborate division of labour grows as the market grows.

5. As the city grows, it becomes impossible to assemble all its residents in a single place. Due to this, increasing reliance is placed on indirect communication as a method of spreading information and opinions, and also meeting decisions.

6. As the density of population in an area increases, extensive differentiation and specialization tend to be the result.

7. Physical contexts in the city are close, whereas most social contexts are relatively superficial.

8. The city pattern of land use is the result of competition for a scarce resource. Those who can derive the greatest economic return from it, own the land.

9. The absence of close, sentimental, and emotional ties between co-workers, and between co-residents, fosters competition and mutual exploitation rather than cooperation.

10. The interaction of persons with very varied roles and personalities breaks down simple class distinctions.

11. City dwellers belong to a variety of groups and their loyalties to these groups often conflict.

12. The division of labour, combined with the emphasis on segmental relationship, exercises a levelling influence.

Although the features and characteristics discussed above were true for American societies (which were relatively more urbanized than the developing countries), they were not quite applicable to the urban set-up in India. Even the Western thinkers criticized Louis Wirth and expressed their apprehensions regarding these features. Indian sociologists have also tried to explain the peculiarities of urban and rural set-up with distinctive social characteristics. The famous sociologist, R.K. Mukherjee, argued that the differences between rural and urban areas reside mainly in the differences in their physical characteristics, density of population, utilization of land and habitation, economic organization, and the material amenities available to the people.[5] Urban societies in India present more an example of a continuum of two social and cultural streams rather than a dichotomy.

The social and cultural life of any city is shaped and influenced by the kind of people who live in the city. How a city has grown over a period of time also shapes the social and cultural fabric of the city. We have seen that various rulers have ruled Delhi. Every ruler left his imprint on the city. Foreigners from other cultures came as merchants, mercenaries, or as rulers with their vassals to the city. They brought with them their culture, customs, dress, religion, and social values. The cross-cultural interaction of various ethnic and social groups led to the emergence of a society with new sets of values, customs, and traditions, in which foreigners became indistinguishable from the local population over a period of time. This trend has continued and has further promoted the assimilation and integration of society through diverse cultural streams with new horizons of communication technology. The presence of the Mughals and British, who ruled Delhi for a long time, was responsible for the introduction of new customs, traditions, and values in the society, remnants of which can be seen even today.

The dominant culture of Delhi before Independence was the culture of Shahjahanabad. This was not true for Muslims only. This was accepted by all communities in Delhi as the epitome of all courtly grace. Khushwant Singh talks of this culture very vividly when he says:

> The whole area behind Jama Maszid up to Ajmeri Gate was where courtesans, dancers and singers lived. Hizras were found in Lal Kuan. Youngmen of upper classes were called Nawabs. They dressed like tops in little clothe caps and chicken Kurtas. They learned manners from certain families of courtesans. It was a cultural life of mushairas and mujras in the evening.[6]

Shahjahanabad culture influenced even the British for a long time. In the late seventeenth and eighteenth century, the British adopted much of the old Mughal lifestyle and attire. However, once the British society was well established in the city and the numbers of Britishers increased, they started distancing themselves from the masses to establish their own credentials as a ruling class, different from the rest of the masses. The presence of the British started influencing the culture and lifestyle of people in the city. By the early decades of the twentieth century, the upwardly mobile middle classes in Delhi began to adopt anglicized modes of behaviour to indicate their modernity and progress, and identify more closely with the ruling establishment.[7]

Delhi's Kayastha community has historically been part of the ruling establishment since the Mughal era. Raja Raghunath Das, for instance, was *wazir* to the emperors Shahjahan Aurangabad and lived in a haveli in Shahjahanabad's Chelpuri Mohallah. The Mathurs were an eminent Delhi Kayastha family with many branches. There were six or seven leading cultural families in Delhi. Sri Rams and Pandits were also among them.

However the post-Independence cultural and social life of Delhi underwent dynamic changes with the Partition and arrival of refugees. The arrival of the refugees was responsible for several changes in the city in the post-Independence period. Very soon, they became the dynamic driving-force behind the enormous transformation of Delhi from its stolid imperial identity of 1947, to the brimming, prosperous, and ferocious city of multiple universes that it is today.[8] After Independence, the city started attracting more and more people from outside, making it a city of migrants over a period of time. There are so many cultures in Delhi today. The migrant communities added new dimensions to the already existing heterogeneous culture, making it truly metropolitan in character.

Delhi as a metropolis has peculiar sociological characteristics that are not very common to other metros. Some of this uniqueness can be characterized as:

1. Despite the fact that Delhi has assumed the status of a growing metropolitan city, it has not completely got rid of the rural population. As we have seen historically, Delhi used to be a city full of villages. The gradual urbanization and horizontal expansion of the city started swallowing up these villages and led to the emergence of new townships. Even today, as per the Census of 2001, there are more than 164 villages located in different parts of the city. At this point of time, a distinction also needs to be made between urbanized villages and other rural segments. Urbanized villages are situated very much within the heart of cities in many localities. Due to their proximity and exposure to the typical urban way of life, these villages are very much part of the existing core city, which is situated around it. However, one finds distinctive differences in the way of life, culture, and attire of the core urban set-up and the urbanized village. Although the villagers have adopted the Western style of life, one

finds difference in their pattern of family and economic occupation. Since they have been living in the villages for ages, the predominant family pattern is that of a joint family and people from two or three generations stay together under one roof. The villagers have different economic activities. The most common source of livelihood in the urbanized village is income through rent. Due to escalating rate of land prices in Delhi, village landlords have constructed multi-storey complexes and given it out on rent to reputed showrooms and individual tenents. The presence of showrooms of Adidas, Nike, and other garment and apparel brands is a common feature in urbanized villages like Shahpur Jat, Haus Khas village, and Kotla Mubarakpur. Several enterprising landlords in the villages of south and south-west districts have become millionaires overnight by selling their land and building premises. However, this may not be true for all the villages of the same nature. The most important thing is the location of the village and the typical core city around it. These urbanized villages also act as a support base for various services to the posh urban localities around it, since domestic help and other service providers stay at cheap accommodations available in these urbanized villages.

Another significant characteristic of the rural set up is the community life. Presence of joint family norms in the rural fabric, community feeling, and dependence and existence of healthy neighbourhood relationships are very visible in the outlying villages. Mobilization of caste/community *panchayats* on specific issues in the capital is the proof of a strong community life. Professor Yogendra Singh[9] has rightly said that cities in India continue to be dominated by the cultural and structural attributes which are far different from those which are considered to be typical for a city, for example, formalization, atomization, lack of familism and kin-bound groupings, predominance of secular ideologies, etc. R. Ramachandran[10] says that rural-urban migration has generated a parallel society in urban areas, in which the *varna* and *jati* systems are perpetuated. He further observes that both the rich and poor from rural areas who migrate to the city use family and social links to establish themselves there. In the city, people congregate in dwellings on the basis of family, village, and jati relationships. In a way, the city, instead of contributing to the loosening of family and jati affiliations, often tends to increase them further.

These observations of Professor Singh and Ramachandran stand corroborated through several other urban studies that have projected the limitations of a typical rural-urban dichotomy in the Indian context. However, the continuous exposure of the younger generation to the Western style of living and consumerism has undermined the traditional role of institutions like the family over a period of time and, particularly, the influence of the elders in the family is waning away. This has led to deviance and criminality, particularly among the unemployed youth in the urbanized villages and other rural segments.

2. Delhi is truly a multi-ethnic and multi-lingual society without exclusive claim of any native. Delhi can be called a city of migrants who have contributed to the overall socio-economic development and prosperity of the city.

3. The profile of rural areas in Delhi is different from the rural areas of any other part of the country. Unlike other rural segments in the country, the average per capita income and overall standard of villagers in Delhi are better. It is precisely because of these reasons that every subsequent census in Delhi has eliminated the villages from the category of typical village and included it in the category of census towns. This logically explains the increase in the number of census towns in every census and the decrease in the number of villages. The day is not far, when practically all the villages will logically come under the category of census towns in Delhi.

4. As compared to a slightly more cohesive and community-based living in the peripheral areas, the pattern of life, culture, and standard of living in core living establishments and posh localities are characterized by individualistic, ego-centric, and anonymous lifestyles. In these areas, neighbours also exist as strangers. If we

look at the physical growth and social life of Delhi over a period of time, it was more compact and cohesive earlier.

This aspect of social and cultural life of Delhi figured very prominently in the poems and *nazams* of the famous Urdu poets. For example, a very famous Urdu poet, Mir, once wrote about Delhi:

Dilli ke na the kooche, aurak-e-musavir the.
Jo shakl nazar aayi, tasveer nazar aayi.

Over a period of time, the same Delhi which Mir described as very simple and homogenous in nature, took a shape and size in its personal and human relations that has been well described in following lines of another Urdu poet, Bashir Badr:

Koi hath bhi na milayega,
Jo gale miloge tapaqq se,
Yeh naye mizaz ka shahar hai
Zara fasle se mila karo

The urban anonymity of the city has also been aptly described in the following lines of Dushyant Kumar, a Hindi poet:

Is shahar mein woh koi baraat ho ya vardat
Ab kisi bhi baat per khulti nahin hain khirkiyan.

THE ADMINISTRATION OF DELHI

The administrative set-up of Delhi has been changing with the change in the set-up of various rulers. The British established their rule in Delhi in 1805 with the operation of general regulations made by the British under the charge of the resident and the chief commissioner of Delhi. The system continued with slight modifications till 1857. In the year 1858, the British made Delhi a provincial town of the Frontier Province and later transferred it to the newly formed Punjab Province under a lieutenant governor. Delhi continued to be administered directly by the Government of India through a chief commissioner till 1950.

The shifting of the capital from Calcutta to Delhi led to the formation of a separate committee known as the Imperial Delhi Committee on 25 March 1913. The basic objective of the committee was to oversee the management of civic affairs of the new capital. In the year 1916, it was notified as the Raisina Municipal Committee under the Punjab Municipal Act 1911, primarily to meet the sanitary needs of the workers engaged in the construction of the capital. On 16 March 1927 it was re-designated as New Delhi Municipal Committee. In 1932, it was upgraded to the status of a first-class municipality entrusted with the responsibility of providing civic services.

Later on, a committee chaired by Dr B. Pattabhi Sita Rammaiya was set up on 31 July 1947 to study and report on constitutional changes in the administrative structure of the chief commissioner's provinces, which also included Delhi. It is on the report of the committee that the Constituent Assembly agreed to incorporate Article 239 and 240 in the Constitution to allow Part-C states, functioning through a chief commissioner or lieutenant governor. Delhi became a Part-C state in 1951 with a council of ministers and a legislature.

In 1953, the States Reorganization Commission recommended that Delhi and the national capital must remain under the effective control of the national government. It also suggested formation of Municipal Corporation of Delhi (MCD). As a result, the council of ministers and the Legislative Assembly of Delhi ceased to exist from 1 November 1956. Delhi, now a union territory, was administered thereafter by the President of India through a chief commissioner appointed under Article 239 till the Delhi Administration Act of 1966 came into force.

The Delhi Administration Act of 1966 (No. 19 of 1966) was enacted by the Parliament to provide for limited representative government for Delhi with the creation of a metropolitan council comprising of 56 elected and 5 nominated members. The President also constituted an executive council and appointed four executive councillors and the chief executive councillor.

The administrative set up of Delhi further underwent changes through the 69th Constitutional Amendment and the insertion of Article 239AA. This led to the enactment of Government of National Capital Territory of Delhi Act 1991. This Act came into force in January 1992. This Act provided Delhi a legislative assembly and a council of ministers to aid and advice the lieutenant governor. The President appoints the chief minister and other ministers on the advice of the chief minister. The Act provides for a 70 member legislative assembly with powers to make laws on matters contained in the state and concurrent lists applicable to union territories, except for those relating to public order, police, and land. The overall developmental activity in different parts of Delhi is carried out by three different civic agencies independent of each other: New Delhi Municipal Committee (NDMC), Municipal Corporation of Delhi (MCD), and Delhi Cantonment Board (DCB). Delhi Police has to coordinate its day-to-day functioning with all the three agencies.

The chronological administrative developments of Delhi reveal the unique features of the city, which are not common to other metros in the country. This uniqueness has a lot of bearing on the overall development of the city and policing.

PECULIAR RESPONSIBILITIES OF POLICING

Like any other police force in the world, Delhi Police has to evolve and shape itself in tune with the overall growth of the city, needs of the citizens, and other challenges of urbanization. We have already seen how, from time to time, the Delhi Police set-up underwent changes. Till 1978, Delhi Police had been governed and was performing various police-related duties under the magistrate system, in which the overall command of policing remained initially with the chief commissioner, and later the DM.

In pursuance of the Khosla Commission Report, commissionerate system of policing was introduced in Delhi on 1 July 1978. It is important to mention that commissionerate system of policing was introduced by the British more than hundred years ago in Calcutta, and some years later in Bombay and Madras. It was gradually extended to some other parts of country. Under the new system, some of the powers vested in the office of the DM were transferred to the commissioner of police as far as maintenance of law and order and crime control were concerned. The new system led to the end of dual authority on vital issues of law and order and governance in day-to-day policing.

The status of Delhi in terms of administrative set-up is peculiar as compared to other states and union territories. Some of these peculiarities can be summarized as:

1. The state has an elected government with a chief minister and a council of minister to aid and advice the lieutenant governor who is also the administrator. The bureaucratic set-up in the city is managed by officers of joint state and union territory cadre officers. The administrative control over the Delhi Police is with the central government. The transfer and posting of the officers within Delhi is done by the administrator, while postings outside Delhi are done by the MHA, Government of India. The overall maintenance of law and order in Delhi remains with the central government, thereby bringing the police machinery under the administrative control and command of the central government. The ambiguous character of Delhi as a state where certain departments are managed by the state, while others are under the administrative and operational control of the central government, does lead to operational constraints on the overall working of these organizations at times. The National Capital Territory Act of 1991 provides for a 70-member legislative assembly to make laws on matters contained in the state and concurrent list. The operational problems were aptly summarized by Srivastava Committee in the following words:

A fast growing urban metropolis like Delhi poses problems for any system of its governance and these have not been eased by the presence of multiplicity of authorities which have a say in the administration of the Union Territory of Delhi. There are three large civic authorities: Delhi Development Authority, which is responsible for the overall planning and development of the Union Territory, the Delhi Municipal Corporation which has jurisdiction over entire union territory including the rural areas and the New Delhi Municipal Corporation which only looks after an area of 42.7 sq. km in New Delhi. Despite the best intentions and will the presence of such a large number of administrative authorities overseeing various aspects of the administration of the city creates situations of conflict, mixing of priorities and delays in decision making.[11]

Delhi Police has to perform its day-to-day duties in close cooperation with these multiple civic bodies.

2. Another significant feature of Delhi is its importance as national capital. Delhi is not only the seat of political power of the state, the entire infrastructural and organizational set of central government machinery is based in Delhi. This is evident from the presence of Rashtrapati Bhavan, Parliament House, Supreme Court, Prime Minister's Office (PMO) and residence, and central government ministries in North and South Block. Delhi police has to provide adequate security cover to these premises in cooperation with the other sister agencies. Although the access control of some of these complexes remains with various paramilitary forces, the overall maintenance of law and order is with the Delhi Police.

3. Being the national capital, Delhi also accommodates the offices and residential complexes of various foreign embassies and high commissions (169 in number). Apart from these establishments, the headquarters and regional offices of various international organizations and bodies are also situated in Delhi. Delhi Police has planned special security schemes for these premises and integrated them with their overall area policing duties. The city is also preferred venue for several national and international conferences. The law and order and traffic management around the venues is carried out by the local police.

4. The Parliament in Delhi meets for nearly 6 months in a year in prolonged sessions, posing additional special responsibilities on the police. During parliament sessions, a lot of movement of the prime minister and other protected persons takes place to Parliament House. Delhi Police has to make elaborate security arrangements on the routes as well as around the venue from overall law and order and security point of view.

5. Being the seat of power, Delhi attracts protest marches and rallies by various political parties on a regular basis. The number of such processions and rallies increase during parliament sessions. The number of persons in these rallies varies from 5000 to 1,00,000. The police have to give permission and handle several political rallies at a time any given day and this has tremendous implications for law and order. The total number of rallies and demonstrations handled by Delhi Police during 2009 are shown in Table 3.1. These law and order arrangements require massive mobilization of manpower and other logistics for foolproof security arrangements.

6. Every year from November to March, the city is visited by several foreign HoSs and HoGs. These protectees arrive in the capital for state visits as well as for bilateral talks with the Indian prime minister, President, other government ministers and officials. The security-cum-law and order arrangement for all these VIPs is made by the Delhi Police. These arrangements include deployment en-route from the airport to the place of stay and different venues for bilateral talks. Arrangements for these events require massive mobilization of manpower and diversion of resources meant for

TABLE 3.1 Total Number of Demonstrations, Rallies, and Dharnas in 2009

Demonstrations	1649
Rallies	246
Dharnas/Strikes	3539

Source: *Annual Review*, 2009.

other aspects of regular policing. Handling of VIP arrangements by Delhi Police has become a very important aspect of policing, unlike other police forces. Delhi Police personnel have acquired professional competence in handling such situations. The sensitivity of these locations and activities are so important that even a minor lapse on part of the law enforcement agency has wide national and international ramifications. Delhi Police handled as many as 1517 such arrangements in the year 2009 flawlessly.

7. People owing allegiance and faith in different religions celebrate festivals throughout the year in Delhi. Many religious processions are taken out as per historical and religious traditions on different occasions. Several such processions pass through communally sensitive areas having implications for law and order. I would like to cite here an example of a Ramlila procession taken out during Dussehra celebrations every year from the walled city of old Delhi for ten days up to Ramlila Maidan. The procession is escorted by a sufficient number of policemen every year. On the last day of Dussehra, the function is attended by the prime minister and other VIPs at three important locations in the walled city. This practice has continued since the time of Jawaharlal Nehru, the first prime minister of the country. I had the privilege of supervising four such functions. The execution of a successful security arrangement on such occasions, particularly in an area which is communally very sensitive, has always been a daunting task for the Delhi Police. This has continued for years without any problem. Religious processions are very common in other parts of the city where members of different communities live together side-by-side.

Apart from these processions, several fairs are also held during the festival season in Delhi all across the city. These fairs attract a large crowd. On a regular basis, Delhi Police has been managing these processions, fairs, and festivals peacefully without disturbing the peace of the area. However, due to increasing terror incidents and volatile situations in neighbouring countries, such gatherings remain very vulnerable. In 2009, 737 fairs and festivals and 1320 processions held throughout Delhi were handled by the Delhi Police.

8. Apart from handling city religious functions, Delhi Police is preoccupied every year, almost for a month, with mass movement of *Kanwariyas* (devotees of Shiva) who travel from Haridwar in Uttarakhand and come up to Delhi in the months of July-August on foot. Most of the devotees travel on one stretch of the road. Even one minor incident with any kanwariya has the potential to disrupt the law and order situation in other parts of Delhi, irrespective of the fact whether the incident occurred in UP, Uttarakhand, or Delhi. On several occasions, the devotees have indulged in vandalism and blocked traffic on the roads for hours. During the Shrawan month, several facilitation and welcome camps are set-up along roadside by different religious and philanthropic organizations with provision for food and overnight stay. Due to large-scale gathering and religious sensitivity, the local police of the respective districts—particularly north-east, east, north, central, south and south-east districts— remain preoccupied with security and law and order arrangements.

9. Unlike other state capitals where Republic Day celebrations are more local in nature and attended by governors and chief ministers, the Republic Day function in Delhi is a big event that is organized at Rajpath in open lawns every year. The function is not only attended by the prime minister, president, cabinet ministers, diplomats, constitutional heads, judges of Supreme Court and High Court, but also by a foreign head of government/state, who is also the chief guest. Apart from the presence of such a large number of VIPs at one place, the celebrations are also witnessed by around 15,000–20,000 people sitting across north and south of Rajpath in various enclosures. The function continues for more than an hour. Being held in an open area with the presence of so many VIPs and public at one place, the function poses additional responsibilities for the police. The security sensitivity of such functions has increased every year. Such a huge gathering is always on the terror radar.

On a slightly smaller scale every year, the prime minister of India unfurls the national flag from the ramparts of the Red Fort on 15 August. This function is also attended by the entire cabinet, and other Indian and foreign VIPs. The security sensitivity of this function is more because of its proximity to more densely populated areas of erstwhile Shahjahanabad. Very few police forces in the country, as well as abroad, handle such law and order arrangements which have tremendous security implications on a regular basis. Delhi Police has been handling such functions regularly since Independence with professional competence.

10. Increasing westernization, modernization, globalization, and consumerism has led to the emergence of many multi-storey shopping complexes which house movie theatres and outer outlets in Delhi. Earlier, such complexes used to be few and far between. Over a period of time, the number of such complexes has increased manifold. These complexes attract huge crowds on a regular basis, particularly on holidays. They all remain high on terror alert as a general target. The overall security in and around these complexes is supervised by the local police of the area.

11. The Delhi Metro Rail Corporation (DMRC) has redefined the whole transportation system in Delhi. It has been able to ease the pressure of vehicular traffic on the roads. Today, lots of people prefer the metros over other means of transport. It has provided a new dimension to the overall transport system in the city. Apart from easing pressure on the traffic, the metro has also redefined the concept of leisure and entertainment. The presence of several malls and shopping complexes in the inner and outer periphery of the metro stations attracts large crowds. Security of these places has become a huge concern for the local police.

12. Unlike other metropolitan cities, Delhi faces a serious problem of a floating population. It is estimated that every day about a million people enter Delhi for regular and odd jobs, business, and commerce. While the affluent sections of the floating population

commuting to Delhi for business purposes are victims of crime in the city, it also contains small time petty criminals who escape the city very conveniently after committing crimes.

13. Unlike other police forces in the country where the constabulary and the sub-inspectors are recruited locally, Delhi Police recruits its constable and sub-inspectors from different parts of the country. Constables serving in Delhi Police hail from as close as Gurgaon in Haryana to as far as Port Blair in the Andaman and Nicobar islands. This heterogeneous character of the force merges with the multi-ethnic and cultural pattern of the city as a whole.

14. Delhi is geographically very close to UP and Haryana. Various parts of Delhi are so closely linked with their neighbouring states that they appear to be in continuity. The horizontal expansion of the city has practically blurred the geographical boundaries. The policing and crime scenario in Delhi is greatly affected by the NCR towns. In other words, they act as a criminal hinterland for Delhi. The rapid development of Delhi in comparison with other NCR towns has attracted criminals from neighbouring towns over a period of time. This was also observed by the Srivastava Committee:

> The constant and daily movement of a large number of people across Delhi borders and to and fro from the adjoining states of UP and Haryana also as neighbouring states, imposes a heavy burden on its administrative and civic services and creates special problems for law enforcement machinery.[12]

The open borders provide very easy escape routes for criminals who operate in Delhi. The surveillance of bad characters, apprehension of criminals, and investigation of offences committed by them is difficult and time-consuming since the administrative system and procedures in the neighbouring states are different from that of Delhi. The overall crime scenario in Delhi, particularly in the south, outer, south-west, west, east and north-east districts is very much affected by the criminal activities and trans-border movement of criminals. (This aspect will be discussed in the following chapters.)

15. The historical development of the city has shown that Delhi is one of the most unplanned cities in India. Several buildings and unauthorized structures have come up on government land. Unauthorized 'colonizers' have encroached upon precious government land over a period of time and built permanent structures. Beautification drives and restoration of encroached land to the original land-owning agency requires removal of these structures. The way the city has grown, every other day the local police is engaged in providing security cover to a demolition squad in one part of the city or the other. At several places, where no alternative place has been provided to the encroacher, the operations have turned violent and kept the police occupied for days.

16. Often the law and order of the city gets influenced, to a large extent, by major socio-political developments in other parts of the country. For example, the Gujjar agitation in Rajasthan over reservation has affected the law and order situation in the city on several occasions due to presence of a sizeable population of members of this community in Delhi. Similarly, the recent mobilization of the Jat community on the reservation issue and the same-gotra marriage issue has posed additional problems and affected day-to-day policing.

17. The day-to-day policing responsibilities of Delhi Police is carried out with close cooperation and coordination of various civil agencies and central paramilitary forces. Unlike other states where the interaction of the local police with the central paramilitary forces is occasional, Delhi Police performs various law and order duties in conjunction with these forces on a regular basis.

In conclusion, it will be clear that the above description of the special and unique dimensions of policing duties in the city of Delhi reflect the changing nature of its problems, the challenges they have posed before the police, and how they have affected the latter's day-to-day working. It also shows that the basic job of the police in Delhi is not only to apprehend the criminals and prosecute them.

Policing in Delhi also means that the traffic on the road moves without any problem and the VIPs get adequate cover during their movement in the city. To ensure that a metro station or a crowded market in any part of the city does not witness any terrorist incident also assumes equal importance for the Delhi Police. All these and many more miscellaneous duties are performed by the Delhi Police in coordination with multiple authorities. Let us remember that these duties are part of regular policing on daily basis. Very few police forces in the country are confronted with such a vast and wide range of typical policing and non-policing responsibilities in day-to-day working as are experienced by the Delhi Police.

4

CRIME IN DELHI

To measure the extent of crime in any city, the most important methodology to rely on is statistics prepared by law enforcing agencies in quantified terms. This is done by dividing them under various heads of offences under existing criminal laws and acts of the land. This is the practice followed the world over for analysing crime. At this point of time, the distinction between cognizable and non-cognizable crime is very important for the actual appreciation of the crime scenario in Delhi. Cognizable crimes are those offences in which the police is legally bound to register a case, investigate, prosecute the criminal, and take the case to its logical end. Non-cognizable cases are the ones in which even if the matter can be reported to the police, the latter is not bound to carry out an investigation and prosecute the offender as per law, without the orders of a magistrate. However, the police have to investigate non-cognizable cases once ordered by the magistrate of any court.

All cognizable offences are classified under various heads and under proper sections, as per the provisions of the Indian Penal Code (IPC). The IPC classifies and defines the basic ingredients of a particular crime. For example, A inflicting injury voluntarily with a knife to B is a cognizable offence. On the other hand if, while walking, I lose my wallet, it is a non-cognizable offence. The basic philosophy in a cognizable offence case is the presence of an accused/ offender who is clearly identified, can be prosecuted, and awarded punishment as per law. However, in several cases of a non-cognizable nature, the actual identity of the accused may not be known. There are almost 511 offences termed as cognizable as per the provisions of the IPC, starting from murder—a serious crime—to simple cheating and counterfeiting of currency. The IPC came into existence during the British rule. Criminal activities have been increasing with urbanization and other processes of social change. Over a period of time, several amendments have been made to the IPC to include new types of crimes which affect the overall order in society.

The analysis of crime in Delhi in this chapter has been done under these broad parameters. The first section deals with the general crime trend from 1912–94. The analysis has been done on the basis of crimes registered on a decade-wise basis. While analysing crime, the focus has been more on violent crimes like murder, robbery, and dacoity. The second section covers the crime scenario in various police districts in Delhi and a comprehensive analysis of the crime scenario of each district in the period, 1995–2006, has been undertaken with special reference to the peculiarities of crime and other crimogenic factors. An attempt has been made to highlight the general trends with the help of the total number of criminal cases registered under various sections of the IPC. The heterogeneous social, economic, and political character of Delhi is also reflected in the nature of criminal activities in different parts of the city.

GENERAL CRIME SCENARION IN DELHI: 1912–94

1912 to 1950[1]

The beginning and closing dates of this period are very important. In the year 1912, the capital was shifted to New Delhi, and the city was separated from neighbouring provinces. Logically, a different type of policing began, and with it, a different compilation of official records. Prior to this, crime figures also included figures of nearby towns/ villages. Again, the year 1950 marks a very crucial period when India got Independence in the backdrop of rioting and migration on a mass scale, beginning in 1947, which affected the growth of the city and changed the pattern of crimes as well. On the basis of crime figures available for this period, a few broad conclusions regarding the crime scenario emerge:

1. The increase in crime from 1912 to 1940 was very gradual. Keeping in mind the decadal gap in each period, the increase in crime up to 1940 is not very significant.

2. A common feature for crime figures up to 1950, is the absence of any crime under the category of rape, snatching, hurt, motor vehicle theft, criminal breach of trust, and even road accidents.

3. In the entire period up to 1940, cases under dacoity, murder, attempt to murder, robbery, riot, burglary, total theft, and arson show a gradual increasing trend.

As compared to previous decades, the period from 1940 to 1950 shows a phenomenal increase in crime under different heads. This is the period which also includes the Partition in 1947. As we all know, the Partition of the country was followed by large-scale rioting, arson, etc. Crime under the heads of murder, attempt to murder, riot, burglary, and total theft also show phenomenal increase. As a matter of fact, figures under these heads are much more than crime figures for the preceding thirty years. As compared to the previous decades, the figures for 1950 shows a two times increase in murder, four times increase in attempt to murder, two times increase in robbery. three times increase in rioting, while figures under total theft show an increase of more than three times. However, the increase in crime during this period needs to be understood in the backdrop of the post-Independence riots and, thus, cannot be considered as a general indicator of crime in the city.

4. If we look at the figures for the total IPC offences under various sections for 1940–50, it is 8563 as compared to 3261 for the previous 10 years. The figures for 1940–50 are also much higher than the entire crime figures from 1912 to 1940.

1951 to 1963

This period shows yearly increase under various heads. While dacoity has been constant, except a marginal increase in the years 1956 and 1960, crimes under every head increased, with a few exceptions. However, total IPC cases have shown a consistent increase every year. The total number of IPC cases during 1953 was 7625; these almost doubled and became 14,445 in the year 1963. A trend evident during this period is the absence of any case under important heads such as rape, snatching, hurt, and motor vehicle theft. But these three heads have started contributing to the overall IPC crime from 1960 onwards when a total number of 33 cases were registered under rape, three under snatching, and 485 under hurt in the year 1960 itself.

The gradual increase in crime can be logically linked to the gradual increase in the population, including the migrant population which came after Partition. The new developmental paradigm of the city and rapid urbanization resulted in ample job opportunities and the process started attracting more and more people, not only from nearby towns but also from different states.

1964 to 1974

This decade has shown an increasing trend under every head, including rape, snatching, hurt, and motor vehicle theft. Under the category of serious crimes, dacoity has shown the highest ever increase in the years 1970 and 1974, with a total number of 29 and

30 cases, respectively. Similarly, murder has also shown a consistent increase in every year, starting from 59 cases in 1964 to 173 cases in 1974. The total IPC cases rose from 17,172 in 1964 to 33,825 in 1974.

A significant departure in crime figures for the entire period up to 1974 is the registration of cases under various local and special laws like Arms Act, Gambling Act, and Excise Act, etc. From 1912 onwards till 1959, no cases were registered under these heads.

1975 to 1985

The perusal of figures for this period shows the same increasing trend of crime under different heads. The total IPC cases registered in 1975 was 28,571, which rose to 30,773 in 1984. The most striking figures for crime under different heads was in the year 1984. This year showed an increase under every head when compared to previous years. Under certain categories of crime, the figures doubled—under dacoity, 30 cases were committed in 1984, as compared to 15 in the previous year.

Apart from other factors, the increasing trend of crime during this period, particularly in 1984, was due to mass-scale rioting, arson, and looting in Delhi after the assassination of Indira Gandhi, the then prime minister of India. The riots which took place immediately after her death led to large-scale violence in different parts of Delhi.

1985 to 1994

A perusal of figures for this decade shows an increasing trend in crime with minor fluctuations under different heads in different years. The total IPC cases registered in 1985 was 33,412, which rose to 38,233 in 1994. The increase in crime in this decade needs to be understood in the context of significant changes in the overall profile of the city.

The increase in the population during this period in the city is, perhaps, the most significant as far as the increasing rate of crime is concerned. The population of Delhi was 70 lakh in 1984; it rose to one billion and four lakh in 1994. The increase in the number of people in the city also led to an increase in the number of vehicles, posing problems of traffic management. The unavailability of proper living space for the increasing population arriving in the city from different parts of the country also saw problems of squatting and unauthorized encroachment of available government space in an unplanned manner. Moreover, JJ clusters and slums came up in and around affluent residential complexes. All these developments in the profile of the city had tremendous implications in different dimensions of policing, and contributed to an increase in crime. It is also important to mention here that there was no proportionate increase in manpower and other resources of the police force to cope with these problems. The shortage of manpower and resources of the Delhi Police emerged as a major handicap in its response to the large-scale riots in 1984.

DISTRICT-WISE CRIME FIGURES: 1995–2006

Between 1995 and 2006, the city witnessed an unprecedented level of urbanization. It had indeed assumed a very huge shape and size. Delhi now comes in the category of megacities, as per the classification of the National Crime Records Bureau (NCRB). Any city having a population of more than 10 lakh (one million) is classified as a mega city.

In order to understand the overall crime scenario during this period in Delhi, it is better to go through the crime figures of different districts, police station-wise, by analysis of important heads of crime.

At present, there are eleven police districts in Delhi. Two districts—outer and south-east—were carved out of the north-west and south districts, respectively, in 2008.

For the sake of better understanding and convenience, the figures only include total IPC cases, and cases registered under local and special laws—in the districts. District-wise crime figures may be seen in Appendices 4.1b and 4.1c.[2]

South District

According to the 2001 census, the total population of the district is 22,67,023. The density of population in the district is 9068 persons per sq km. The decadal growth of population (1991–2001) is 50.27 per cent, the second highest after north district. The district is a mixture of rural and urban population. In fact, it has sixteen villages. All the villages are inhabited and equipped with basic amenities and infrastructural facilities. There are three important religious groups in the district; Hindus constitute the majority, followed by Muslims and Sikhs. The population of scheduled tribes is nil, while the scheduled castes constitute 15.63 per cent of the total population.

From a sociological point of view, the district has a mixture of all categories of people. Elite and posh localities like Panchsheel Park, Malviya Nagar, Sarvapriya Vihar, Safdarjung Enclave, Safdarjung Development Area, West End, Vasant Kunj, and Vasant Vihar are located in this district. The physical boundary of the district extends up to Aya Nagar border near Gurgaon on the one hand, and Rajokri on the other. More than 2000 spacious farmhouses are also located within the jurisdiction of a few police stations in this district. Shahpur Jat and Hauz Khas villages are the prominent urbanized villages of the district.

There are fifteen police stations in the district. This district has been considered as one of the 'heaviest districts' of Delhi from the crime point of view. After an analysis of the geographical boundaries of the district and its overall crime, a new district, south-east, was carved out in 2008. The creation of the new district saw the reorganization of boundaries of several existing police stations, as well as the creation of new police stations. The basic philosophy was to optimize and rationalize the policing responsibilities, so that they are in tune with the number of inhabitants in a particular area, and the existing manpower and logistics of the police station. In the process of reorganization of the district, several existing police posts got elevated to the status of police stations, and a few new ones were also created.

The crime figures for the district from 1991 to 2006 can be seen in Appendix 4.3. On the basis of the crime figures, the following broad conclusions can be drawn about the district:

1. A total number of 9603 cases were registered under various sections of the IPC. From the year 1996 onwards, till 1998, the district has shown an increasing trend in crime. However, from 1999 onwards, the total number of IPC crimes in the district started declining. The decreasing trend in crime has continued till 2003. An increasing trend emerges from 2004 onwards again.

2. On the basis of crime figures, five police stations can be identified as more crime-prone. These are Hauz Khas, Malviya Nagar, Lajpat Nagar, Kalkaji, and Srinivaspuri. Police stations like Ambedkar Nagar also emerged as crime-prone in some years.

3. Head-wise, crime for the district, particularly for serious offences, reflects that Ambedkar Nagar, Okhla Industrial Area, and Mehrauli police stations are very prone to crimes like dacoity. It is important to mention here that dacoity is a crime which is committed by a group of more than five people. Far flung areas and less densely populated residential complexes are more prone to such crimes. A common feature of all dacoity-prone police stations is their geographical location and topography. All the three police stations cover very wide areas. The jurisdiction of one police station, Mehrauli, extends up to the border of Haryana, making it more vulnerable

for crime. Multiple entry and exit routes in these police stations act as fertile ground for the commission of crimes like dacoity. Police patrolling and presence in these areas is not adequate due to the geographical vastness of the area.

4. The posh localities of the district are very crime-prone. They are vulnerable due to urban anonymity and the lack of healthy neighbourly relationships. People are more egocentric and status conscious and neighbours are hardly bothered about the activities of each other. Although they physically share houses next to each other, they hardly ever interact. Strangers and anonymous characters move around in posh colonies without anyone questioning them. Since next-door neighbours in various localities live like strangers and are indifferent to activities happening around them, anonymous criminals have committed crime in these localities very easily and have also managed to escape safely. The initial inputs received by a police officer regarding the commission of any crime at a particular place are very important. In such localities it is difficult to gather any inputs about any assailant from the neighbours. One important case that demonstrates the magnitude of anonymity and indifference towards neighbours concerns a Romanian diplomat. In 1993, this diplomat was abducted by a Punjab-based terrorist group from Delhi. The Delhi Police launched a massive hunt for the release of the diplomat. In desperation, the abductors finally released him at New Delhi Railway Station. The accused wanted in this case were also apprehended later on. The interrogation and questioning of one of the accused—the one who actually abducted the diplomat—revealed that before the actual operation, he stayed in a rented house in a posh colony in south Delhi, with a woman posing as wife, for more than a month. Many suspicious movements and activities took place at the rented premises. However, the next-door neighbours were completely ignorant about the activities of this couple.

5. R.K. Puram, Sarojini Nagar, Netaji Nagar, Laxmi Bai Nagar, and East and West Kidwai Nagar accommodate the maximum number of government servants from lower and upper middle class,

with the maximum number of working couples. The absence of members from the house, and the numerous entry and exit points to various sectors of these colonies have led to the easy commission of crimes. A very peculiar feature of crimes committed in these colonies is that they are being committed during the day, as most of these houses remain locked due to the absence of residents who are at their place of work.

6. The criminal activities in the district, particularly in posh localities, get affected by the proximate presence of affluent colonies and slum/unauthorized colonies. Many areas within the jurisdiction of Vasant Kunj South and Mehrauli police stations are also prone to attacks by criminals from Haryana due to their close proximity to the border. Additionally, adjoining urbanized villages like Kishan Garh, Masood Pur, Mahipal Pur, Rangpuri, Ghitorni, and Rajkori act as criminal hinterlands for police stations such as Vasant Kunj.

South-West District   The south-west district was initially carved out from the south district in 1988. Thereafter, some changes in the territorial jurisdiction were made in 2008. At present, the district comprises four sub-divisions and thirteen police stations. The district shares an inter-state border with Haryana. The satellite township of Dwarka is located in this district. Once fully developed, this will be one of the biggest residential areas in Delhi. Busy market complexes exist in Sectors 4, 7, 11, 12, 6, and 10. There are eight metro stations within the jurisdiction of the police station located in Sector 23, Dwarka. The area is expected to see further expansion with the coming up of offices of several Public Sector Undertakings (PSUs), shopping malls, university campuses, and five star hotels.

As per the 2001 census, the total population of the district is 17,55,041. The density of population per sq km is 4169. As compared to the south district, south-west district is less densely populated. The decadal growth of population in the district (1991–2001) is 61.29 per cent. The district is a mixture of rural and urban population. It has the second highest number of villages (51), after the south district. The largest religious communities in the district are Hindus, Muslims, and Sikhs. Hindus constitute the majority group, followed by Muslims and Sikhs.

On the basis of crime figures of the whole district, the following broad conclusions can be drawn:

1. From 1995 till 2001, the crime trend of the district has shown a marginal increase. From 2003 onwards, the crime trend of the district shows an upward trend.

2. The analysis of crime at the police station level shows Najafgarh and Dabri having registered the maximum number of cases under different sections of IPC, every year. The main reason behind the increasing trend of these police stations can be attributed to the geographical location and typical demographic profile of the police stations. Both the police stations cover very wide and open areas.

3. As far as the vulnerability of police stations for serious crimes like robbery and dacoity is concerned, Najafgarh, Dwarka, Kapashera, and Dabri take the lead. Of all the police stations, Dabri and Najafgarh have constantly shown an increasing trend in these crimes.

4. A very important sociological characteristic of the district is the presence of members of denotified tribes, particularly within the jurisdiction of the police stations of Dabri and Uttam Nagar. Many members of these communities are habitual criminals. They specialize in bootlegging and illicit liquor. Their share in robbery and other property offences is also very common. Their area of operation is the entire district, as well as the adjoining west district. These communities are also known for attacking police parties with lethal weapons during raids of their hideouts. They largely survive in the city on the proceeds of crime only.

West District   This district is situated next to the south-west district. It includes important colonies like Rajouri Garden, Punjabi Bagh, Vikas Puri, Paschim Vihar, etc. It also includes the urbanized villages of Nangoli and Mundka. As per the 2001 census, the total population of the district is 21,28,908 and the density of population is 16,503 per sq km. As compared to the south and south-west districts, the density of population in west district is much higher. The district also shares a border with Bahadurgarh district of Haryana. The district is a mixture of rural and urban population with nine inhabited villages. The three important religious communities— Hindus, Muslims, and Sikhs—are scattered over different areas. Hindus constitute the majority, followed by Sikhs and Muslims. The population of Sikhs is the highest in this district as compared to other districts. Tilak Vihar, inhabited by the victims of the 1984 riots, is a very sensitive area.

On the basis of crime figures of the district, the following conclusions can be drawn:

1. The district has shown a marginal increase in crime every year from 1995 to 2006. In some years, the figures have shown only minimal increase. As a whole, the district has shown a constant pattern of crime as far as the registration of IPC cases is concerned.

2. In terms of serious crimes, this district registers many property offences, while dacoity is not a very common crime. This is very evident from the yearly registration pattern. The most important reason for the lesser number of dacoities is the densely populated nature of the colonies. In fact, the terrain and topography of the maximum number of areas within this district do not provide a very easy access and escape after the commission of crimes like dacoity. Moreover, since the minimum number of persons involved in crimes like dacoities is five or more, the identification of such a large group in a densely populated area is easier than in other open areas.

3. On the other hand, body offences like murder are common in all police stations. Police stations like Uttam Nagar and Nangoli have registered the maximum number of cases on a yearly basis. Another property offence, robbery, is very common in all the police stations, with an increasing trend in Uttam Nagar, Nangoli, and Paschim Vihar. A very significant reason for the increasing trend in

body and property offences is the presence of criminal elements in the nearby police stations areas. Most of the time, one police station has acted as the criminal hinterland for another police station. Criminals from police stations like Dabri, Uttam Nagar, and Tilak Nagar keep operating in the whole district. This is quite different from areas like Greater Kailash or Vasant Vihar where criminals travel a long distance to commit crime. The district is communally very sensitive.

North District   This is a district which is situated on the banks of the Yamuna. It covers almost all the important areas of erstwhile Shahjahanabad. The famous police station, Kotwali, is situated in this district. All famous gates like Delhi Gate, Ajmeri Gate, Kabul Gate, which once acted as entry points during the Mughal and British periods, still exist, surrounded by different kinds of structures. The district also includes areas like Civil Lines, which was developed by the British after 1857 to accommodate the ruling elite. Even today, the spacious bungalows of Civil Lines accommodate the affluent and rich sections of the society. The district is the hub of wholesale markets for various products. All famous markets are located in the district. Owners of shops in the area reside in posh areas like Civil Lines, Greater Kailash, and Vasant Vihar, etc., and commute everyday for business purposes. As per the 2001 census, the total population of the district is 7,81,525, while the density of population is 13,246. The overall population of this district is lesser than that of south, south-west, and west districts, while the density of population is higher than the south and south-west districts. An important reason behind less population is the presence of commercial establishments. The district is essentially urban in nature. There are only five inhabited villages in the district. There are three important religious groups in the district; Hindus constitute the majority, followed by Muslims and Sikhs.

1. Except in the year 1996, the normal trend of crime in the district is constant. After 1998, the district shows a declining trend,

which continues till 2006, with a slight yearly variation as far as the registration of IPC cases is concerned. A very important factor contributing to decreasing crime in the district has been the removal of JJ clusters situated along the banks of the Yamuna. These used to be the reservoir of criminals, national as well as international. This is very much evident in the crime figures for the home police station, that is, Kotwali.

2. A perusal of crime figures for different police stations shows that Kotwali and Kashmere Gate police stations reflect an increasing trend from 1995 to 1998. After 1998, the crime figures for both the police stations have shown significant decline, till 2006. The lowest crime registered was in Maurice Nagar police station. The important reason behind lesser crime here is the presence of educational institutions. Apart from the existence of the Delhi University campus, all important colleges of North Campus are situated within the jurisdiction of Maurice Nagar police station. As compared to other police stations, the residential composition of the police station is also different.

3. An analysis of serious crime shows that dacoity is not a common crime in this area. The very topography and the density of population goes against this kind of crime. For example, Civil Lines is one police station where only one case of dacoity was registered in 2004. However, all the police stations in the district are vulnerable to robbery, with Kotwali, Kashmere Gate, Sabzi Mandi, and Lahori Gate leading the figures. A very significant feature conducive to robbery is the presence of commercial institutions and overall affluence. This has always attracted criminal groups from different parts of the city.

North-West District Beyond the congested domains of north district starts the boundary of the north-west district. This district is a mixture of upcoming posh settlements as well as relocated resettlement colonies. Except for few police stations, the socio-economic profile of the people, particularly those in Mangol Puri, Jahangirpuri, and Khanjawala, is in stark contrast with the socio-economic profile of police stations like Mukherjee Nagar, Model Town, and Ashok Vihar. The district extends up to bordering areas spread over the far flung pockets of Bawana, Alipur, Narela, and Rohini. As the result of a beautification drive, several JJ clusters and slum areas existing in New Delhi, central, and north district have been relocated to Bawana and Narela. Of late, the area has also emerged as the new face of the horizontal development of the city. Several new DDA residential complexes, district centres, shopping malls, and industrial establishments are coming up in this district. This district has always been very heavy in terms of crime.

Keeping in view the geographical vastness and incidences of crime, the district was divided into two districts in 2008: north-west and outer. The bifurcation led to the reorganization of boundaries of various police stations and creation of new police stations. As per the 2001 census, the total population of the district is 28,60,869. As compared to other districts, the north-west district has the highest population. The density of population is slightly higher than New Delhi and south-west districts. This is primarily due to the fact that the area is still being developed, as compared to other parts of the city. The decadal growth of the population (1991–2001) is 60.12 per cent, second highest after the north-east district. The district is a mixture of rural and urban population. It has the highest number of villages in Delhi (62). There are three important religious groups in the district; Hindus constitute the majority group, followed by Muslims and Sikhs.

Crime figures for the district help us in drawing the following conclusions:

1. Except in the year 1997, the crime figures for all other years show an increasing trend.

2. Of all the police stations, Sultan Puri has consistently shown an increasing trend of crime every year, with the highest number of cases registered in the year 2005. After Sultan Puri, Mangol Puri police station also shows an increasing trend in crime. As soon as

the population started increasing in Rohini, it also started showing an increase in the number of crimes.

3. From the point of property offences, police stations like Samaipur Badli, Saraswati Vihar, and Alipur show vulnerability to dacoity cases. The reasons that these police stations are vulnerable to dacoity are similar to those already cited for Nangoli, Mehrauli, and Kapashera in other districts. A distinguishing feature of police stations like Alipur and Badli is the involvement of cross-border criminals from neighbouring states.

The rate of crime in this district has been less since 2007, as a separate outer district has been carved out from the original district.

Central District This district also covers few areas of erstwhile Shahjahanabad, like Jama Masjid, Daryaganj, and Chandni Mahal. It is a mixture of densely-populated areas like Jama Masjid and Chandni Mahal, and the wide, open areas of Prasad Nagar, Karol Bagh, and IP Estate. As per the 2001 census, the total population of the district is 6,46,385, while the density of population in the district is 25,855—the second highest after the north-east district. A few police stations have a predominantly Muslim population, particularly Jama Masjid, Chandni Mahal, and Hauz Qazi. This area had accommodated a large number of Muslim emigrants after Partition. The high density of population here can be attributed to an interesting fact. Owing to the paucity of space in the houses, people sleep in shifts. This can be deduced from the fact that the number of persons in one dwelling house is more than the available space inside the house. Streets in this part of the city are never deserted. Even at midnight, the area is full of activity, unlike the deserted streets of posh localities like Greater Kailash and Vasant Vihar. A very distinguishing feature of the district—which is not common to other districts, except New Delhi—is the absence of rural areas. It is essentially an urban district where the three largest religious groups are Hindus, Muslims, and Sikhs; Hindus constitute the largest, followed by Muslims and Sikhs.

The district has the third highest population of Muslims among all the Delhi's Police districts.

On the basis of crime figures for the district, the following broad conclusions can be drawn:

1. The crime figures for the whole district during the entire period shows a constant trend with very slight variations in some years. A typical feature of policing in this district—which is not true for other districts—is its preoccupation with VIP arrangements, public meetings, and rallies on a daily basis. The presence of various *samadhis* on the western bank of the Yamuna attracts many VIPs during particular periods of the year.

2. A perusal of crime figures for different police stations reflects very few cases of dacoity under property offences. IP Estate and Prasad Nagar police stations have registered more cases compared to other police stations. Unlike dacoity, robbery is very common in almost all police stations. Kamla Market, IP Estate, DBG Road, and Prasad Nagar police stations reflect particular vulnerability to robbery. Several police stations in the district act as a hinterland for various crimes in other police stations. Recorded criminals are prime suspects for any crime, not only in the district but also for the home police station itself. Several dreaded and recorded criminals of the district have been found to be involved in crime in other parts of Delhi.

Police stations Daryaganj, Paharganj, Karol Bagh, and DBG Road can be identified as crime-prone police stations.

3. Apart from the normal policing duties, the district is preoccupied with different kinds of law and order and security duties. Many political rallies are held in the Ramlila Maidan. Elaborate security arrangements are provided by the district police at various samadhis of national leaders on their birth and death anniversaries. Organizing safe cricket matches at Feroz Shah Kotla also falls under the normal policing duties of the district. As a whole, the district has to handle

various law and order arrangements and religious processions on a normal basis.

A few communities prone to crime also reside in some pockets of this district. For example, within the jurisdiction of Paharganj police station, several persons belonging to the Ghera community survive on the proceeds of crime on day-to-day basis. They are involved in small time pick pocketing as well as big robberies. After committing theft or robbery, they immediately dispose of the stolen property to fulfil their daily needs.

New Delhi District This is a district which has historically been known as Lutyen's Delhi. The overall profile of the district is radically different from other districts. Prominent government buildings like the Parliament, Rashtrapati Bhawan, Supreme Court, and High Court are located in this district. Places like South Avenue and North Avenue accommodate MPs, while spacious bungalows on various roads within New Delhi district belong to the cabinet ministers of the Government of India. Senior bureaucrats also reside in various colonies like Chanakya Puri, Kaka Nagar, etc. All foreign missions/embassies are situated in the district. In a nutshell, the socio-economic profile of the district is very high.

The basic data sheet of the district highlights the following important features:

1. As per the 2001 census, the population of the district is the lowest as compared to all other districts. It is 1,79,112, with a density of 5117 per sq km—slightly more than south-west district.

2. A very important feature of the district—not common to any other district—is the proportionately larger deployment of policemen in the area due to the presence of vital installations and the residences of VIPs.

3. Second, there is no rural population in the district. The district is completely urban in nature.

4. The geographical location, the layout of the houses, and the demographic profile of the district has a very strong impact on the overall crime pattern of the district.

5. The three important religious groups in the district are Hindus, Muslims, and Christians. Hindus constitute the majority, followed by Muslims and Christians. The Muslim population in this district is the lowest compared to other districts.

6. The overall literacy rate in the district is 83.24 per cent, with male literacy at 88.62 per cent, followed by female literacy at 76.33 per cent.

7. There is no ST population in the district while SC population stands at 22.22 per cent of the total population.

Crime figures for this district help us in drawing the following conclusions:

1. In comparison to other districts, the overall registration of IPC cases from 1995 to 2006 is very low. Except in the years 1997 and 1998, the figures are below 3000 cases for the whole year. As explained earlier, a very important reason for the fewer number of cases in the district is the adequate deployment of policemen, along with private security persons. Since the houses are owned by individual owners, private security guards have been deployed to control access round the clock. Houses occupied by cabinet ministers and other protected persons are covered by the special deployment of armed guards as per threat perceptions. Over and above this, there is more deployment of police resources in this district in terms of patrolling and area policing schemes.

2. At the micro level, the Connaught Place police station takes the lead in the registration of IPC cases. It shows an increasing trend of cases every year, with the highest number of cases, 1423, in 1997.

3. As far as property offences are concerned, the registration of cases under dacoity shows a negative trend in all the police stations of the district. In police stations like Chanakya Puri, no such cases

were registered. Similarly, the Tughlak Road police station shows zero figures for dacoity cases after 1995. However, this is not true for cases like robbery. Connaught Place, Tilak Marg, Mandir Marg, and Chanakya Puri police stations are very vulnerable to robbery. A typical physical feature of the district which is conducive to robbery is the sizable presence of the ridge area within the jurisdiction of the Chanakya Puri and Mandir Marg police stations.

4. The overall profile of the district is law and order oriented. On an average, the district has to handle four to five sensitive processions everyday at Janta Mantar, near Parliament Street. The frequency of the law and order arrangements increases during Parliament sessions. These heavy arrangements keep the whole district preoccupied from morning to evening. Several political protests also end up in violent activities. The volume and magnitude of the law and order arrangements can be judged by the following figures, spanning three years, as shown in Table 4.1 below. It also gives an indication of the increasing burden on the district over a period of time.

East District This district is situated across the Yamuna river, which divides the city into two parts. The area is very close to the borders of UP and other satellite towns like Noida, Greater Noida, and Ghaziabad. Like the north-west district, this district is also undergoing tremendous horizontal expansion.

The basic data sheet of the district throws light on following features:

1. As per the 2001 census, the overall population of the district is 14,63,583 while density of the population is 22,868 per sq km.

TABLE 4.1 Public Gatherings in the New Delhi District 2006–8

Year	Nature of Crowd	Incidences	Approximate Gathering
2006	Demonstration	942	2,15,342
2007	Demonstration	1173	2,70,664
2008	Demonstration	1105	2,09,895

2. This area has substantially accommodated the migrant population over a period of time. Apart from the presence of various co-operative multi-storey housing societies in Mayur Vihar and Patparganj, several posh localities like Preet Vihar, Vivek Vihar, and Madhuban Enclave are also situated in this district. The overall socio-economic profile of the district is a mixed one. Apart from the presence of resettlement colonies, housing accommodation in this district varies between 25 sq ft to 200 sq yds independent houses. The density of population is very high and several areas are highly congested. Due to the presence of a substantial migrant population, several pockets in the district act as the hinterland for many crimes in the district.

3. The district is predominantly urban in character with the existence of only three inhabited villages.

4. There are three important religious groups in the district; Hindus constitute the majority, followed by Muslims and Sikhs.

5. The overall literacy rate of the district is 84.91 per cent. Male literacy is 89.65 per cent and female literacy is 79.26 per cent.

6. There is no ST population in the district, while the SC population is 16.33 per cent of the total population.

On the basis of the crime figures, the following broad conclusions can be drawn:

1. The district shows an increasing trend in crime on a yearly basis. Total IPC cases registered in the year 1995 was 2890, which almost doubled to 5483 in 2006.

2. Pandav Nagar, Shakar Pur, and Kalyan Puri have emerged as crime-prone police stations till 1997. However, 1998 onwards, three more police stations joined the rank of crime-prone police stations.

3. Police stations like Krishna Nagar, Vivek Vihar, and Preet Vihar show vulnerability to property offences like dacoity. Except for Farsh Bazar police station, almost all police stations show vulnerability to robbery cases, with Kalyan Puri leading the figures in 2006, with 16 cases.

4. Due to the proximity of the district to neighbouring states, the involvement of criminals from nearby villages and the areas of UP is also very high. This is very evident from the figures of crime under robbery, snatching, and auto-lifting for a period of three years (2005 to 2008 [up to 31 August 2008]). These figures show that the share of criminals, particularly snatchers, robbers, and auto-lifters belonging to the NCR towns is more than the share of home criminals. This is clear in all the subdivisions of the district. Vivek Vihar, which is very close to the UP border, has shown the highest numbers of NCR auto-lifters in the period in question, followed by Preet Vihar.

If we look at the figures of the individual police stations, police stations closer to the borders have registered more cases compared to police stations far off from the border. For example, Anand Vihar, Vivek Vihar, and New Ashok Nagar police stations have shown a greater involvement of NCR criminals. The primary reason for more involvement in these police stations is the physical proximity to the NCR border. The criminals in these police stations enter Delhi within ten minutes and, by the time the crime is reported in these police stations, they are already beyond Delhi's borders.

North-East District This district used to be part of the east district and was carved out as an independent district in 1987. The district includes areas like Shahadara, Bhajanpura, and Gokul Puri.

The basic data sheet of the district reveals some very interesting features:

1. As per the 2001 census, the population of the district is 17,68,061, while the density of the population is 29,468, the highest in all the districts.

2. As a matter of fact, the district has also registered the highest decadal growth (1991–2001) of 62.52 per cent.

3. There are a lot of similarities in the demographic profile and socio-economic characteristics between the east district and the

north-east district: it shares borders with Haryana and UP, and cross-border criminals have a large share in the crime of the district. In fact, a few pockets like Seelampur are dens of notorious criminals having direct as well as indirect links with notorious gangsters and criminals of UP and Haryana. In many ways, the crime culture of the district reflects the criminal behaviour of cults of nearby western UP cities, where gun battles are very common on very petty issues. The possession of fire arms increases the status of the criminals within their wider networks and provides a psychological edge over other groups. Offenders can be located in the criminal hinterland of the police stations at the micro level, and in the district or across the border at the macro level.

4. There are three important religious groups in the district; Hindus constitute the highest numbers, followed by Muslims and Jains. It is also significant that the population of Muslims is the highest in this district compared to other districts. There is no Sikh population in the district. On the other hand, Jains have preponderance in only this district in Delhi.

5. The ST population is nil in the district, while the SC population is 16.69 per cent.

6. The district has both rural and urban population. There are 12 inhabited villages in the district.

7. The overall literacy rate in the district is 77 per cent. Male literacy stands at 84 per cent while female literacy is 68.94 per cent.

The crime figures for the district reflect the following important features:

1. With minor fluctuations every year, there is an increase in the figures of IPC cases. The year 2006 has shown the highest registration of cases—5389—as compared to previous years.

2. Seelampur, Gokul Puri, Bhajan Pura, and Seema Puri are more crime-prone police stations as compared to other police stations.

3. In terms of serious property offences, all the police stations mentioned above take the lead, particularly in robbery and dacoity

cases. Seelampur registered the highest number of cases of dacoity in 1998.

The description of the crime scenario in the various districts given above reflects the different dimensions of criminal activities, as well as the Delhi Police's preoccupation with various aspects of policing duties. Crime in each of the districts is affected by various crimogenic factors such as the proximity to neighbouring NCR towns, the presence of affluent and under-privileged settlements side by side, unauthorized colonies, floating population, the nature of business, and other activities. The preoccupations of various traditional police stations in the city have also changed with rapid urbanization. Except districts like north-west, west, outer and north-east, all other districts in Delhi are preoccupied with several VIP security as well as law and order related duties on a regular basis.

THE INTER-STATE AND TRANSNATIONAL CONTEXT OF CRIMINAL ACTIVITIES IN DELHI

Delhi is a preferred and safe hunting ground for criminals, not only from the neighbouring states but also from several South Asian Association for Regional Cooperation (SAARC) countries.

Crime patterns in Delhi are very much affected by the criminals of other states, particularly the adjoining towns of the NCR region. Certain criminals hailing from nearby states, and notorious for their criminal activities, regularly commit crime in Delhi. For example, criminals hailing from the Mewat region of Haryana and Rajasthan regularly strike in various localities of Delhi. These groups specialize in burglary and house-breaking cases. They have decamped with valuable electronic goods from reputed showrooms of Delhi during the night. They always commit crimes using big tempos. The apprehension of such criminals is not very easy. They have often held various police teams captive in their hide outs, and have even inflicted serious injuries to police teams of Delhi, forcing them to retreat.

Apart from burglaries, criminals hailing from the Mewat region are also expert cattle thieves. They move around in big tempos in urbanized villages in various parts of Delhi during the night and pick up cattle. One gang member sits in the rear of the tempo and throws chilli powder into the eyes of police patrolling parties in case they face resistance from them. They have even indulged in firing on police teams in case they have been chased by them while committing crime. In the month of May 2007, one policeman was killed and another critically injured in the south-west district when the gang was asked to stop. Criminals hailing from the region commit all kinds of crime. They are also notorious for automobile thefts. Two wheelers are picked up in big tempos and disposed of at very cheap prices. It will not be out of place to mention that the sensational sexual assault case of Dhaula Kuan in 2010 was committed by members of this group.

The vulnerability of the border districts like south and south-west to criminals hailing from Mewat is due to two factors. Firstly, these districts are very close to their area, as a result of which, their escape routes and movement beyond the Delhi border is very fast. Secondly, most of the big showrooms of electronic goods are located in these two districts.

The overall share of criminals hailing from NCR towns in important crimes committed in Delhi during the period 2007–9 (see Figure 4.1).

Investigations of criminal activities in Delhi have also shown the involvement of criminals from SAARC countries. Nepal, Bangladesh, and Pakistan are very important from this point of view. While criminals from Nepal and Bangladesh have committed all sorts of crime, criminals from Pakistan (and also Bangladesh) have, directly and indirectly, committed and abetted terrorist activities in the capital. This has been corroborated by the arrest of a number

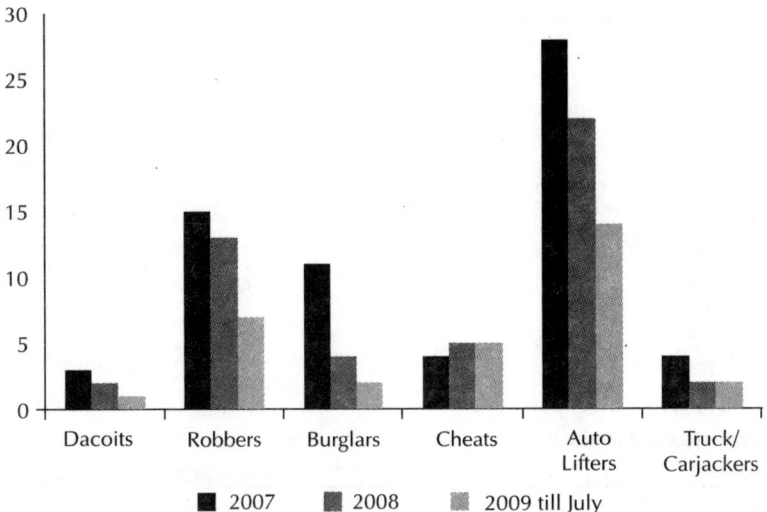

FIGURE 4.1 Inter-state Gangs Arrested by Delhi Police (last 3 Years)

of Bangladeshi and Nepali criminals during 2005–07 as is evident from Tables 4.2(a) and (b) which list the arrested criminals under different heads of crime. The apprehension of such criminals is also very difficult as they immediately escape to their respective destinations after committing crimes. In some cases, by the time the crime has been detected in Delhi, the accused has already reached his/her native village. I still remember a quadruple murder case in Vasant Kunj in which four members of a family were brutally killed by a Nepali domestic servant who had locked the house from the outside after committing the murders. By the time the local police was informed, the servant was already in his native village in Nepal.

A perusal of the above tables shows that the share and participation of Bangladeshi criminals is more when compared to criminals hailing from Nepal. The participation of foreign nationals in different crimes has continued at a similar rate in the last two years, as well. The year 2007 saw the involvement of 70 Bangladeshis, 54 Nepalis, and 11 Pakistanis in criminal activities in India. In 2008, 67 Bangladeshis,

TABLE 4.2(a)   Nepalese Criminals Arrested (2005–7)

Crime Heads	2005	2006	2007
Murder	2	3	1
Theft	2	0	-
Hurt	0	1	2
Economic offences	5	19	2
Burglary	2	4	3
Misc. IPC	1	1	4
Arms Act	2	4	1
N.D.P.S Act	1	0	4
Exp. Sub. Act	0	0	–
Cheating	–	–	36
Other Act	–	–	1
Passport Act	–	–	1
Rape	–	–	1

TABLE 4.2(b)   Bangladeshi Nationals Arrested (2005–7)

Crime Heads	Number of Persons Arrested		
	2005	2006	2007
Dacoity	16	8	12
Robbery	15	4	1
Murder	2	–	–
Burglary	24	24	7
Preparation of dacoity	–	–	23
Theft	7	26	–
Other IPC	34	34	4
Total IPC	98	96	47
Local & Special Laws	43	10	13
Total	141	106	60

52 Nepalis, and 6 Pakistanis were arrested for their involvement in crimes committed on Indian soil. In 2009, 42 Bangladeshis, 55 Nepalis, and 3 Pakistanis were arrested and in 2010 (up to 31 October), 35 Bangladeshis, 7 Nepalis, and 3 Pakistanis were arrested.

5

INFRASTRUCTURE
CONSTRAINTS
AND CRIME

The whole of Delhi will become an overcrowded slum buried under rubbish unless immediate measures to contain pollution, overcrowding, crime and traffic chaos are implemented. The slums will encroach on all available space within two years. Fifty-seven per cent of Delhi inhabitants will have no water, 41 per cent no sewerage and 40 per cent no power.[1]

The major impetus to urbanization in modern times has seen a shift from primary to secondary and tertiary-based occupation for livelihood. It places economic, social, infrastructural, and environmental strain and pressures on both rural and urban areas leading to serious concerns about its sustainability. The problem of sustainability and gap in resources can be seen in key infrastructure areas like food, energy, water, raw materials, housing, transport, etc. Today, almost half of all people living in cities in the developing world have no access to basic services. Furthermore, even where the installations exist, the quality is not always guaranteed—for example, power cuts, low water pressure, etc.[2]

The pre-Independence growth of the city and the shifting of capital to Delhi had been largely gradual. Although the pace had increased subsequently, the administrators had a choice to plan the expansion of the city in a better manner, keeping in view the availability of land and other resources.

The Independence of the nation followed by Partition posed several infrastructural constraints for the overall development of the city. The unprecedented movement of people from Pakistan in large numbers led to the foundation of unhealthy parameters and dimensions in urban development. The basic objective was to accommodate the new arrivals. There was no time to plan their dispersal in the city in an organized manner. This led to the development of rehabilitation colonies all across the city. The purpose was to provide shelter to the people as early as possible. There was no time to design the architecture and aesthetics of the upcoming colonies all across the city. Apart from the movement of people from across the border, the emergence of Delhi as a capital city and its growth as a major commercial town in north India with lots of prospects for the future further facilitated the movement of the people through internal migration.

The onslaught of migration led to development of the city by squatters. People started encroaching available land for their shelter, irrespective of the availability of basic infrastructural and civic facilities. In fact, the basic amenities followed later without any approved design or planning. By 1957, the situation had become so grim that the government realized the necessity and importance of some sort of scheme for the development of the new capital. To meet the challenge of rapid urbanization and to prevent future haphazard development, Jawaharlal Nehru, the first prime minister of India conceived the idea of setting up a single planning authority for the entire metropolitan region. This prepared the base for enactment of Delhi Development Act in 1957, and DDA was entrusted with the responsibility of the formulation of the 'Master Plan' for the city.

The First Master Plan (1962–81) tried to build and design the city after taking into account the existing infrastructural gaps between the population and housing, community facilities, water, power, transport, etc., and future requirements. To meet the requirements of a projected population of 46 lakh, the plan envisaged the urbanization of about 1,10,000 acres of land up to 1981, as against 42,600 acres in 1960. It also stipulated that 42 per cent of the area should be earmarked for residential use, 23.7 per cent for recreational and green use, 8 per cent for public utility, 7.4 per cent for government offices, 5.4 per cent for industrial use, 2.3 per cent for commercial use, and the remaining land for circulation, institutional use, and other community facilities. Thus, the planned approach to the city visualized various dimensions and needs of human beings in a developing city, and made adequate provisions for those basic facilities and services under the plan through a rational distribution of resources. Theoretically speaking, provision of land for basic facilities like roads, bridges, schools, hospitals, etc. were accounted for, and was not left as unused to be squatted as had happened in the past.

Another significant development from a better planning point of view during the drawing up of the Master Plan was the preparation of Squatter Resettlement Scheme in 1960 to deal with the problem of slums and squatting on public land. The squatter resettlement scheme visualized allotments of 80 square yards of land to each eligible squatter on a 99-year basis. The plot included a package for provision for a latrine, a water tank, and a plinth on which the allottee could build a hut or house according to his/her needs. It was under this scheme that squatters were removed from core areas and prime locations, and were accommodated in several parts of north, west, north-west, east, and other districts. The basic objective of this scheme was to decongest the core area and relocate the displaced persons in peripheral areas where the person could be part of a healthy living habitat.

All these developments in the city put extra strain and pressures on basic infrastructure services like water, electricity, and housing. These services could not cope up with the pace of increasing numbers in the city. As a result, a gap emerged between the increasing numbers and the distribution of water, housing, and electricity in the city. The gap could also be understood through the Malthusian paradigm, which tried to explain the relationship between an increase in the number of people in the society with an increase in the resources to support the population, using the concepts of arithmetical progression and geometrical progression. He believed that population in a society increases in geometrical progression, that is, in a 2, 4, 8, 16, 32, 64... series, while resources on which the population survives increase in arithmetical progression, that is, in a 1, 2, 3, 4, 5, 6, 7, 8... series. Over a period of time, this gap becomes very wide and unmanageable. Let us see the gap in Delhi in terms of increasing number of people and the availability of housing, water, and electricity.

HOUSING

Increasing population and continuous migration to cities has affected the availability of housing. To meet the requirements of a growing population, several years back, it was anticipated that within the period, 1981–2001, over 20 lakh acres of urban land will be required.[3] More demand and less supply of land for housing purposes has led to increase in land prices, thereby making it difficult for the poor to buy land.

The prices of land have been increasing in Delhi since Independence. As per an official estimate, the price of land in suburban areas in Delhi increased by over 145 per cent within four years (1955–8). In some other areas within the city, the increase was as high as 350 per cent over a period of 10 years (1948–58).[4] The increasing urbanization and horizontal expansion of the city kept on increasing the land prices. According to an analysis of data from a 19-year period in Delhi (1963–82) reveals that in the residential colonies of Delhi, the land prices increased from Rs 15.75 per sq mtrs to Rs 2000–4000 per sq mtrs, that is, an increase of 40–60 times.[5]

The increasing trend of land prices continued. In some areas in Delhi, the cost of land has gone up to Rs 40,000–60,000 per sq mtrs. While the increasing prices of land have made it difficult for the poor sections to own land, several landlords have become multi-millionaires by selling the land they had bought earlier. As a matter of fact, the increasing prices of land have added a new dimension to the building architecture of the city. Several owners of the spacious plots/flats in posh localities in south Delhi have sold their plots at exorbitant rates to private builders for construction of multi-storey flats.

This development has increased the density of many colonies. The change in building style is very evident in Chittaranjan Park, Greater Kailash I and II, and Vasant Vihar. B.K. Roy Burman, a famous anthropologist who lives in Chittaranjan Park in an independent house once told me that the architectural beauty, land space and aesthetics of this beautiful colony, which was allotted to all the displaced persons of East Pakistan after Partition by the Ministry of Rehabilitation, are being ruined by the builder mafia.[6] The colony which accommodates a sizeable Bengali population is completely changed today. The independent houses have been replaced by multi-storey flats. However, this has become the latest fashion in almost all parts of the city as a result of roaring land prices.

The increasing price of land in several parts of the city has resulted in the forced occupation of vacant lands and construction of temporary hutments. Since this arrangement has been made beyond the formal and planned housing schemes, there are no basic facilities like drinking water, drainage, and electricity. In order to survive, people have to access these facilities on a day-to-day basis by whatever means possible. This has further led to other illegal activities like theft of electricity and water from any available sources. The resource gap between land and aspirants for land had led to the growth of JJ clusters and slum population in Delhi.

Towns and cities have been in a constant state of flux ever since their existence. The process of urbanization affects the city in many ways. Fernand Braudel has rightly said that town are like electric transformers. They increase tension, accelerate the rhythm of change, and constantly recharge human life .... Towns generate expansion and are themselves generated by it.[7]

The emergence of slums in different parts of the cities has led to the emergence of different social set-ups and sub-cultures within the city, which are different from the mainstream culture. This new social set-up within the city has promoted social imbalance for the inhabitants and has led to the emergence of a culture of violence in day-to-day lives. The new slum culture in Delhi reflects the typical characteristic of a 'Street Corner Society'.[8]

While describing the characteristics of people in Cornerville, an Italian neighbourhood in Boston, Whyte dispelled the then current notion that slum areas were by definition disorganized and were organized more on the basis of small gangs and racketeers. He actually traced the origin of the gangs to the breakdown of the existing social rules of the immigrant peasant societies.

According to the Census of 2001, the total slum population in Delhi is 20,29,755, which is 15.7 per cent of its total urban population. Of the three metropolitan cities, Greater Mumbai has the highest slum population of around 6.5 million followed by Delhi (1.5 million) and Kolkata (1.5 million). Rural urban migration has been considered the major factor for growth of slums in urban areas. The UN has warned that rapid urbanization and migration would lead to a tripling of the slum population by 2050.[9]

The city continues to struggle with the problem of space for accommodating the growing numbers. A recent report indicated that there are an estimated 1 lakh people in the city without proper homes. They spend the night in the open spaces in the city. Only

10,000 of them could be accommodated in temporary shelters erected by the government.[11]

ELECTRICITY

The disequilibrium in the demand and supply of power in the city has increased over a period of time. Power supply has not kept pace with the increase in the per capita power consumption in the city. As a matter of fact, power generation has failed to keep pace with the growth of the city over the years. The increasing demand for electricity in the city over the years from 1998–9 till 2007–8 are shown in Table 5.1.

On an average, Delhi faces power shortage with a 4.4 per cent peak demand deficit. The existing power plants of Delhi are not able to cope with the increasing demand for electricity in the city. The total production of electricity by various existing plants in Delhi is only 1400 Megawatts (MW). Delhi is dependent on electricity from

TABLE 5.1 Power Demand in Delhi from 1998–9 to 2007–8 (in MW)

Year	Demand (MW)
1998–9	2509
1999–2000	2580
2000–1	2670
2001–2	2879
2002–3	3097
2003–4	3289
2004–5	3490
2005–6	3626
2006–7	3736
2007–8	4030
2008–9	4500 (expected)
2009–10	5000 (expected)

Source: Hindustan, New Delhi, 22 March 2008.

other states for its additional requirement of 3400 MW. The situation of power supply is likely to improve with some more power plants being developed in Bawana (1500 MW) and Rithala (108 MW).

Truly speaking, the power situation is grim in the entire NCR including Gurgaon, Noida, Greater Noida, and Ghaziabad. For example, the total demand for electricity in Noida is 470 MW, while the supply is only up to the tune of 320 MW; Greater Noida has a supply of 50 MW against a demand of 75 MW. Similarly, as against a demand of 525 MW, there is a supply of only 375 MW in Ghaziabad. Gurgaon, which is expanding at a very rapid rate also faces power shortage. As against demand of 1074 MW, the supply is only 525 MW. The situation in the satellite towns in NCR is likely to improve by 2011–12 when additional power plants come up at Dadri (7480 MW), Jhajjar (1500 MW), and Bamnauli (750 MW).

WATER

The gap between demand and supply of water in Delhi is also very grim. As against Delhi's per capita demand for 240 litres, the per capita supply is only 96 litres. Delhi's overall demand for water is 950 MGD (millions of gallons per day), there is a supply of only 475 MGD. Like power, Delhi is dependent on supply of water from Haryana and Uttar Pradesh to meet the increasing demand. Haryana releases 360 MGD of Yamuna water daily for Delhi. The water situation in the city has been summed up in a recent economic survey of Delhi in the following words:

> In spite of best efforts made by the government, water supply front remained a matter of concern due to various reasons like raw water scarcity and related problems, transmission and distribution losses, supply with less pressure, uneven distribution, depleting ground water level, non recharge of ground water due to rapid urbanization, increasing cost of water treatment and increasing gap between water supply cost and tariff, etc.[12]

The increasing gap between demand and supply for basic necessities like housing, power, and water has often promoted deviant behaviour among residents in different parts of Delhi. During summer season, this gap has resulted in serious law and order problems in various parts of the city. Inadequate supply of electricity in various parts of the city has led to road blockades, dharnas, and demonstrations by the residents. The wide gap between demand and supply for water and power has led to serious law and order problems in unauthorized colonies and slums as well. In several localities, the scarcity of water and electricity has led to the flourishing of private contractors whose business is supplying electricity and water through generators and water tankers respectively. Fights among the residents, particularly in slums and resettlement colonies, centred on water and electricity shortage are an everyday affair. The analysis of reasons for murders committed during 2010 in the city revealed that two murders took place in trans Yamuna area over this issue: one over taking water from a water pipeline (in Karawal Nagar), and another over the issue of filling of water in a bucket (in Geeta Colony area). It is not out of place to mention that both these areas of Delhi exhibit an acute gap between the number of people and availability of basic civic amenities.

The overcrowding of people and the density of population in certain areas has facilitated several kinds of criminal activities in the city. A correlation could also be established between busy commercial markets, district centres, effluent business establishments, shopping malls and markets, and the rate of crime. The increasing rate of crime in such areas is due to heavy transactions of cash and influx of a floating population on a daily basis. In several areas in Delhi, the criminal elements in the floating population have disappeared after committing the crime. Moreover, these areas also demonstrate the commission of specialized crimes, particularly cheating, fraud, embezzlement, bag lifting and snatching, etc. Crime figures for police stations like Paharganj, Connaught Place, Gandhi Nagar, Kalkaji, and Lajpat Nagar could be understood within this framework. There is also a correlation between the rate of crime and socio-economic composition and distribution of the population in the concerned district/police station. Areas having the existence of rehabilitation colonies, JJ clusters and slum pockets have reported a greater number of crimes, as compare to areas where there is less or no existence of slums, JJ clusters, and rehabilitation colonies. New Delhi district, with the least number of crimes, is a good example as no such pockets are located inside this district. On the other hand, increasing crime in the north-west district could be attributed to the existence of low income group pockets, JJ clusters, resettlement colonies, and slum areas. Districts like south, which has a mixture of all groups and ethnic communities, have also reflected an increasing trend of crime. The peripheral area of the district, like Badarpur, Sangam Vihar, part of Okhla Industrial Area, Dakshin Puri, Mehrauli, Saidlajab, and Jamia Nagar, is full of JJ clusters, slum areas and unauthorized establishments, along with the existence of posh localities within their jurisdiction. It is not unusual to find squatter huts next to modern highrise buildings or five star hotels, or in the nooks and crevices of the posh colonies of Delhi.[13] These areas have also affected the crime graph of the home police station as well as the neighbouring police stations in the district. The existence of such a pattern is also visible in districts like south west, east, and north-east.

STRUCTURAL CONSTRAINTS OF ROAD, PARKING SPACE, AND CRIMINALITY IN THE CITY

The uniqueness and diversity of Delhi as a metropolis is also reflected by the transport fleet of the city. One can find the presence of the latest low floor red (AC) and green (non-AC) Delhi Transport Corporation (DTC) buses on Delhi's roads adjacent to handcarts and horse carts. There are as many as fifteen different varieties of transport available in the city which caters to different classes of people. Some of these are TSRs (three-wheeler scooter rickshaws), goods cycle rickshaws, Phut-Phuts, taxis, tempos, school Maruti vans, trucks, three-wheeler goods carrier, etc. Apart from this commercial fleet of vehicles, the city is full of private cars. The city registered as many as 6.5 million vehicles in the beginning of 2010. Road experts believe that practically 1000 vehicles are added every day on Delhi roads. The problem in Delhi is further aggravated with the movement of another 8 lakh vehicles from the satellite towns situated around Delhi. According to the findings of Centre for Science and Environment (CSE), there has been a 132 per cent increase in the number of cars in Delhi in the last ten years, whereas the total road length has increased by only 20 per cent during the same period. Although Delhi's average length of roads per 100 sq. km (1992 km) is still way above the national average, the scenario reflects that Delhi has more vehicles than can be accommodated on the road. The increase in the number of vehicles in the city has three important implications.

First, it has led to congestion and affected movement patterns on the road. Since there is a scarcity of parking space, it has led to encroachment and congestion in the residential localities. People own cars despite the fact that they do not have enough space for parking. In several posh localities, where there are more than four cars in a single family, the parking is done on the lanes and by-lanes.

Second, the huge numbers of cars in the city and inadequate parking space has also increased motor vehicle theft in the city. It is always easy to steal a car from an open space, as compared to closed premises. The paucity of parking space has also reflected deviance and criminal behaviour on the part of citizens in several localities. Minor scuffles, at times leading to serious injuries to owners of cars, over parking in front of houses on public roads often get reported in the local police stations. Delhi has also witnessed the worst forms of road rage where errant drivers have indulged in the killing of people over minor issues like parking, overtaking, and lane driving. The recent death of a hotelier in Khan Market in New Delhi after being dragged gruesomely under a car driven by an airline pilot, reflects the driving culture and ethos of a driver in the city. Such drivers have, at times, even assaulted the on duty traffic cop who dared to prosecute him for a driving offence. Last, the increasing number of vehicles has also promoted pollution in the city.

Thus, infrastructural constraints do play a very important role in shaping deviance and criminal behaviour in fast growing metropolitan cities, where overall development creates a gap in the process of availability of basic resources to its increasing numbers. Reflecting on the peculiar dilemma of development and how it affects crime, the Prime Minister of India, Manmohan Singh very rightly said:[14]

> With development, there are also tensions. Because the capacity for development is not uniformly distributed to all our citizens. There are variant capacities. There was an old system, the caste system, when a person was left behind, he could always blame it on his birth. But now we teach in our schools that we are citizens of a unique Republic which prides itself on providing equality of opportunity to all our citizens. But that is the norm. But whether it is in fact the case or not, I think very often reality is different from norms, even then we are getting growth rates of 8–9 per cent per annum, and there are people who believe they are left out. When they are left out, I think the grievances against the system multiply and some of them take the form of challenging the authority of law and order. The crime rate grows up probably it is inherent in the processes of urbanization that incidents of urban crimes will be a problem for quite some time to come and it may be an increasing problem.

Keeping in tune with ground realities, some of these factors were also considered as very important factors for crime in urban areas by the seventh report of the National Police Commission (NPC). The report, while discussing crime in urban areas observed:

> the existence of a large floating population, the presence of gullible rural migrants, give rise to crimes involving cheating, confidence tricks, etc. Large population and heavy densities increase anonymity, the flow of large cash in the handling of business through banks, cinema houses, and major retail outlets increase the temptation as well as the opportunity for crime.[15]

6

TERRORISM

Several acts of terror in recent years—hijacking of an aircraft (1999), attacks on the Parliament in New Delhi (2001), on Akshardham Temple in Gujarat (2002), and at the Indian Institute of Science, Bangalore (2005), bomb blasts in market places in Delhi (2005) and in Varanasi (2006), serial bomb blasts in Mumbai (2006) and Malegaon (2006), massacre of labourers in Assam (2007), etc.—demonstrate that terrorism is not confined to a few pockets and that almost every part of the country is vulnerable.[1]

Terrorism has emerged as one of the most serious challenges before law enforcing agencies in the country as a whole, today. It has emerged as a major challenge to internal security. The perpetrators of terrorist violence are choosing their targets globally and indulging in violence everywhere. According to a 2007 report on terrorism by the National Counter Terrorism Centre (NCTC) in the USA, approximately 14,000 terrorist attacks occurred in various countries during 2007, resulting in over 22,000 deaths. Compared to 2006, the attacks remained approximately the same in 2007, while death rose by 1800, a 9 per cent increase from the previous year. The largest number of deaths occurred in the near east and south Asia. These regions accounted for about 87 per cent of the 355 casualty attacks, each of which killed 10 or more people.[2] Expressing concerns regarding the problem of terrorism, the union home minister of India observed: '[W]e live in a troubled world and a troubled neighbourhood that has witnessed numerous acts of terror last year. In 2010, there were at least 35 major acts of terror in a number of countries. India is no more—but no less—vulnerable than any other country.'[3]

Unlike other metropolitan cities, Delhi has been always on the radar of various terrorist groups. Before the scenario of terrorism in Delhi is discussed in detail, a brief discussion regarding conceptual aspects of the problem and the way it has been changing, is necessary.

It is very difficult to define terrorism today; more so in the light of so many kinds of definitions. One international expert has rightly said that the phenomenon of terrorism is shrouded in terminological confusion.[4] Without going into the polemics regarding the conceptual definition of the term terrorism, Bruce Hoffman has provided a very broad definition of terrorism which covers all the dimensions of the problem today. Terrorism, he argues, is

> the deliberate creation and exploitation of fear through violence or the threat of violence in the pursuit of political change. All terrorist acts involve violence or the threat of violence. Terrorism is specifically designed to have far reaching psychological effects beyond the immediate victim(s) or objects of terrorist attack. It is meant to instil fear within and thereby intimidate a wider target audience that might include a rival ethnic or religious group, an entire country, a national government or political party or public opinion in general. Terrorism is designed to create power where there is none or to consolidate power where there is little. Through the publicity generated by their violence, terrorists seek to obtain the leverage, influence, and power they otherwise lack to effect political change on either a local or an international scale.[5]

The basic objective of terrorism is to frighten, scare, terrify, and deter. This is actually the English meaning of the Latin word 'terrere' from which the word terrorism is derived. The methodology used for creating terror is violence. A very celebrated police officer credited with handling and controlling terrorism in Punjab, Julio Riberio,[6] has equated the menace of terrorism with that of a man eater. The man-eating tiger or leopard strikes unsuspecting victims miles away from the scenes of its previous kills. Nobody knows when it will strike or who it will strike. Hence, everybody lives in the mortal fear of instant death and this built-up fear makes life in the surrounding areas extremely uncomfortable and miserable.

Terrorist violence is manifested in diverse forms today. The various forms have different ideological and motivational patterns which triggers a particular group to indulge in terrorist violence with proper justifications for its perpetrators. The Second Administrative Reforms Commission has identified some important forms of terrorism in the country as

- Narco-terrorism
- Religious terrorism
- Ideology-oriented terrorism
- State-sponsored terrorism
- Ethno-nationalist terrorism

Every terror group has an operational target for violence. In this sense, terrorism can be understood at two levels: 1. specific and 2. general.

1. Specific Level of Terrorism: The focus in this approach of terrorism is important individual leaders who are considered as threats and road blockss for the ideology of the terror group. The basic objective of the terror group is to harm such individuals first, so that there is no opposition to their agenda. Individuals falling in this category occupy very important political positions in the ruling establishment. The assassination of the former Prime Minister of India, Rajiv Gandhi, by the Liberation Tigers of Tamil Eelam (LTTE) is a glaring example of specific level of terrorist violence. Several prominent political leaders in the country face threats from various terrorist outfits due to their overt and covert opposition of the demands and ideologies of the groups. Terrorist groups have targeted individual VIPs or their family members for release of their fellow members who are facing criminal charges in the target

country. For example, an Indian Airlines plane from Kathmandu was hijacked by a Pakistan-based terrorist group (Harkat-ul-Mujahideen) in 1999 for the release of their terrorist friends lodged in Delhi's Tihar Jail. Similarly, the daughter of the then chief minister of J&K, Mufti Mohd. Sayeed, Mehbooba Mufti, was kidnapped by a terrorist group for release of their fellow members. These are few examples of specific targets which terrorists chose in the past as a part of their strategy. Over a period of time, specific targets started getting private as well as government security cover, making it very difficult for terrorist groups to strike. As a result, out of desperation the terrorist groups changed their focus from specific persons to general targets. However, specific targets still persist in their hit list.

2. General Level of Terrorism: At the initial stage, a terrorist group develops its hostility towards individuals who are opposed to their interests. Gradually, this hostility turns into hatred towards a particular race, ethnicity, and, at a broader level, towards nation states. Since individual targets operate in a protective environment due to their official and political position, a terror group adopts the methodology of targeting innocent civilians. The basic objective of civilian killings is to gain publicity, recognition, and create panic in the minds of rulers in particular and the ruled in general. Terrorist incidents in hotels, restaurants, market places, and in public transport system are very good examples of general level of terror targets. Incidents like 9/11 in USA, 26/11 in Mumbai, and other such incidents across the globe including our country are examples of general level of terrorism.

Terrorism in Delhi

Delhi as a capital of the country and the centre of power has always been on the target list of terror groups. The city has witnessed both forms of terrorism in the past. The problem of terrorism in Delhi can be classified into the following phases.

Early Phase (till 1997)

This phase actually started in the 1980s. The genesis of terrorist incidents in Delhi can be traced with important political developments in Punjab. The early phase terrorist incidents in Delhi were actually the by-product and retaliation of political developments in Punjab, where the Sikh community was demanding for a separate state called, Khalistan. The Khalistan movement in Punjab also got support from Pakistan-based militants. In 1984, the militant activities in Punjab were curbed through Operation Blue Star which was carried out in the holy Sikh shrine, the Golden Temple, in Amritsar. After a fierce battle between the army and the militants led by Bhindranwale, the Golden Temple was taken under control by the army. The whole operation witnessed the death of eighty-three army personnel with injuries to more than 249 others. On the other hand, more than 493 militants were killed, and eighty-six were injured. The incident in the Golden Temple became a solid ground for various militant groups to retaliate. Their anger and protest led to terrorist incidents not only in Punjab but also in other places, particularly Delhi. The immediate fallout of the incident was the assassination of Indira Gandhi, the then Prime Minister of India, by her own bodyguards in 1984. This incident witnessed a major riot in Delhi in which several Sikhs were killed. Both these incidents played a very important role in the early phase of terrorist incidents in Delhi. This period also saw the emergence of various new terrorist groups in Punjab. Prominent among these groups were Babbar Khalsa International, Khalistan Commando Force, Khalistan Liberation Force, and Khalistan Zindabad Force. These groups carried out tragic terror incidents after 1984. In 1985, Air India's Flight 182 from Canada to India was bombed by Sikh militants, in which more than 329 people on board were killed.

In 1985, Delhi witnessed serial transistor bomb blasts in various parts. These blasts were carried out by Khalistan sympathizers who used transistors like contraptions with an explosive mixture of picric acid and ammonium nitrate added to dry batteries. Sixty-nine people were killed and 127 people were injured in different incidents that took place in buses and public places. The number of terrorist incidents that happened in Delhi shown in Table 6.1. The early phase of terrorist incidents in Delhi were initially carried out by Punjab-based terrorist outfits with logistical and other support from across the border. The methodology and technology used in these blasts were not very sophisticated. The targets were both specific and general, but the causalities were mostly innocent people, rather than specific targets. The maximum number of terrorist incidents in this phase took place in the year 1997 when the city was rocked by as many as 21 incidents. These incidents happened in different parts of the city. Most of these incidents took place between July and December. It happened in areas like Punjabi Bagh, Karol Bagh, Sadar Bazar, Kingsway Camp, and Red Fort. Incidentally, all these areas are prominent market places and always remain crowded. The most number of causalties occurred in the bomb blast in Chandni Chowk on 30 November 1997 in which three people were killed and seventy-three others were injured.

Intermediate Phase

The period from 1998–2000 can be considered as an intermediate phase of terrorist activities in Delhi. Although terrorist incidents did take place during this period, the intensity as compared to 1997 was less. These incidents were also significant in the sense that the death toll was less as compared to previous years.

New Phase

The beginning of this phase starts with the attack on Indian Parliament on 13 December 2001 when five gunmen infiltrated the Parliament

House in a VIP car bearing home ministry and Parliament car labels. While both the Rajya Sabha and Lok Sabha had been adjourned forty minutes prior to the incident, many MPs, including the then Home Minister L.K. Adwani were reportedly inside the house. The gunmen rammed their vehicle into the car of the Indian Vice President Krishna Kant and started indiscriminate firing. The security officials detailed with the vice president retaliated. In a fierce battle between the security forces and the militants, all the terrorists were killed including five policemen on duty. This incident was carried out by the Pakistan-based terrorist groups, Lashkar-e-Taiba and Jaish-e-Muhammad. This incident was an indirect attack on the democratic institution of the country. It was quite different from the earlier attacks in terms of methodology. This was carried out by a dedicated suicide squad (*fidayeen*). Another significant feature of the attack was its cross border connection. In this sense, terrorism assumed an international dimension. The new phase saw the emergence and participation of Muslim terrorist groups. This also coincided with the emergence of a dreaded phase of international terrorism across the globe. Just two months before this incident, on 11 September 2001, al-Qaeda terrorists hijacked four commercial passenger jet airliners in USA. The hijackers intentionally crashed two of these airliners into the Twin Towers of the World Trade Center (WTC) in New York, killing everyone on board and many others present in the buildings. Both buildings collapsed within two hours, destroying nearby buildings and damaging others. The hijackers crashed a third airline into the Pentagon in Arlington, Virginia, just outside Washington, DC. The fourth plane crashed into a field near Shanksville in rural Pennsylvania after some of its passengers and flight crew attempted to retake control of the plane, which the hijackers had redirected toward Washington, DC. There were no survivors from any of the flights.

Nearly 3000 victims and 19 hijackers died in the attacks. According to the New York State Health Department, 836 responders, including fire-fighters and police personnel, have died as of June 2009. Among the 2752 victims who died in the attacks on the WTC, 343 were fire-fighters and 60 were police officers from New York City Police and Port Authority. Another 184 people were killed in the attacks on the Pentagon. The overwhelming majority of casualties were civilians, including nationals of over 70 countries.

This phase of terrorist incidents continued with a renewed vigour and strength, and several planned incidents occurred not only in Delhi but in other parts of the country as well. This phase also saw the consolidation of several countries in Europe for a joint international plan for action on terror across countries. As a result, several countries came together to provide a unified stand against terror. A paradigm shift in the strategy to fight terror emerged across nations as more and more developed nations became victims of this menace.

The new phase of terrorism saw another paradigm shift in terms of targets chosen, as demonstrated by the deadly attacks in Taj Mahal Hotel and Oberoi Hotels in Mumbai in 2008. For a change, the terrorists targeted the elite section of society. These attacks were also significant as they reflected overt participation of cross border terrorists in the country. The incidents in Mumbai further increased the vulnerability of five star hotels and other important eating joints, particularly in metropolitan cities. Logically, Delhi became further vulnerable to terrorist attacks after these incidents.

The new phase of terrorism also became significant because terrorists started using new technological tools to achieve their targets. This phase of terrorism marked the advent of suicide squads who sacrificed their lives for the cause. This phase saw the use of liquid bombs, detected in Europe, which increased the vulnerability of air travel followed by an international ban on carrying liquids (and gels) as a preventive strategy.

CYBER TERRORISM

By this time, information technology had assumed newer heights globally. Terrorists were very prompt in using this technology as a part of a new methodology of terror. Law enforcing agencies all over the world were further confronted with the problem of cyber terrorism. Cyber terrorism has acquired new dimensions today. The World Economic Forum[7] has considered cyber terrorism as a global risk in a recently published document. The report considers that cyber terrorism is perhaps less understood and is fuelling concerns over the openness of the Internet, security, and privacy. It observed that many have inferred a high risk of cyber terrorist attacks from terrorist organizations' extensive use of the Internet in recent years for doctrinal, recruitment, and operational communication purposes, as well as some occurrences of cyber theft.

Terrorist incidents have affected different parts of the city. Table 6.1 shows that except 2002–3, bomb blasts have been taking place in Delhi every year with the highest number of bomb blasts occurring in year 1997.

TABLE 6.1   Bomb Blasts in Delhi

Year	Number of Incidents
1991	12
1992	11
1993	5
1994	2
1995	6
1996	3
1997	21
1998	5
1999	2
2000	4
2001	5
2002	
2003	
2004	1
2005	5
2006	1
2008	5

The actual breakup of terrorist incidents in various parts of Delhi since 1997–2008 are shown in Table 6.2.[8]

TABLE 6.2 Bomb Blasts in Delhi, 1997–2008

Date	Place	Killed	Injured
27 September 2008	Flower Market, Mehrauli	3	21
13 September 2008	Karol Bagh, Connaught Place, and Greater Kailash	25	150
14 April 2006	Jama Mosque, Walled City, Old Delhi	0	14
29 October 2005	Sarojini Nagar/Paharganj/ Govindpuri	59	155
22 May 2005	Liberty/Satyam cinema	1	60
13 December 2001	Parliament	11	30
11 August 2001	South Extension	-	2
20 May 2001	CGO Complex	-	-
9 May 2001	Army Headquarters/Dalhousie Road	-	1
18 June 2000	Red Fort	2	-
16 March 2000	Sadar Bazar	-	7
27 February 2000	Paharganj	-	8
6 January 2000	Old Delhi Railway Station	-	20
3 June 1999	Chandni Chowk	-	27
16 April 1999	Holambi Kalan Railway Station	2	-
19 December 1998	Bhajanpura Temple	-	Unspecified
31 August 1998	Turkman Gate	1	17
26 July 1998	Interstate Bus Terminal	2	3
9 January 1998	ITO	-	40
30 December 1997	Punjabi Bagh	4	30
30 November 1997	Chandni Chowk	3	73
26 October 1997	Karol Bagh	1	34
18 October 1997	Rani Bagh	1	23
10 October 1997	Kingsway Camp	1	18
1 October 1997	Sadar Bazar	-	30
1 October 1997	Frontier Mail Train	3	Unspecified
14 July 1997	Red Fort	-	18
4 January 1997	Sonepat Road	1	11

Source: www. satporg.org.

The analysis of various terrorist incidents, investigations, and apprehension of terrorists over a period of time have reflected cross border dimensions. The socio-political situation in the neighbouring countries, particularly Pakistan, has very important consequences for India. Terror outfits in Pakistan have always cultivated bases in different parts of the country and have triggered off terror attacks with the help of local recruits. Conspiracies to carry out terror attacks in the country as a whole and Delhi in particular are being carried out by various terrorist outfits abroad.

Recent trends have revealed an ideological convergence of diverse terror outfits for pragmatic purposes to execute terror incidents in the city. The socio-economic and demographic profile of Delhi has been very conducive for pre-planning of terror targets by groups. Urban anonymity and the floating profile of the city have proved to be a boon for terrorist outfits in the past. The international dimension of terrorist incidents in Delhi is evident from the arrest and killing of the following Pakistani nationals in the past few years as shown in Table 6.3.

TABLE 6.3 Pakistani Nationals and Criminals Arrested/Neutralized

Year	Arrested	Killed
1997	4	
1998	14	
1999	1	
2000	19	2
2002	2	4
2003	7	
2004	13	1
2005	6	
2006	4	
2007	11	
2008	6	
2009	3	

This aspect has been recognized world over and stands substantiated through various reports. This is evident from the following text:

> Pakistan has given sanctuary to 20 principal leaders of Sikh and Muslim Terrorist groups, including hijacker of an Indian aircraft and transnational criminals colluding with terrorists. Despite strong evidence of their presence in Pakistani territory and active cooperation from there, its government has denied their presence and refused to act against them. It has also ignored Interpol notices for apprehending them and handing them over to India.[9]

A recent example of cross-border terrorism has been the 26/11 attack in Mumbai in which a Pakistani national Ajmal Kasab was apprehended red-handed by the security forces, and has recently been sentenced to death by a Mumbai court. A very significant feature of terrorist incidents in Delhi has been that civilians or common citizens have been the usual targets. Despite futile attempts on very specific targets, the terrorist groups have more or less not been able to harm important political functionaries in past, with a few exceptions. This is precisely due to adequate security cover and deployment of round-the-clock armed personnel. As a result, various groups have targeted crowded places like markets where innocent citizens have lost their lives. The overall topography, vastness, and multiple entry and exit points at prominent places in the city always pose operational problems for law-enforcing agencies making foolproof security arrangements.

MODUS OPERANDI ADOPTED BY TERRORIST GROUPS

Investigations carried out and the scrutiny of scenes of crime has revealed various modus operandi adopted by the terrorist groups in different incidents. Of late, it has been observed that the terrorist groups have been adopting modern technology in carrying out incidents. Changes have been seen in the kind of explosives and improvised explosive devices used from time to time. The initial blasts carried out in the early phase of terror attacks in Delhi were low intensity explosives. These explosives were planted in commonly use articles, which would not arouse suspicion. In such cases, the perpetrators of crime used to abandon bombs in crowded places and disappear. Bombs have been planted in items like tiffin carriers, containers, bicycles, and briefcases with timer devices. In such cases, the assailants used to operate from behind the scene. These terrorists took full advantage of fluid security at the target places and could easily mingle with the anonymous crowd. The basic aim was to create terror in the minds of ordinary citizens.

The year 2000 saw a gradual change in the technology and methodology used by terrorist groups. They stated making use of modern means of communication like Internet and mobile phones for coordination of their activities. Gradually, more lethal explosives like Research Department Explosive (RDX) came into use by terrorist groups. This phase also saw the emergence of suicide squads and use of sophisticated weapons like AK-47 rifles, hand grenades, and rocket launchers by the terrorist groups. They were more overt and wanted publicity for their actions. Suicide squads are considered to be the most lethal form of terrorism. The attack on the Indian Parliament was carried out by such a group. This phase also saw use of different objects and articles for planting of explosives. For example, on 29 October 2005, three explosions took place in three different places in Delhi. The first explosion took place outside New Delhi Railway Station near Paharganj. The explosives in this case were planted in a two wheeler. In the second blast, the explosives were kept in a plastic bag in a Delhi Transport Corporation (DTC) bus, while the third and the most powerful explosion took place at the busy Sarojini Nagar market, where the explosives were planted in a second-hand Maruti car. All the three blasts together saw 62 dead and more than 210 injured.

The investigation of various cases and interrogation of the apprehended terrorists over a period of time has revealed the following
important dimensions of their overall strategy in the execution of
their assigned tasks:

1. The key members have carried out complete survey of their
target area much before the actual operation. During the survey, they
have identified possible entry and exit routes. They also established
the vulnerability of the proposed target from the security point of
view, and also assessed the logistical requirements for the operation.

2. Immediately after survey of the proposed target, they have
taken a hideout within the city on rent. The members have tried to
take houses on rent on rates higher than the market rate. Several
group members have stayed in guest houses as well. It is at this
stage that they try to mobilize the resources required for the actual
operation. It includes procurement of second hand cars, scooters,
etc.

3. They have used nearby PCOs and cyber cafés for getting in
touch with their leaders as well as coordinating of other details related
to the operation. They have also used cyber cafes for communicating
and claiming responsibility for a particular incident immediately
after the blast.

4. The groups have also recruited local carriers for carrying out
supplementary jobs by paying them handsome amounts. This is a
very significant and alarming trend in terrorist strategy. Showing
concerns about local modules and the sympathizers of terrorist
activity, Manmohan Singh, the prime minister of India has observed
that the

> growing problem we face [is] of terrorism, sometimes supported by forces
> outside our countries, but we must also recognize that today I think there
> are dangers that terrorism can become an internal intruding problem as
> well. If it is terrorism driven by outside forces or sent to our country, it is
> in some way easy. But if terror modules are to be found in our country
> and some misguided elements of our society take to that path, I think we
> have to tackle this problem with all sensitivity that it requires.[10]

RESPONSE TO TERRORISM: METHODOLOGY AND STRATEGY

The problem which emerged in the 1980s posed a major challenge to Delhi Police. The police machinery at the initial stage was not at all prepared to handle this menace. Theoretically speaking, this is a special type of crime which requires special treatment by a specialized force, rather than a general preventive and detective police organization. A former Delhi Police Commissioner, Ved Marwah,[11] rightly said: 'The police in India are not recruited, trained or equipped to combat terrorism.' As a city police force responsible for the overall maintenance of law and order and crime control in the city, Delhi Police had to address itself to the problem of terrorism in Delhi and tune its ground machinery accordingly. In the recent years, this has assumed a central place in the overall policing scheme in the city. All major functions in Delhi are on the radar of terror groups. They look forward to the most opportune time to launch attacks during such functions and derive the maximum mileage out of it. Anti-terror preventive measures have become part and parcel of day-to-day policing in Delhi today. Taking cue from the various incidents over a period of time, Delhi Police has been able to devise meaningful preventive strategies for combating the menace of terror-related incidents. The preventive strategy is a mixed package which includes awareness and participation of the civil society, apart from pro-active executive actions initiated by the local police as a whole. The measures can be classified into two categories: preventive and detective.

Preventive Measures

These measures are based on inputs received from earlier incidents. Such measures have been further classified in two categories.

1. **Preventive Measures Initiated by Delhi Police**: The following constitute important aspect of these measures. These are measures where the local police seek the active cooperation and participation of citizens.

a. **Regular Checking of Hotels and Guest Houses in Delhi**: In order to establish the credentials and authenticity of the residents, periodic surprise-checks of all the guest houses and hotels are carried out by the local police as well as the centralized anti-terrorist cell of Delhi Police.

b. **Regular Checking of Cyber Cafés and PCOs**: All the cyber café owners have been directed to maintain registers regarding use of the café by various clients under 144 CrPC (Criminal Procedure Code). They have also been directed by the police to obtain valid identity proof of the users before allowing them to use the Internet. In a recent directive by the police, all cyber café owners are supposed to install CCTV cameras at their premises. The compliance of all these directions is checked by the local beat officers on a regular basis.

c. **Regular Tenant Verification**: In order to prevent misuse of rented premises, all house owners in Delhi are directed to furnish the details of the proposed tenant to the local police before letting the house on rent. This is enforced through the issuance of an order under 144 CrPC. The compliance of these directions is also checked through a sustained tenant verification drive launched by individual police stations in their areas.

d. **General Awareness towards Suspicious Objects and Persons**: All the stakeholders and citizens in general are sensitized regarding general safety measures to be adopted in day-to-day lives. Such awareness is created by Delhi Police through centralized issuance of advertisements in leading national dailies in Hindi and English and different channels of All India Radio (AIR). Such advertisements also mention the do's and don'ts to be followed in case of terror incidents. Stakeholders like vendors, *chowkidars*, scrap dealers, and other vulnerable groups are motivated to share information with the local police regarding suspicious objects and persons through a very meaningful scheme called 'Eyes and Ears Scheme'.

e. Regular Meetings with Market Associations and other Crucial Stakeholders: Taking cue from earlier incidents and vulnerability of markets in Delhi, regular meetings are held with various market associations and their cooperation is sought in implementing certain basic safety measures from an anti-terrorist point of view. Regular announcements related to anti-terror precautions are conveyed to general citizens on public announcement systems in prominent markets.

2. Proactive Anti-terror measures adopted by Delhi Police: Immediately after the 26/11 incident in Mumbai, one out of the three inspectors in every police station has been designated as an Anti-Terrorist Officer (ATO). The basic job of the ATO is to take stock of the preparedness of the police station for any possible terrorist strike. He/she is supposed to ensure and supervise the ground implementation of various anti-terrorist measures in the police station under the overall supervision of SHO.

a. Deployment of Mobile Quick Reaction Teams (QRTs): In order to prevent and retaliate quickly during a terror incident, every police station has deployed QRTs in and around vulnerable places. These places include shopping complexes, crowded markets, metro stations, and other locations which attract large crowds on a regular basis. These mobile QRTs contain specially trained commandos who are supposed to react during an incident and chase the culprits.

b. Special Weapons and Tactics (SWAT) Commandos: They are commandos, specially trained from an anti-terrorist point of view. This group of commandos came in existence after the Mumbai incident. They work under the direct control and command of the Anti-Terrorist Cell of Delhi Police. They act as back-up during anti-terrorist operations and provide support to the existing resources of the local police.

Detection Aspect

Collection of Intelligence, Coordination, Dissemination, and Execution of Various Terror-related Inputs: The special cell of Delhi Police is the nodal agency to coordinate various inputs related to terror with other sister agencies. The investigation of all terrorist-related incidents is carried out by this cell only. This cell is also instrumental in apprehending the militants and prosecutes them as per the law. They also coordinate and supervise various anti-terror exercises carried out by the local police in day-to-day policing. They have been instrumental in solving all important terrorist-related incidents in past. Their proactive approach has also neutralized several terrorist modules in past. Commenting on the performance of the cell in neutralizing various modules, the then commissioner of police,[12] in the foreword to the Annual Review of 1998, said: 'We can reasonably feel proud of our achievements in neutralizing ISI backed terrorist modules operating in the country. Out of total detection of 28 modules we accounted for 17—a rare feat by any standard.' This is also evident from the seizure of explosives and apprehension of militants from time to time by the sleuths of the special cell. In 2010, as many as 18 terrorists belonging to various groups were apprehended by Delhi Police (see Table 6.4).

In instances of terror strikes, Delhi Police has shown rare professionalism and ability for efficient investigation of cases, some

TABLE 6.4   Organization-wise Breakup of Arrested Cross-border Terrorists

Organization	No. of Terrorists
Lashkar-e-Taiba (LeT)	9
Jammu Kashmir Islamic Front (JKIF)	9
Babbar Khalsa International (BKI)	2
Others (Kashmiri militants)	1
Total	18

of which have ended up in conviction. The cases of terrorist attack on the Parliament and Red fort were solved very quickly in a record time.

PUBLIC-PRIVATE PARTNERSHIP FOR COMBATING TERRORISM

The fight against terrorism in the city requires constant awareness and participation of the citizens in Delhi. An alert citizen can always avert an incident by adopting certain basic precautions and sharing information with the local police. We all know how a child averted a bomb blast in Connaught Place in 2008 when a bomb was planted in the dustbin near Regal cinema. Timely sharing of the input by the child with the area beat officer helped in diffusing the explosives and saving human lives and property. This requires the breakdown of a feeling of anonymity among residents and fostering healthy community living. We all know that a terrorist needs a place to live in the city to coordinate logistics and various operational aspects of his plan. Terrorist groups have often taken houses on rent for short periods in prominent localities by paying very high rentals. A landlord should take such instances with a pinch of salt and inform the local police. In an urban set-up, we are less sensitive to our surroundings and tend to ignore some very unusual things in day-to-day life. The importance of community policing in combating the menace of terror was highlighted by the union home minister while delivering a lecture on the eve of IB Centenary Endowment Lecture. He said:[13]

> More often than not, intelligence is provided by the citizen who would wish to remain faceless and nameless. It is therefore important that state governments adopt community policing and establish a toll free service under which a citizen can provide information or lodge a complaint. It is the myriad bits of information flowing from different sources that when sifted, analysed, matched, correlated and placed together, become actionable intelligence.

It will not be out of place to mention that Delhi Police has made available a toll-free phone number (1090) for citizens to share information regarding suspicious objects and persons.

The role of the civil society in combating the menace of terrorism was also recognized by the Administrative Reforms Commission report on combating terrorism. The report[14] observed:

> Civil Society could also be of immense help in the prevention of terrorist acts. They could play an advisory and educative role in making the community at large aware of the basic precautions to be taken because in most terrorist strikes, the common citizens are the target. It is therefore necessary that the citizens are themselves well equipped and trained to handle any such incident, as apart from being the victims they are also often the first responders in any crisis. Civil societies and NGOs can partner with law enforcement agencies to develop targeted programmes for cooperation, focusing, for example, on spreading awareness and understanding of the diversity of local cultures, religious customs and traditions of certain communities and in developing outreach activities for healing community rifts and tensions. An alert citizenry is perhaps the best way to ward off terrorist strikes. Civil society in conjunction with the agencies of the State can help in developing this capability among the citizens.

Today, terrorism has assumed an international dimension and posed itself as a major challenge before every nation. Even more developed nations are gradually becoming the victims of terrorist violence. The new trend of terrorist violence has acquired a multnational dimension in terms of planning, recruitment, target, and logistical support. Any meaningful strategy to combat the menace of terrorism has to take into account this reality and plan counter-terrorist measures accordingly. Emphasizing the international dimension of terrorist violence the then secretary general of United Nations, Kofi Annan, proposed that there is a need for a principled, comprehensive strategy which the entire world can support and implement. He proposed the 'five Ds'.[15] They are:

1. First, we must *dissuade* disaffected groups from choosing terrorism as a tactic.

2. Second, we must *deny* terrorists the means to carry out their attacks. That means making it difficult for them to travel, to receive financial support, or to acquire nuclear or radiological material.

3. His third D is the need to *deter* states from supporting terrorist groups.

4. The fourth D focuses on *developing* the capacity of states to prevent terrorism. Terrorists exploit weak states as havens where they can hide, train, or recruit personnel.

5. The fifth D highlights that human rights and rule of law be *defended* at all costs.

Notwithstanding the constraints in fighting the menace of terrorism in a billion-plus city like Delhi, Delhi Police has done a commendable job in meeting the challenge of terrorism headlong in the city. By cracking several terrorist modules in time, Delhi Police has been able to avert havoc in the city. The successful completion of the recently held XIXth Commonwealth Games in the city in the backdrop of a heightened security threat is a testimony to the overall efforts in this direction.

7

CRIME AGAINST
WOMEN AND JUVENILES

Crime against women has assumed an important place in the analysis of crime in metropolitan cities for law enforcing agencies. In Delhi, even a small incident involving women attracts a lot of media coverage. Crime against women has taken different forms with the changing socio-economic profile of the city. It is important to mention that till 1959, no case related to crime against women was registered in Delhi in any police station. It is only in 1960 that the registration of rape cases became part of the official crime statistics. The non-registration and non-reporting of rape or sexual assault cases need to be seen in the overall framework of the existing social norms and status of women during that time in society. Historically speaking, the offences related to women have a strong social stigma attached to them. Even if incidents may have happened, they were not reported due to social inhibitions attached both to the offence and its formal reporting at police stations.

However, as soon as society became more open and women got educated, participation of women in various activities increased. The upward social mobility, exposure to formal education, and contact with outside world in different spheres increased the vulnerability of women and children to crime. Westernization, consumerism, education, and economic independence of women further contributed to this problem. Globalization and the culture of metro cities have made women more and more susceptible to crime.

The offences against women can be broadly classified into following broad categories:

- Rape
- Kidnapping and abduction for different purposes
- Homicide for dowry (dowry deaths) or their attempts
- Torture (mental and physical)
- Molestation
- Sexual harassment
- Importation of girls
- Other offences against women under provisions of various local and special laws like Immoral Traffic (Prevention Act), Dowry Prohibition Act, Child Marriage Restraint Act, Indecent Representation Prohibition Act, Commission of Sati Act, and the latest Domestic Violence Act.

However, of all the cases, the cases under rape and molestation of women, dowry deaths, kidnapping, and abduction of women get reported in large numbers and also attract wide publicity. The figures under various categories during 2003–7 may be seen in Appendix 7.1. In the discussion that follows, detailed case studies of various rape cases registered in Delhi over the years will be presented. The analysis attempts to demystify some of the popular misconceptions attached with such offences in Delhi. The second part of the chapter is an analysis of kidnapped/abducted women and girls through an organized network of traffickers from different parts of the country for the purpose of commercial sexual exploitation in the organized sector. This analysis has been done on the basis of personal interviews with victims who have been rescued from brothels located at G.B. Road in Delhi.

DOWRY DEATHS

Historically speaking, issues related to dowry have always been a personal affair between two families where things used to get resolved through mutual consent. The death of young girls immediately after marriage by suicide or through brutal killings following demands for dowry in urban areas became a serious concern, which led to provisions of a separate section under the IPC, specifically to deal with dowry-related cases. Over a period of time, dowry deaths have been increasing in metropolitan cities and have indeed become a matter of serious concern. Perusal of figures under dowry deaths in Delhi during 2003–7 shows a gradual increase except 2004 and 2005.

Dowry deaths have sociologically affected the age-old institution of marriage and led to serious social tensions within the family in the urban set-up. This has actually led to the diminution of marriage as an institution of social equilibrium and security, especially in urban areas. This has also affected the incidence of juvenile crimes in families where matrimonial disputes exist. In several cases, the demand for dowry becomes a potent tool to enhance economic prosperity of the groom's family. Since many families are not able to enhance their economic status in the city due to competition and lack of legitimate resources, among other factors, dowry has emerged as the quickest means to be rich overnight

The peculiar dimension of this crime is the involvement of the whole family and their criminal conspiracy in pursuing their illegitimate demands, up to the extent of murdering newlywed girls or creating situations where married women are left with no option but suicide. Normally, marital disputes have been solved by the senior members of the family. Unfortunately, such disputes are now solved through police intervention and courts.

I had the opportunity to interact with many such couples and families during the course of the official discharge of duties in various field postings. As a student of sociology, it was shocking for me to see the behaviour of parents of couples. In many cases, it was either the parents or some other members of the family who were themselves responsible for the breakdown of marital relations between newly-married couples.

EVE TEASING AND MOLESTATION

Analysis of crime (up to 30 April 2008) under this head has shown that a maximum number of cases are committed by school dropouts in the age group of 18–25. This age group is very vulnerable to deviant activities. The important reason for involvement of this age group is exposure to unhealthy print and visual literature, consumerism, lavish lifestyle, loose parental control, and unhealthy socialization. Broadly speaking, the commission of such crimes in metropolitan cities also reflects the attitude of society towards women in general.

RAPE

Analysis of Rape Cases (2003–7)

An analysis of rape cases in the capital during the period 2003–7 reflects some very important findings. The details of these cases may be seen in Appendix 7.2. The analysis was done using the following parameters (which have been explained in detail below):

- Relationship of the accused with the victim
- Number of accused involved
- Elopement
- Age group of accused
- Education standard of accused
- Social status of accused
- Education standard of victims
- Age group of victims
- Social status of victims

1. Relationship of the Accused with the Victim: The analysis shows that in the year 2003, a total number of 50 cases were committed by relatives of the victim. Relatives included father, step father, grandfather, brother, ex-husband, uncle, cousin, brother-in-law, and father-in-law. Out of these categories of relatives, the maximum number of cases (18) were committed by the brother-in-law, followed by the father. Both these categories have a larger share every year till 2007. Commission of incest-rape, and also those by other relatives of the victims, reflects the breaking down of some strong family norms in an urban set-up. Moreover, it also reflects the loosening of healthy family ties in urban areas. The category of relatives is followed by neighbours, friends, and other persons known to the victim. As a whole, in 2003, an overwhelming majority (93.06 per cent) of the cases were committed by known persons. This has been the trend throughout till 2007 when 98.33 per cent cases were committed by known persons. This pattern is also common in some of the advanced nations. For example, an analysis of sexual abuse cases in the USA revealed that rapes and most sexual abuse cases are committed by individuals with whom the victims are related or otherwise acquainted. Such relationships can discourage the victims from reporting the incidents to law enforcing agencies, thus failing to bring the culprit to justice. In the long run, such trends allow the offenders to get away unpunished, leaving them free to commit the offence again.[1]

2. Number of Accused Involved: The analysis shows that most cases were single accused every year till 2007, when 88.96 per cent cases were committed by single accused.

3. Age Group of Accused: The maximum number of cases were committed by persons in the age group of 18–25, followed by 22–35 and 35–50 years. However, the share of persons below 18 years is also very significant. A very important reason for involvement of youth in such cases is their continuous exposure to unhealthy print and visual literature, consumerism, western style of living, and loose control of family.

4. Education Standard of Accused: The maximum number of cases every year were committed by school dropouts and illiterate persons, followed by persons educated up to 10th or 12th standard.

5. Social Status of Accused: The maximum number of cases were committed every year by poor persons (79.80 per cent in 2003 and 2007 followed by middle class people). The share of upper class is minimal. The most important reason for the involvement of poor persons is due to sexual deprivation caused by long absence from family and unhealthy exposure to print and visual literature.

6. Education Standard of Victims: In a maximum number of cases, the victims were illiterate, followed by school dropouts or those educated up to 10th standard.

7. Age Group of Victims: The maximum number of victims were in the age group of 12–16 years followed by 16–18 years and 18–25 years. In few cases registered from 2003–7, the victims were also up to 2 years of age.

8. Social Status of Victims: In a maximum number of cases, the victims were from the lower strata of the society followed by middle class victims. The year 2005 showed the maximum number of victims (13) from the upper class, as compared to previous and subsequent years.

Analysis of Rape Cases Registered in 2010

These findings of the rape analysis are also true for all rape cases registered in Delhi in the first half of 2010. In the year 2010 (up to 30 June), there is an increase of 16.88 per cent in rape cases (277 against 237). Out of these cases, 93 per cent cases were solved by the police. A further analysis of case police station shows that no case of rape was registered in 54 police stations, while 139 (over 50 per cent) cases of rape were reported in 27 police stations. Out of these 27 police stations, 25 fall outside the Ring Road. Moreover, 85 (50 per cent) police stations recorded 89 per cent of all rape cases in Delhi. Out of the 155 territorial police stations, 61 police stations (39 per cent) registered an increase in rape cases, while 94 police stations (61 per cent) registered decline or remained at par. Out of all persons arrested on the charges of rape, 28 were relatives, 41 were friends, 100 (36 per cent) were neighbours, and 94 (34 per cent) were other known persons. In only 14 (5 per cent) of rape cases the crime was committed by a person previously unknown to the victim. Additionally, 84 per cent of the accused arrested were illiterate, school dropouts, or educated up to class 10. Among the accused, 56 per cent were below 25 years and 67 per cent belonged to the lower economic strata.

A close look at the rape statistics for the last ten years (2001–10) reveals that the rape per lakh of population has been declining in Delhi since 2005. This may be seen in the graph in Appendix 7.3a. Delhi has been often portrayed as an unsafe place for women by the media. However, if we compare the rape statistics of Delhi with some of the major cities of the world, it emerges that the portrayal of the city at times as the 'rape capital' is not based on true assessment of facts. Comparison of available figures of rape per lakh of population in eight cities all over the world revealed that except Islamabad all other cities have fared worse than Delhi.[2] In United States, often portrayed as an example of gender equality, has a much worse rate of incidence of rape than Delhi. As against 3.6 percent cases of rape per 1 lakh of population in Delhi, New York has figures of 10.6, while in Washington DC these figures are at 32.6. The same ratio (of rape per lakh of population) in two Australian cities (Brisbane and Cairns) stand at 87 and 83, respectively, as against 3.6 of Delhi.

WOMEN AND CHILDREN COMMERCIAL SEXUAL EXPLOITATION: A CASE STUDY OF SEX WORKERS[3]

Commercial sexual exploitation, also known as prostitution, has been an integral part of society since ages—sometimes as deviant social behaviour and at others as an accepted norm in certain societies. Simone de Beauvoir[4] has rightly said: 'That prostitution has followed humanity from antiquity to the present day; so have many other phenomenons which have not created such emotional and vitriolic responses.' Globally, prostitution has emerged today as a new industry based on demand-supply and other market force mechanisms. End Child Prostitution Asia Tourism estimates prostitution to be a $5 billion-industry.[5] The victims in this profession have landed up under different pretexts through an organized network of traffickers operating in different parts of the country in different forms. The fundamental aspect of the modus operandi has revealed prior acquaintance of the victim or his family with the initial contact person who traffics her from the point of origin to the final point of destination.

Some significant dimensions of trafficking of women and children for commercial sexual exploitation, which emerged through analysis of individual accounts of various victims rescued in Delhi, have been summarized below. These observations are based on personal interview of more than 200 minors rescued from the Garstin Bastion Road (G.B. Road) brothels in Delhi during 2002–4. G.B. Road is Delhi's 'red light' area, the same as Sonagachi in Kolkata and Kamathipura in Mumbai.

1. Delhi was actually a place of delivery for the victims who hail from different parts of the country. These victims came to Delhi from the point of origin through known persons. Out of 270 victims rescued in 2002, there was only one victim who was resident of Delhi. These could be called the source areas of the victims. The actual distribution of the victims across different parts of the country may be seen in Appendix 7.3c.

2. There was no involvement of an organized gang at a national level, which was responsible for the trafficking of all the victims from different parts of the country.

3. The local trafficker followed the following drill for choosing his victims.

Trafficking Cycle[6]

a. Locating Source Area: A trafficker first locates a fertile source area from where the victim can be easily trafficked.

b. Locating Vulnerable Families in the Source Area from an Economic Point of View: After locating the source area, the trafficker tries to locate vulnerable families and from an economic point of view. They also hunt for abandoned, neglected, and step children who can be easily trafficked without much resistance.

c. Getting Friendly with the Victim's Family and the Process of Brainwashing: This is the stage where the trafficker tries to establish rapport with the proposed victim's family and the process of brainwashing, with promise of better economic opportunities, is extended to the victim.

d. Victim is Trafficked: If the trafficker has been able to convince the victim and her family meaningfully, and she readily agrees to the request put forward, she is trafficked. Minor reluctance of the victims is taken care of through clandestine methods.

e. Victim reaches Destination and kept in Transit Stay: In order to avoid suspicion and easy detection by local police due to probable revolt by the victim, traffickers keep them in a transit accommodation which could be a residential area or a hotel.

f. Contact with the owner of the brothel house.

g. Delivery of the victim at the transit place after taking money.

h. The victim finally lands up at the brothel premises and confined.

i. Initial socialization by senior members and exposure to the trade.

j. Surrender to the situation.

4. The analysis also revealed that in some cases the old victims themselves facilitated the movement of fresh girls to the brothel houses in the disguise of being a relative.

Rescue Operations

The rescue operations in Delhi and subsequent investigation by local police were appreciated by all the stakeholders, including Delhi High Court. Some of the important features of the investigation are:

1. Delhi Police took the lead in treating the victims as complainants in several cases, rather than as offenders. This was an important paradigm shift in the strategy of a law enforcing agency. As many as 75 criminal cases were registered on the statement of the rescued victims against traffickers, touts, and *kotha* owners under various sections of IPC and Immoral Traffic [Prevention] (ITP) Act, including sections for confinement, kidnapping, rape, and criminal intimidation. The registration of criminal cases followed by arrests really made a difference in the situation in the red light area. The focus of traffickers shifted from trafficking of victims to organizing legal relief for them. As a result, there was a substantial decrease in the number of fresh victims in the red light area.

2. Due to the intervention of the high court's speedy trial of these cases started while the victims were housed in observation homes.

3. Despite the abortive designs of the kotha owners to win over the victims during trial, the prosecution was able to secure conviction in several cases and exemplary punishment was awarded against the traffickers and brothel owners.

4. Sealing of various kothas on conviction was another milestone which the local police achieved during the trial of these cases. Delhi Police was the first police force in the country to take lead in this regard. Several premises were sealed through court orders without any law and order problem. A similar exercise in Mumbai led to a major law and order problem forcing the police to retreat.

The efforts of Delhi Police in curbing the menace of trafficking in Delhi, through sustained rescue operation followed by effective criminal action, was appreciated not only by the judiciary but was also cited as an example in various official records and reports of Ministry of Women and Child Development in that period.

Interviews of various victims revealed a well organized social structure existing in the red light area. The internal social set-up of the kotha consisted of the following key persons who, apart from discharging important roles in the whole trafficking cycle, also managed day-to-day affairs of the brothels.

1. Madam: She is the actual owner of the brothel house. She could be the real owner of the premises or could have hired the premises on rent. Her basic job is to coordinate the procurement of minor and new girls into the brothel houses. The procurement of minors or young girls is more due to increasing demand. She assigns the day-to-day management of the brothel house to a full-time manager from among the prostitutes (who is slightly older and an expert) to manage the affairs without constant support of the madam.

2. Manager: Manager could either be male or female. The basic job of the manager is to arrange logistics and other support services and resources for all the inmates on a daily basis. The first contact for any customer visiting the brothel house is the manager. It is the manager who allots a particular prostitute to the customer after taking money from him.

3. Touts: This is a floating lot whose essential job is to trap customers from outside the brothel house and drop them to a particular kotha. Every kotha has its own paid touts. They get commission on every customer from the kotha owner. Several *panwallas*, tea-stall vendors, and rickshaw pullers of the area also act as touts as per their convenience. Clash over same customers often results in brawls.

On the basis of the interactions and personal interviews, the victims could be classified into three broad categories:

1. Bonded: These victims have been procured for the kotha from various traffickers. They have landed up in the kotha without being told about it at any stage by the traffickers. As a matter of fact, these victims have been sold by the traffickers to kotha owners directly at a handsome price. In a sense, they are personal properties of the brothel house owners and are entirely at their disposal. They are allotted a particular space to live, which is so inhuman that under normal circumstances anyone would run away. All living expenses of the victim in this category is borne by the management of the kotha. They cannot escape till the amount with which they were bought is realized from them. On top of that, everyday expenses are also added to the overall amount, creating a vicious circle of debt, which makes it very difficult for the victim to be free in the long run. It is a kind of perpetual indebtedness. Every new victim has to pass through this stage at the initial entry into the trade.

2. Nayikas: Every senior prostitute after some point of time patronizes a few younger victims and uses them for her own purposes, precisely because she has been able to facilitate their entry into the brothel house through her own contacts. These victims are known as their pet ones by name. They are also called *nayikas*. However, nayikas do not enjoy the status of kotha owners. They are still under her overall patronage. Senior prostitutes survive on the earnings of the nayikas as they lose their charm for the customers due to age.

3. Commission-based: This status is acquired by the victim once she has become very old in the profession. It is practically impossible for her to go out of the premises. She gets a space to operate.

During rescue operations, it emerged that while in the same premises the owner of the kotha had a well furnished room with all modern amenities, the victims did not even have a bed to sleep on. The normal business activities inside the premises were carried out in partitioned wooden cubicles. The cubicles were also safe hideouts for confining and concealing victims during police raids. I still remember a rescue operation in 2002 when we had a specific tip off regarding the presence of 10 minor victims from a particular state at a particular kotha. During the raid, the entire premises was searched by several police teams, but the trapped victims could not be located. While I was going out with the police team after a sense of disappointment, I saw a strand of long hair coming out of a false wooden ceiling. I tried to pull the hair and to my horror I could find a live source for the hair. The place in question was searched again and the assistance of the owner of the premises was sought. The owner of the premises was questioned regarding the topography of the house. We were finally able to rescue ten minor victims in the age group of 15–17 from the false ceiling. A delay of half an hour would have led to the death of all the victims due to suffocation.

The profile of various rescued victims revealed that the maximum numbers of victims were brought to the premises on the pretext of a better job through contacts known personally to the victims. Several victims also came to the premises by themselves.

JUVENILES

Urbanization, industrialization, and westernization have affected the behavioural pattern of various social groups, particularly in developing societies. Juveniles have always been vulnerable to the negative influences of the various social processes of change since time immemorial due to their innocence and dependence on adults in the formative phase of their life. It is this dependence which has made them vulnerable to several illegal activities. A juvenile needs care and protection against these evil influences at the initial stage of life. If proper care and protection is provided, it reduces the vulnerability of the juvenile to crime in the long run. Before juvenile delinquency and crime in Delhi is discussed, it would be proper to understand the evolution of the concept in the Indian context and the way it has been changing.

A basic question that arises is who can legally be called a juvenile. The perusal of various legal documents reveals that it is the age of a child which acts as a crucial parameter for defining a juvenile. The basic age has been undergoing changes in various documents. To be precise enough, the concept of child has always been suffering from the lack of a uniform legal definition. Under the 1860 IPC, child usually refers to a person less than 12 years of age. The Central Children Act, 1960, which was amended in 1978, defined a child as a boy who had not attained the age of 16, and a girl who had not attained the age of 18. The discrepancy and variation in defining a child in various acts was taken care of through Juvenile Justice Act, enacted in 1986. Under this Act, a delinquent juvenile is defined as one who had committed an offence. It considered a boy who had not attained the age of sixteen and a girl who had not attained the age of eighteen as a juvenile. The act also exempts all children between seven and twelve years of age from all kinds of criminal responsibility. This act underwent further changes with a lot of new modifications in the year 2000. The new act was called Juvenile Justice (Care and Protection of Children) Act, 2000. Under the new Act, the minimum age criteria for defining a child changed yet again and a juvenile or child now meant a person who has not completed the age of eighteen. The changes brought in the new Juvenile Justice Act 2000 were in tune with the UN standards. Another significant theoretical change in the act was deletion of the word delinquent. The Act introduced twin concepts of 'juveniles in conflict with law' and 'juveniles in need of care and protection'. This act also laid down different methodologies to deal with both the categories of juveniles.

In pursuance of the directions of the central act, further rules were also framed by respective states and union territories. The state of Delhi has recently published 'The Delhi Juvenile Justice (Care and Protection) Rules, 2009'.

Juveniles in Conflict with Law

Chapter III of the above rules deals with juveniles in conflict with law. As per section 4 of the rules, there will be one or more

Juvenile Justice Boards (JJBs) to deal with cases pertaining to juveniles. Section 11 of the rules lays down pre-production and post-production formalities to be carried out by different agencies while dealing with juveniles in conflict with law. The rules very clearly state that under no circumstances will the police register a case or FIR against a juvenile, or file a charge sheet except where the offence committed by a juvenile is of serious nature such as rape, murder, or cases which have been committed by juveniles jointly with adults. In the rest of the cases, the police will only record details regarding the offence in the police station diary, which would be followed by a social investigation report. Both these reports will be forwarded to the concerned JJB for further necessary action. The rules also say that every police station will have a Juvenile Welfare Officer (JWO) who will only handle cases related to juveniles. Every police station in Delhi now has two, or more than two, JWOs who deal with cases related to juveniles. The basic philosophy behind such measures is to treat the juvenile differently from normal adult offenders. This emanates from the basic premise that juveniles come in conflict with law due to various reasons beyond his/her control. The attempt of the JJB is to understand the reasons responsible for bringing a juvenile in conflict with the law. They get comprehensive feedback regarding the background of a juvenile through the probation officers of the JJB, as well as initial social investigation reports filed by the police.

Juveniles in Need of Care and Protection

These are cases in which juveniles have not come in conflict with law as yet. They have been found abandoned and recovered under adverse conditions. If immediate care of the child is not taken, he is vulnerable to further abuse by adults in different forms. Such juveniles are also prone to come in conflict with the law because of various reasons beyond their control. Since these juveniles fall in a different category as per the act and rules, they require different handling. As per the rules, juveniles who are recovered by the police or NGOs should be produced before a child welfare committee. As per the orders of the child welfare committee, such juveniles will be sent to juvenile homes for proper care and protection.

A scrutiny of the recent Juvenile Justice Act, 2000 reveals two important features of the act. First, the act treats juveniles differently from the adult criminal, and intends to understand the causes and circumstances responsible for bringing them in conflict with the law. This is done through a detailed analysis of the social background of the juvenile. Second, the act intends to reform the habits of the juveniles coming in conflict with the law by providing them a child-friendly atmosphere by placing them in observation homes.

As a large metropolitan city, Delhi has seen its juveniles coming in conflict with the law in various ways. These juveniles come from both affluent and under-privileged families. However, the reasons for both the categories of juveniles coming in conflict with the law are different. While the former comes in conflict with the law to fulfil his/her luxury and comfort, the latter comes in conflict with the law to fulfil his/her basic survival needs. Juveniles in Delhi are brought up in indifferent socio-economic circumstances. Various studies have explained the inadequate and improper social ambience in urban areas that have forced juveniles to come in conflict with the law over a period of time. In the initial stages of their lives, they are exposed to unhealthy habits. Their initial process of socialization suffers from an unhealthy environment. Delhi has seen increasing numbers of juveniles coming in conflict with the law in the last few years. Total number of juveniles who came in conflict with the law over the years may be seen in Table 7.1. The decrease in the number of juveniles coming in conflict with the law from 2009 onwards is primarily due to the increase in the age of juveniles from 16 to 18 as per the legal definition.

Apart from various other factors like rapid industrialization, urbanization, gradual break-down of joint family norms, emergence of nuclear families, loss of parental control, cases of broken homes, overall family circumstances, growth of consumerism, emergence

TABLE 7.1   Juveniles in Conflict With the Law
(up to 31 August 2010)

Year	Arrests
2001	858
2002	1192
2003	802
2004	909
2005	1250
2006	1513
2007	970
2008	523
2009	586
2010	360

of unhealthy print media, and unhealthy visual exposure in peer group interactions are some of the important sociological factors responsible for the increasing trend of juvenile coming in conflict with the law in Delhi. Experts also feel that depression among children is mostly fuelled by parental anxieties, which have risen to an unprecedented 8–10 per cent in contrast to 2–3 per cent thirty years ago.

According to a recent study by the British medical journal, *Lancet*, Indian teenagers have the world's highest suicide rate, accounting for 50–75 per cent of all deaths among young women in the age group of 15–19, and one-fourth of boys between 10 and 19.[7]

The increasing trend of juveniles coming in conflict with the law is a growing concern for law enforcing agencies everywhere in the world. The Home Office in the UK has listed troubled home life, poor attainment at school, truancy and school exclusion, drug or alcohol misuse, mental illness, deprivation such as poor housing or homelessness, and peer group pressure as some of the important risk factors contributing to the increasing trend of youth crime in England and Wales.

8

TECHNOLOGY AND POLICING

Technology has affected the different dimensions of human lives today in a very big way. It has also affected the policing dimensions in several ways. It has not only affected the law enforcing agencies, but also affected the methodology of crime. The director of Australian Institute of Criminology has aptly summarized the menace of crime induced by rapid technological advancement. He says, 'As we approach the 21st century, our efforts to tackle crime will be significantly assisted by developments in technology. Along with this, however, some contain down side risks.'[1] The impact of technology with implications for policing can be analysed at two levels.

TECHNOLOGY AS FACILITATOR FOR CRIMINALS

Cell Phones

Criminals have been very prompt in adopting new methods and technological tools for crime. They were the first to lay their hands on mobile phones as soon as it emerged as an effective means of communication. Every criminal wants to avoid being caught and also wants to be in touch with his group. Mobile phones proved a boom for them as they could commit and facilitate crime, with less chances of being caught. Today, almost all crimes of kidnapping and abduction for ransom revolve around the cell phone. Starting from the initial demand of money to fixing of the final delivery of money is all through communication on cell phones.

The mobile phone is widely used today by national and international criminals. Since there is no direct physical contact between the victim and the criminal, actual apprehension by the police is also very difficult, unless he is caught red-handed. Shrewd and notorious criminals have recruited henchmen to carry out kidnapping operations, keeping themselves in the background. Even if the actual perpetrators of the crimes are nabbed, the 'Don' behind the scene remains miles away from the clutches of the law. Today, various anti-national and terrorist groups are resorting to bomb blasts and other forms of killings, all of which are planned on cell phones. Although law enforcing agencies have been able to succeed in nabbing criminals through investigation, there are several such gadgets like wireless or satellite phones in the possession of criminals, which are beyond the network of formal investigation. Criminals may shrewdly change their cell phones at the last moment, particularly in kidnapping for ransom cases. I remember a case in which a kidnapper changed the cell phone number for delivery of ransom money in the last minute, so that his actual location is not known to the police. This has become a common modus operandi for seasoned criminals.

Cell phones are also being used today by anti-social elements for sending lewd and obscene messages to women and girls. It has become an effective tool for eve-teasing and harassing working women and young girls in Delhi.

Cyber Crimes

The Internet has emerged as another very popular method to commit sophisticated crimes. Broadly, these crimes can be called Cyber Crimes. The peculiarity of this crime is its international dimension. It is essentially a by-product of a global technological revolution in the field of communication and technology. Every advanced nation today is facing the menace of this crime. According to UK Cyber Crime Report in 2006, more than 3 million online crimes were carried out in the UK alone. These included fraud, blackmail, sexual offences, and computer hacking. The study concluded that out of three million reported online crimes, more than 8,50,000 were sexual offences, 2,00,000 were cases of financial fraud, 90,000 were cases of identity theft, and 1,44,500 were cases of hacking into a person's personal computer. Emails have become preferred means of communication for terrorist groups, for communication and coordination of terrorist modules. Terrorist groups are claiming responsibility for major terror incidents across the world through emails sent directly to the media. Today, criminals trap innocent email users through mails regarding lottery wins. The mail sounds so authentic in terms of the content that several persons have been tempted to proceed with the directions provided by the originator. Lots of people have even sent cash cheques and got themselves cheated.

The increasing trend of cyber crimes in India led to enactment of the Information Technology Act of 2000. Cyber refers to an imaginary space which is created when the electronic devices communicate. A cyber crime refers to anything done in cyber space with a criminal intent. These could be either a criminal act in the conventional sense, or could be activities that have evolved with the growth of the new medium. Cyber crimes include crimes such as hacking, uploading of obscene content on the Internet, sending of obscene emails, and hacking into a person's bank account to withdraw money, among others. The importance of the increasing trend of cyber crime has been emphasized by the Government of India. Through a recent advisory on prevention of crime, MHA has very categorically stated the need for building adequate technical capacity in handling cyber crime. The state governments must create necessary technical infrastructure, including establishment of adequate number of cyber police stations and post-technically trained manpower for detection, registration, investigation, and prosecution of cyber crimes.

According to IT Act, 2000, the following three kinds of offences are important:

1. Tampering with Computer Source Documents: An act without authority or who exceeds authorization of use commits computer tempering by accessing, altering, damaging or destroying any computer, computer program, computer system, and computer network.

2. Hacking with Computer System: This is an act where the intention is to cause, or knowing that it is likely to cause, wrongful loss or damage to the public system.

3. Publishing of Information which is Obscene in Electronic Form: This includes actions where the person publishes or transmits or causes to be published in the electronic form anything which is lascivious.

Technological innovations and new paradigms in the criminal activities have proved that there is no direct link between poverty and commission of crime, as most of these crimes are committed by people who are otherwise very well-off. As a matter of fact, it is the urge for more money which propels persons to commit crimes through sophisticated technological methods. Second, it also demystifies the conventional wisdom that crime is committed by illiterate people only. On the contrary, cyber criminals are sophisticated and intelligent. It requires a certain standard of proficiency and intelligence in handling the tools for the commission of crime. It

TABLE 8.1 Total Number of Cyber Crime Cases
Registered in Delhi

Year	No of Cases
2007	09
2008	06
2009	05
2010 (till 31 October)	36

also requires a certain level of education and expertise in the field. Third, cyber crime has abolished the conventional contact between the victim and the criminal. It has become anonymous in character, where establishing the identity of the real culprit is a herculean task for law enforcers and investigators.

Cyber crime cases have been increasing in Delhi over a period of time. Total number of cases registered in Delhi in the last three years may be seen in Table 8.1, which clearly reflects the increasing trend of cyber-related crimes covered under various sections of IT Act, 2000.

TECHNOLOGY AS FACILITATOR FOR BETTER POLICING

In order to be in tune with recent trends in crime and criminal activities, Delhi Police started making use of new tools and technologies in day-to-day detection of crime and criminals. Since more and more criminals have started using sophisticated tools for the commission of crime, the police had to use technology to counter such moves by the criminals. Apart from adopting appropriate technology to counter criminal activities, Delhi Police has started the use of new tools and technology in a big way as compared to other police forces. Some of the areas where technology has been used extensively are enumerated below:

1. Extensive use of Computers: Every police station in Delhi has more than one computer for use in day-to-day policing. All the reports and diaries which used to be sent through *dak* and in manual handwriting are being sent in computer typed format on emails.

2. Computer-generated First Information Reports (FIRs): Delhi Police is still in possession of those precious and important FIRs in Urdu and Hindi written years back. Till a few years ago, all the FIRs for cognizable and non-cognizable cases were handwritten and delivered to the complainants. Today, any complainant lodging a report in a police station in Delhi gets a computer-generated FIR. In February 2011, Delhi Police became the first police organization in the country to start uploading all FIRs, registered in police stations in Delhi, on the Delhi Police website. Citizens can download copies of all FIRs except those that have been categorized as sensitive by the respective DCP's of the police districts from the website without needing to visit the police stations. This is another milestone that the organization has achieved in community-friendly policing.

3. Computerized Case Diaries and Charge Sheets: Nowadays all the case diaries (proceedings of investigation carried out in a particular case by the investigating officer) are computer generated. The final charge sheets, which are filed before the criminal courts for further prosecution, are also computer generated.

4. Registration of FIRs and Complaints on email, SMS: Several cases are registered in Delhi police stations on the basis of emails that have been sent to them. Copies of FIRs have also been delivered to them through email. Citizens of Delhi send several complaints to various senior officers, including the commissioner of police (CP) on email today. Thus, the senior supervisory officers are accessible to the citizens of Delhi through technology.

5. Uploading of Useful Forms Information including Citizen's Charter on Website: Several useful information and forms which could be accessed only through personal contact by visiting police stations are a mouse click way. Citizens can now know the status of their stolen vehicle, missing children, etc. on the Delhi Police

website. Various licensing-renewal forms are available on the website which can be downloaded at one's leisure.

6. Video Conferencing: Under the most ambitious modernization project, very soon all the police stations will have a video conferencing facility in which senior officers in the district can be directly in touch with the SHOs through video link. The system will facilitate one-to-one interaction between the CP and all the field officers up to the level of SHOs directly.

7. Digitalization of Police Station Records: Delhi Police intends to digitalize all the police station records very soon.

8. Fingerprint Analysis and Criminal Tracking System (FACTS): The fingerprint bureau in Delhi has a comprehensive, fully-computerized fingerprint database of approximately 1,97,692 criminals in FACTS. The system helps the area police to go for a quick and instant check of the previous criminal records of the arrested offender through touch screen method. FACTS systems are installed at strategic locations in Delhi. This important input helps the local police know more about the arrested criminals.

The Use of Close Circuit Television Cameras (CCTVs)

A very popular technological gadget which is widely used today by police world over is the CCTVs. This is a technology that is not only popular with the police, but shopping malls, mosques, temples, markets, airports, banks, railway stations, and schools have adequate coverage of CCTV. It is now being considered to be an agent of silent policing.

In North America and Europe, which make up over 65 per cent of the global CCTV market, cameras have emerged as effective means of prevention and detection of various kinds of crime. They are used to monitor traffic flows and deter public offences, and have proved to be very helpful crime-solving tools. Several parking lots in the

UK are under CCTV surveillance. British Police presented CCTV footage of the 2003 rape and murder of British teenager Hannah Foster by the fugitive Maninder Pal Singh Kohli. The cameras also caught the four bombers behind the July 2005 terror attack, strolling with bomb-laden backpacks into the London Underground.

The most well known terror attacks of 9/11 also received a breakthrough on the basis of footage of CCTV. A Frost and Sullivan report on the Indian electronic security business estimates that the Indian video surveillance and CCTV market is worth about 333 crore. It forms about 29 per cent of the Rs 1150 crore electronic security market in India, which is growing at 14 per cent per annum.

The Delhi Police has started using this technology on a large scale. All the police stations in Delhi are fitted with CCTV cameras. Crucial places like lockup, reporting rooms are under CCTV coverage. It provides an opportunity for the supervisory officer of the police station to keep track of activities from his office itself. Through a very ambitious plan, Delhi Police intends to cover all of Delhi's more popular, famous markets through CCTV. Over 300 street cameras are functional in seven busy markets including Chandni Chowk, Karol Bagh, and Khan Market. CCTV has indeed emerged as an useful tool for information regarding the scene of crime, identification of the accused, and reconstruction of the crime.

The Delhi Police has been able to achieve success in several blind cases of theft through CCTV footage. Recently, a gang of cheats were apprehended in Karol Bagh market on the basis of CCTV footage. There are similar success stories in other police stations. CCTV cameras have been able to act as effective psychological deterrence for many persons with deviant instincts. The Government of India has recently approved the installation of CCTV system in 58 more markets in Delhi and border check points. The cyber highway plan of Delhi Police intends to get the feed of all such CCTV cameras centrally in the Central Command and Control Centre (C4i) at the Police Headquarters.

Zonal Integrated Police Net

We have seen that the crime scenario in Delhi is very much affected by the activities in NCR towns. Proper coordination with the neighbouring police districts in NCR towns is an integral part of day-to-day policing in Delhi. Prevention and detection of cases in Delhi at times also depend on timely exchange of critical inputs with the neighbouring police stations of NCR towns. Conventionally, this exchange of information between NCR police and Delhi Police has been taking place through office modes like papers, TPM and wireless communication. The advent and accessibility to new information technology led to formation of Zonal Integrated Police Network (ZIPNET) in the year 2004. This became an IT platform for the exchange of crime and criminal information among NCR towns. It was initially a collaborative effort of the police forces of Delhi, Haryana, Uttar Pradesh, and Rajasthan. In the year 2008, Punjab and Chandigarh also became members of this IT club. The latest state to enter ZIPNET is Uttarakhand. ZIPNET contains following modules in the police and public domain:

- FIRs (Heinous Cases: murder, dacoity, robbery, and snatching)
- Arrested Persons (heinous cases only)
- Most Wanted Criminals
- Missing Children
- Children Found
- Missing Persons
- Un-identified Dead Bodies
- Un-identified Persons (found unconscious, minor, abandoned, or mentally challenged)

- Stolen Vehicles
- Unclaimed Seized Vehicles
- Missing/Stolen Mobiles
- Police Alerts
- Daily Police Bulletin (for authenticated users only)
- Jail Release (for authenticated users only)
- Bail out (for authenticated users only)
- Press Releases (for authenticated users only)
- Messaging (for authenticated users only)

Crime and Criminal Tracking Network and System (CCTNS)

In a more ambitious plan, MHA, National Crime Records Bureau (NCRB) has initiated computerization of police stations through projects like Common Integrated Police Application (CIPA) and Crime and Criminal Tracking and Networking Information System (CCTNS). P Chidambaram, union home minister of India, mentioned the role of CCTNS during the Intelligence Bureau (IB) Endowment Lecture at Vigyan Bhawan, New Delhi on 23 December 2009 in the following words:[2]

> The Police Stations in the country are, today, virtually unconnected islands. Thanks to telephones and wireless, and specially thanks to mobile phones, there is voice connectivity between the police station and senior police officers, but that is all. There is no system of data storage, data sharing and accessing data. There is no system under which one police station can talk to another directly. There is no record of crime or criminals that can be assessed by a station house officer, except the manual records relating to the police station. Realizing the gross deficiency in connectivity, the central government is implementing an ambitious scheme called 'Crime and Criminal Tracking Network System'. The goals of the system are to facilitate collection, storage, retrieval, analysis, transfer and sharing of data and information at the police station and between the police station and the state headquarters and the central police organizations.

The basic philosophy of CCTNS is the creation of a comprehensive and integrated system for enhancing the efficiency and effectiveness of policing at the police station level, through adoption of principles of e-governance and creation of a nationwide networked infrastructure for the evolution of an IT-enabled state of-the-art tracking system around investigation of crime and detection of criminals.[3] Crime and Criminal Network Tracking System is an advanced software application which would empower police organizations and take policing to the next level. Under this project, a national databank of crime and criminals, and their biometric profiles will be maintained. This database will have a handshake with databases of other agencies of the criminal justice systems like courts, jails, immigration, passport authorities, forensic labs, transport department, mobile companies, and central agencies in a phased manner. Some of the important features of CCTNS system are:[4]

1. Provide the investigating officers of the civil police with all the tools, technology, and information to facilitate investigation of crime and detection of criminals.

2. Improve police functioning in different areas like law and order, traffic management, etc.

3. Facilitate interaction and sharing of crime and criminal's information among police stations, districts, state/UT headquarters, and other police agencies.

4. Keep track of all the cases under investigation, including the one's in courts.

5. Make police functioning citizen friendly and more transparent by automating the functioning of police stations.

6. Improve delivery of citizen-centric services through effective usage Information and Communication Technology (ICT).

It is important to mention that all the police stations in Delhi use CIPA module.

9

THE TYPOLOGY OF
CRIMINALS

To classify criminals into different categories in a city like Delhi with a
heterogeneous population of 177 lakh with an element of 20–5 lakh
floating population and approximately 40 lakh slum population has
its own theoretical and operational limitations. It is more so when
crimogenic factors vary from area to area. Crime is a by-product of
multiple factors. It is very difficult to identify watertight categories of
criminals in Delhi. Every criminal has a typical profile, compulsions
for committing crime, and has a peculiar modus operandi as far
as the commission of crime is concerned. I have tried to classify
the criminals of Delhi on three broad parameters. However, these
categories are not mutually exclusive and operational overlapping
cannot be ruled out. These categories are:

1. Statistical analysis of criminals arrested over the years under
various categories.
2. Sociological factors behind commission of crime (this is
based on my personal experience during interrogation and exposure
to arrested criminals).
3. Criminals who have specialized in a particular type of crime.

Statistical Analysis of Criminals Arrested over the Years Under Various Categories

Criminals on Record (History Sheeters)

Criminals in this category are very much part of the mainstream society and are known for their criminal background. For them, crime has been a profession for years. Their details are available with the local police. Their activities are under constant police surveillance. They are the first suspects for the local police for any crime which is committed in their locality. In some cases, they even have a family history of crime. They survive on commission of crime or acting as agents against criminals (popularly known as informers in the police language). They are also known as 'history sheeters' and 'bad characters' in police stations. A criminal comes in the category of a history sheeter after he has committed a series of serious offences. In other words, he has emerged as a repeat offender. In order to prevent the activities of such criminals who may prove themselves dangerous for the overall security and safety of citizens in the society, the area police may decide to put his activities under constant surveillance. This is a very major decision, which in a way also infringes the fundamental rights of the criminal. There are elaborate written procedures for bringing any criminal under regular formal surveillance. In the first stage, complete details are obtained about the profile of the proposed criminal under surveillance as per standard format. The initial proposal is moved by the SHO of the concerned police station in writing, projecting the criminal profile of the person and proper justification why his activities require surveillance. The proposal is further recommended by the ACP of the area. It finally reaches the SP/DCP of the district who finally orders and approves it in writing, giving proper justification for surveillance. It is only after the approval of the DCP that formal surveillance is mounted by the local police on the criminal. Details regarding the criminal are also reduced in a register called Register Number 10. That is why such criminals are also known as *dus numberis*. There is a very popular hindi film named after this term, in which the famous actor Amitabh Bachchan has played the role of a local goon. As per established procedure, a police station in Delhi maintains three categories of dus numberis: A, B, and C. The categorization has been done according to the desperateness of the criminal. Good behaviour of a particular criminal over a period of time entitles him, as per law to be shifted, to category C with the approval of the DCP concerned, on the recommendation of the SHO. Due to constant surveillance by the area police and over exposure, their share in overall crime in Delhi has gone down over the years. Apprehension of criminals in this category is easier for the police because of their previous records and also because their place of stay is known to the police, as compared to new criminals who keep on changing to their place of stay and whereabouts with every crime.

This takes us to another category of criminals known as 'First Timers'.

First Timers/Anonymous Characters

This is a category of criminals which emerged in Delhi in the year 1990. Logically speaking, this is a category which is the product of the urbanization of the city. They are called first timers in police language because they have no previous criminal record. Theoretically, they are different from the category of recorded criminals we have just talked about. They can also be called anonymous because even after committing a crime they lead a normal life like an ordinary citizen of the city till they are apprehended. They have taken full advantage of urban anonymity and the heterogeneous relationship between individuals in a metropolitan city like Delhi. Since their previous record is not available with the police, their apprehension after commission of crime is also a herculean task for the police.

This category has a sub-group which can be called 'nomads'. Nomad criminals keep on changing their base and area of operation from one part of Delhi to another till they are apprehended by police. Operationally speaking, this group has preferred to commit crimes in anonymous and less densely populated localities which lie beyond their area of temporary night halt or residence. I still remember a case in which a criminal, after committing a crime in a posh locality in south Delhi, stayed in one of the resettlement colonies in north-west Delhi till he was apprehended on the basis of intelligence inputs received from his peer group after a gap of six months. Since the actual profile, details, and hideouts of first timers are not known to the local police, they take easy shelter and lead a normal life and commit crimes with impunity in other parts of Delhi.

As a matter of fact, the share and participation of first timers or novice criminals is increasing in Delhi every year. Let us see, for example, Table 9.1, which reflects the analysis of crime under seven major heads starting from murder to kidnapping for ransom for the period 2006–10 for the whole of Delhi. A comprehensive analysis of crime pattern under these heads from 2006–10 (see Table 9.1).

If we analyse Table 9.1 carefully, it is evident that the participation of novice criminals has been increasing over the years in all the important heads of crime. Crimes like kidnapping someone for the purpose of ransom money, which used to be the specialized activity of seasoned and underworld criminals years back, has seen involvement of new persons who want to make quick money overnight. Several ex-employees who were thrown out of their jobs have also targeted their employers through anonymous letters and threats of underworld criminals and demanded money.

In this context, I would like to narrate a very interesting case. A very rich person in Greater Kailash received an anonymous letter saying that he should arrange to pay 20 lakh of rupees or his school-going son would be kidnapped by members of Dawood Gang. The letter also mentioned the exact date and time of delivery in Jahanpanah City Forest near Chirag Delhi. The worried citizen got

TABLE 9.1 Comprehensive Analysis of Crime Pattern in Delhi (2006–2010)

Heads	2006			2007			2008			2009			2010 (till 31 October)		
	BC	PI	NOVICE	BC	PI	NOVICE	BC	PI	NOVICE	BC	PI	NOVICE	BC	PI	NOVICE
Dacoity	1	7	44	3	28	104		16	90		1	168	1	7	112
Murder	14	45	713	17	50	753	18	32	878	9	42	823	23	35	716
Att Murder	28	86	915	31	96	944	21	45	612	10	41	654	5	28	480
Robbery	19	101	982	24	118	939	25	93	984	16	77	973	27	91	885
Riot	3	10	781	3	14	888	3	16	517	2	2	402		6	388
Rape		13	764	6	14	711	3	6	564		3	551	1	4	494
Kidnapping for Ransom	A	2	67		2	50		2	68			72			29
Snatching	24	214	1354	10	177	1125	18	122	1146	24	127	1232	5	82	1203

in touch with me. We persuaded the resident to arrange the currency in a bag. Everything was planned. He was waiting at the designated place along with the bag in the park, where there was sufficient police presence in plain clothes around him.*

At around 5 pm a young boy on a bicycle approached that area and began looking for his target. Very quickly, he spotted the man with the bag. He abandoned the bicycle in one corner and stated moving towards the person. As soon as he approached and tried to take the bag from the hands of the resident, he was overpowered by the surrounding police team. During interrogation in the police station it emerged that the person has worked in the house of the resident as a domestic servant and was thrown out of the job based on some complaints. He was aware about the whole profile and economic status of the person. He actually wanted to take revenge. As a police officer, I could see a trend emerging in the city. There are several cases in Delhi where this kind of modus operandi has been adopted by criminals. With improvement in the means of communication and technology, the criminal now prefers to intimidate his target on cell phones and landline phones.

SOCIOLOGICAL FACTORS BEHIND COMMISSION OF CRIME*

Marginal Man

This category reflects those criminals who have their own attitude towards society. They are not well integrated in the mainstream social milieu. They have various personal and social reasons to stay away from the social fabric. They do not mingle with people. They don't have a permanent source of livelihood and lead their daily life

---

* This is based on my personal interrogation and exposure of criminals arrested.

under miserable circumstances. In order to survive, they are forced to commit crime. To use R.K. Merton's terminology, they actually fall in the category of 'retreats'. They reject the established cultural goals and the institutional means to achieve them. Drug addicts, vagabonds, alcoholics, and pavement dwellers broadly fall under this category. According to Merton, they are in the society but not of it.[1] They share an ambivalent relationship with society. In the context of Delhi, several unemployed youths of urbanized villages fall in this category. Drug addicts squatting near Kauriya Pul in north Delhi and around temple complexes in various parts of Delhi are very good examples of this category. They commit crimes to support their drug needs. They indulge in petty crimes like stealing of water taps to lifting of bags. Sociologically speaking, they are not part of the mainstream society and always remain in the periphery. This category of criminals may or may not have previous police records. Most of the petty crimes committed by these groups also remain unreported.

Deprived Lot

This is a very important category of criminals. It is a by-product of the overall growth of the city itself. This category has emerged due to an imbalance between Malthus' concept of arithmetical progression (increase in resources for survival) and geometrical progression (increase in the number of people in the city), as has been discussed earlier. This group epitomizes and symbolizes the hiatus which has emerged between the growing numbers and supporting resources. People falling in this category share their habitats and settlements in the city side-by-side with people who are otherwise better off with resources. It is typical human psychology that every individual intends and aspires to lead a good life. This can be achieved only through institutionalized means prescribed by the society. The persons in this category are otherwise deprived of better opportunities, amenities, and luxuries of life. As a human being, he is inclined to and even aspires to lead the life of his neighbour. This is possible only if, in the long run, he accumulates wealth and acquires the so called better amenities. But, he is impatient and cannot wait and also wants to overcome the structural shortcomings by the quickest means possible, whether right or wrong. To use R.K. Merton's phrase, this group becomes innovative in achieving its cultural goals. These innovative means are not always legal. The cultural goals are achieved mostly through commission of crime. Usually, there is no scarcity of targets; they are readily available, very much in the neighbourhood itself.

Commission of crime by slum dwellers and residents of JJ clusters in nearby posh localities is a very good example of crimes committed by such category of people. These areas have always acted as criminal hinterlands for various crimes committed in posh localities.

Theoretically speaking, there are no objective or compelling circumstances for this group to commit crime. Commission of crime is a means to achieve better resources and luxuries in life. It is not for dire survival. The district profile of various districts has revealed that each district has such JJ clusters and slum population, which contributes substantially to the crime figures of the district. In some areas, urbanized villages have also generated such category of youths who have graduated to crime to meet their growing needs, otherwise not supported by family, particularly those families in the urbanized villages that do not have a permanent or alternative source of livelihood. Such families have produced youths who are not well educated, do not get enough financial support to pursue their ambitions, and thereby fall prey to criminal activities. Extortion of innocent people in the far-flung farmhouse areas of Mehrauli, Najafgarh, and Nangoli by such category of youths belonging to urbanized villages, is very common. The booty in this case is utilized by the person to support his daily needs. The criminal activities of such people get a very ambivalent treatment from his peers, family, and society as a whole. I still remember a very sensational case committed in one of the farmhouses in Mehrauli years back, in which some youths from a nearby urbanized village killed three people and injured many more by forcibly entering the premises, precisely because they were refused liquor and denied entry into the premises by the innocent labourers staying in the complex.

Vulnerable Lot

This category of criminal refers to that section of society which is very vulnerable and prone to criminal activities. The vulnerability of this section is due to negative socialization, loosening of maternal and paternal control, breakdown of joint family system, peer group, and other social pressures at very early stages of life. Lack of homogeneity and social cohesiveness and stability in the family and households produce neglected children and youths. The worst affected group in this category is juveniles and youths. We have witnessed a growing incidence of crime in this category in Delhi. Of late, juveniles have even committed serious offences one could never imagine a few years back. Shooting a peer group member on a minor altercation is a very common crime being committed by juveniles and youths in urban areas. Their crimes include stealing of cars for joyrides, sexual assault for lust, and even murder for vengeance or supremacy of authority. Members of this group form and develop their own ideological orientation towards their family, peer group, and society as a whole. The vulnerability of this group to crime is a by-product of the consumerist culture, westernization, and exposure to unhealthy social relations.

Over-ambitious Lot

This category refers to those criminals for whom there are no valid reasons for violating the law of the land and committing a crime. In this category, the urge to commit crime emerges from greed. The people under this category are not satisfied with the present state of affairs as far as their life is concerned. Although they possess everything they need to lead a normal and respectable life, they are not satisfied because they feel that their consumption level is not up to the mark. If others can have more, why can't they? Here, once again, a dilemma between cultural goals and institutionalized means emerges. People in this category want to achieve the cultural goals at any cost. Unlike other categories of criminals, they are well educated, cultured, and intelligent. They don't want to commit a crime in such a way that they are easily caught. The extreme manifestation of this category is reflected in the white collar criminals who operate with innovative methodologies and designs to commit crimes. Financial frauds, cheats, and other organized networks of swindlers are high profile members of this group. Unlike the deprived lot which intends to acquire limited assets to support themselves, members of this group intend to acquire much more, since greed has no limits. This group is very intelligent, articulate, and expert in befriending and fooling the law enforcing agencies. They don't hesitate to promote non-professional means to avoid the pressures of law and apprehension in the long run. This group has increased in number with the overall expansion and development of the city and economic liberalization. A very nebulous category which has emerged out of this group can be called the 'neo-rich class'. Members of this group have become millionaires overnight by selling land or dealing in the real estate business. A section of this neo-rich class violates the basic ethics of a healthy human relationship and has no respect for law. They intend to judge everything in terms of money.

Over a period of time, Delhi has seen the involvement of educated youths and young professionals, working in very good companies, in crimes. This is a group of criminals who have studied in the best schools and professional institutions in the country and come from very good family backgrounds, and otherwise lead a good life. But this lot is not satisfied. They want swanky cars, frequent trips abroad, and anything that money can buy. This is a lot which is over-ambitious. The analysis of the profile of criminals arrested under various categories in 2010 revealed that 24 Master of Business Administration (MBA) graduates or aspirants, 17 Bachelor of Business Administration (BBA) graduates, 11 hotel management students, and at least 71 students pursuing various courses in Delhi University (DU) were caught for offences like cheating, snatching, robbery, and murder. This category demystifies the conventional wisdom that crime is only committed by the poor. The emergence of this over-ambitious group can be logically linked with growing westernization and consumerism in metropolitan cities.

CRIMINALS WHO HAVE SPECIALIZED IN A PARTICULAR TYPE OF CRIME

The heterogeneous character of Delhi is also reflected in the heterogeneity in the types of crime committed. Some of the crimes committed in the city are the by-products of urbanization and have a peculiar modus operandis. The changing dimension of crime has been very beautifully described by Woody Guthrie[2] in the following lines:

Well, as through this I've rambled.
I've seen lots of funny men,
Some rob you with a six gun
Some with a fountain pen

The profiles of the following gangs who have operated in Delhi and specialize in a particular crime merge with the unique profile of Delhi as a metro.

Auto Lifting

The analysis of motor vehicle theft in Delhi and the apprehension of various criminals in this category has revealed the involvement of local, interstate, as well as, international criminals. This is a crime which is committed on the principle of supply and demand. Criminals steal cars as per the demand of particular makes of cars made by receivers of stolen property. What follows is the profile of a gang of car lifters and has interesting characteristics: each member has assigned responsibilities in the whole operation; the share of the booty is to be distributed on the basis of the role and risk involved; there is no overlapping role for different members and after one part of the job is over, the second person will take over.

1. Locating Target Area: The kingpin will identify a parking lot in New Delhi area where businessmen park their cars, handover the key to the attendant, and collect the vehicle in the evening. The leader of the gang analyses the maximum duration a car would be parked in the parking lot. It is here that the leader, along with his associate, will identify the car as per demand.

2. Rapport with the Parking Attendant: One of the members establishes a good rapport and friendship with the parking attendant. After taking him into confidence, they will procure the original key of the identified car for making a duplicate key. They will borrow the key for a few hours after paying handsome money to the attendant. Once the duplicate key is ready they would hand back the original key.

3. Making of Duplicate Key: The duplicate key is made with the help of a key maker after paying him more than the usual charges.

4. Actual Operation: The actual operation of lifting the car used to take place in two phases. The first phase involved following the target till its actual night-parking location. In this phase, the gang assesses the level of police surveillance and patrolling during night, the route for escape, etc. They use preferred routes where no obstruction comes in the way. The second phase involves the lifting of the car. In one of the cases, the targeted car and victims were followed by the gang from the workplace till the residence of the owner in south Delhi. The car was taken by this group within ten minutes of parking of the car by the owner, while he could locate the

theft only in the morning. By that time, the stolen car had crossed Delhi's borders.

5. Handing Over to the Representative of the Receiver: Once the demanded car has been stolen, the gang leader informs the actual buyer to collect it. The arrival of the representative could take a day or more. Till that time, the stolen car would be parked in some safe parking spot, meant only for the transit period, under proper day-and-night surveillance by designated gang members. Once the representative arrives, the car is handed over after taking the money. The cost of the car could vary with make and model, somewhere between 50 thousand to a lakh. Once the car has been handed over to the carrier, the responsibility for its custody rests with him, and the gang is out of the picture. The booty of the crime is shared by gang members as per role and risk involved.

This is a typical profile of one of the gang which used to steal cars from Delhi and send it to far-off places like the north-east. There are other gangs with different modus operandi. One of the gangs recently caught in south Delhi has a very organized networking for car lifting. To avoid police suspicion, they used to prepare forged papers and send it to the respective destination through the railways. The disposal of two wheelers and four wheelers vary. One of the rag-pickers in Meerut used to receive stolen vehicles and cut it into pieces beyond recognition.

It is important to mention that motor vehicle theft in Delhi has always shown an increasing trend. It accounts for 27 per cent of registered crime in Delhi. However, the increasing trend of this crime also needs to be seen in the backdrop of the total number of vehicles. Delhi tops the list of motor vehicles in India (70 lakh) and has more vehicles than the combined figures of the other three metros—Kolkata, Chennai, and Mumbai—put together.

The Thak-Thak Group

This is the profile of a gang which used to lift bags and valuables from cars by diverting the attention of the car owners. They mainly targeted vehicles parked in parking lots or outside on the road, and even vehicles in which driver was still sitting inside. They used to break open the windowpanes of the vehicle with the help of a *gulel* and take away the bags, valuables, or laptops from inside the car in a very short span of time. They used to pass the stolen items to other members of the gang who would be standing very close to the target. They had a very unique modus operandi to commit the crime. They would break open the window of the vehicle and then open the door of the vehicle. In this process even the anti-auto theft devices installed in the car used to be ineffective.

Another peculiar modus operandi was that of a gang in which one of the members would drop 5–6 notes of 10 or 20 denomination near a car and another person would tell the driver that his/her money has fallen out. As soon as the driver gets down to pick up the fallen notes, a juvenile in the age group of 10–12 years would quickly pick up the laptop, valuables, and other things from the car. One of the active gang leaders of the group, Shiv Kumar, a notorious bag lifter was arrested in June 2009 in the south district. He was found to be involved in more than fifty case of bag lifting. Sunny, his younger brother, is also a very active member of the gang, which was assisted by other relatives. This gang has a wide network across different states. They were earlier arrested by Punjab and Gujarat Police. They are active in different NCR towns, are illiterate, and belong to a particular denotified criminal tribe of southern India. This group would to visit the city from a different state, take a place on rent, commit crimes for a few days, and disappear for a few months. The group consisted of women, adults, and juveniles. In the morning itself, the group would divide itself in two-three smaller groups. Each group would move to different parts of Delhi, but never their own area of residence. They would commit three-four such cases in a day and move to their rented accommodation in the evening. The distribution of booty would take place at night. Once a handsome amount would be collected, they would move on to other states.

Pardhi Community[3]

In Delhi, urban anonymity, unplanned growth, and squatting have provided several criminals, from other states, shelter in different parts of the city, enabling them to commit crime at convenience. The members of certain criminal communities visit the city during specific times of a month, commit crimes, and escape immediately afterwards. One such community, which created a sense of insecurity among the residents of Delhi during the 1990s is the Pardhi community, a denotified ex-criminal tribe. The members of this community are known for their brutal killings of innocent people in their sleep. To refresh the memory of Delhi's citizens, I would like to mention few gruesome murders committed during 1990–1: on 12 May 1990, Mrs Veerawali, an 85 years old lady was found clubbed to death in her South Extension Part 1 house and her valuables were looted; on 22 December 1990, Mrs Shradha Khetrapal, a young girl aged 24, was found clubbed to death in the bedroom of her house in Hauz Khas; on 18 April 1991, Mr and Mrs O.P. Mittal, both aged over 70 years, were found battered to death in their sleep in their Panchsheel Park house, with their valuables missing; on 11 October 1991, Maj Gen (retd) Bakshi was found lying dead in a pool of blood in his house in Saket; on 18 November 1991, Maj Gen (Retd) S.S. Kalhan and his son Surendra Kalhan were killed in their sleep, and a young girl Anjali was injured, in their Delhi Cantt house. All these cases happened in the posh and elite colonies of south Delhi. These cases were covered in media for days till the culprits were nabbed. The initial inspection of the scene of crime and peculiarities revealed it to be the handiwork of criminals belonging to the Pardhi community.

With a painstaking and systematic investigation undertaken by the south district police, all the cases of gruesome murder were solved in March 1992. The detailed interrogation and investigation of the cases revealed the following important features related to the modus operandi and base of the criminals belonging to the Pardhi Community.

1. These criminals have their original base in Jhansi and Guna in Madhya Pradesh. The term Pardhi is actually derived from the word 'Pardah' which means hunting. The earliest reference of this community in Indian history is perhaps when Chhatrapati Shivaji used them as guerrillas to harass the Mughal armies. The Maratha chief utilized their intimate knowledge of topography and hunting skills to his advantage. After Shivaji, the Pardhis were left to themselves. Old habits die hard. The instinct to brutal killings once acquired by the Pardhis continued, and the same came handy in commission of brutal killings for the sake of money.

2. There are different kinds of Pardhis: Advichinehers, Phans Pardhi, Harn Pardhis, Chita Pardhis, Gayake Pardhis, and others. Each one of them has distinctive characteristics. But of all the Pardhis, the Langoti Pardhis are known to be the most desperate. They are called Langoti Pardhis as they cover their genitals with a langoti. They are also known as members of the Kachha Baniyan gang, specifying their special attire. They are the most dangerous lot.

3. The Pardhis are essentially wanderers. They are not used to leading a settled life. Living in open is a salient feature of their life. During the summer, they sleep under trees or under mats suspended from bamboo poles.

4. They are one of the scheduled tribes and enjoy the benefits of reservation. Despite governmental assistance in terms of agricultural land and other things, they are addicted to crime and continue to support their lives through the proceeds of crime.

5. Pardhis operate in various groups. They operate around Jammu, Batala, Ludhiana, Himachal Pradesh, and Delhi. Each group

has monopoly in their area. They mostly live on the outer fringes of railway platforms. They do not carry enough belongings with them. They have an extremely dirty appearance. They never wear shoes and are protected by the blessings of the goddess Devi against any injury from reptiles. They also eat uncooked meat.

Modus Operandi   They normally commit crimes after finalizing a reunion point, usually during dark nights after watching a late night movie. They also carry the torn parts of cinema tickets, which are shown to the police patrolling teams during late night to provide legitimate justification for their movements during late nights. They remove all their clothes and move only in kachha and baniyan. The remaining clothes are left at the reunion point.

They also apply oil on their body and tie stones around their waist with the help of a cloth. These stones are weapons of assault in case they are chased and detected during the commission of crime. It is a double-edged weapon, which has also been used to injure the inmates of the houses they rob.

One of the members of the gang carries a multipurpose sharp edged tool called 'daulatiya'. Daulatiya is not only used to break into the house but also to assault and injure the victim. They normally choose their targets close to deserted places which are normally not covered through police patrolling. They also carry small torches and screwdrivers with them. A feature common in most of the cases discussed above revealed that they pick up wooden leg posts of abandoned cots at the spot itself and use it for injuring the victims. They never hesitate to kill ladies if they are wearing jewellery.

The members of this group are addicted to alcohol. They are used to commit crimes in an inebriated condition. They do not easily confess about their crimes and would always like to mislead the police during interrogation.

The women folk of the Pardhi community are equally active in participating in crimes with their male counterparts. They organize lawyers and other logistical support for their male counterparts when they are caught by the police.

The Pardhi criminals have acquired several properties in their ancestral villages through the proceeds of crime.

Courier Bag Robbers[4]

Rapid industrialization and urbanization have led to division of labour, specialization, and occupational diversification in services on a large scale. Several agencies and occupational groups have stated providing specialized services as per the needs of citizens in metropolitan cities like Delhi. This has also changed the conventional mode, delivery mechanism, and profile of pre-existing service providers. Services of cyber cafes, public call offices (PCOs), and subscriber trunk dialling (STD) booths can be seen in this backdrop. Faster and quick delivery of mails and parcels with an element of urgency across the world has led to the emergence of courier companies in the unorganized sector. The delivery mechanism of these courier companies have promoted criminal groups which specialize in commission of crimes specific to the courier companies.[5] Robberies have been committed in Delhi with different modus operandi. Every group adopts its own methodology to deprive the person of his belongings through use of criminal force. The following is a case study of a gang which used to deprive individuals of their valuable properties sent through courier companies. During year 2002, employees of few courier companies reported the robbery of courier packets by a group of people to the local police in the central district. Several of these packets contained bank drafts, which were subsequently cashed at banks. A systematic investigation identified the group which was later apprehended. The detailed interrogation of the gang members revealed the following important dimensions regarding their modus operandi. Commission of crime has three important stages:

1. Planning Stage: This stage consists of following important inputs related to the target:
   a. Receipt of information by the gang members
   b. Leader of the gang organizes the operation
   c. Recee of the proposed place
   d. Assessment of the vulnerability and route followed by the target
   e. Locating the specific target
   f. Following the target
   g. Robbing the courier employee at a secluded place
2. Post-commission Stage:
   a. Immediate shifting of the robbed property to a safe hideout
   b. Sorting and sifting out of the valuables and drafts from the courier packets
   c. Safe custody of the valuables and drafts
   d. Destruction of the rest of the loot
3. Disposal of Drafts and Valuables:
   a. Leader of the group contacts disposal person
   b. Hands over drafts and receives commission in advance
   c. The first contact hands over their drafts to the second party after taking commission
   d. Second party hands over the drafts to third contact and receives his own commission
   e. Third party hands over the drafts to fourth party and takes his commission
   f. The chain goes like this and the cheque or draft is encashed by one of the contacts

The apprehension and detailed interrogation of the group revealed that there was perfect division of labour in the commission of crime. Each individual was assigned a specific role in the whole incident. The whole gang was divided into three groups.

1. Core Group: This is the group which actually commited the crime. It included experienced people, even some of the ex-employees

of the courier companies. This group was well aware about the actual distribution points of the courier bags. They also had intimate knowledge about the contents of the bags in specific instances.

2. Intermediary Group for Transit Custody of the Stolen Properties: The basic job of the members of this group was to take temporary custody of the robbed property. All the robbed courier bags were opened at a safe hideout, where all the bank drafts and cheques were taken out separately from each courier packet. The rest of the baggage was destroyed by the group members at times by burning and at times by throwing it in Yamuna river. The members of this group would not actually participate in the actual commission of crime. However, they played an active role in identifying targets, passing on important inputs, and motivating the active gang to commit crime. They would also identify prospective persons for disposal of property.

3. Peripheral Group: This group actually helped the active members in disposing and cashing of bank drafts. The members of this group operated at the periphery and received robbed bank drafts for disposal through their contacts. They handed over fixed commission to the contact person for the drafts much before it got encashed.

The disposal of bank drafts used to take place in a much disorganized manner. At the end, it became a herculean task to link the drafts with the actual person who handed it over. The group used to commit crime after taking proper care. They would normally target courier employees who used bicycles. It is important to mention that the sorting out of courier bags takes place at several locations in Delhi. This group would target the courier employees from Shankar Market in Connaught Place where the sorting out of courier packets used to take place. The gang members used to rob the courier company employee after establishing rapport and engaging him in conversation. Some of the members also used chilli powder during robbery.

The broad profile of the group emerged to be that of school dropouts with very poor economic status. The key members of the group used to recruit unemployed migrant youths by alluring them with promises of a better living. Detailed interrogation of the group revealed that several members were outside the formal control of their families. In some cases, the family members were aware of the activities and protected them. A key member of the group was working as an assistant in a lawyer's office. The apprehension of the group helped solve more than fifteen cases, which were reported in different police stations of Delhi. This is a very good example of how the growth of the city, urbanization, and development provided scope for new service providers to emerge and also led to the simultaneous emergence of a new category of criminals.

10

PREVENTION OF CRIME

Crime is a threat to freedom and democracy. Reducing crime is an imperative necessity for stability, security and development. Crime cannot be totally eliminated. What a society with an effective system of governance can hope to achieve is to reduce the incidence of crime to reasonable limits, and to manage the detection and punishment of crimes in an effective manner in order to maintain the rule of law.[1]

The simplest meaning of prevention of crime is to prevent a crime from happening. The Global Report on Crime and Justice has provided a very comprehensive and broad-based definition of crime. According to the report, crime prevention is defined as anything that reduces delinquency, violent crime, and insecurity by successfully tackling the scientifically identified causal factors. It gives special attention to activities that are 'problem solving partnerships', that is, measures developed as a result of careful effort to identify causal factors while mobilizing the agencies able to influence those factors.[2] Prevention of crime is very closely linked with the crimogenic factors that are responsible for crime and overall functioning of the criminal justice system. There are many stakeholders in the exercise of prevention of crime. While talking about prevention of crime theoretically, it is also important to understand the relationship between penology and crime prevention.

Penology has actually originated from the Latin word *'ponea'* which means punishment. It is concerned with the process devised and adopted for the punishment, repression, and prevention of crime, as well as the treatment of prisoners.

APPROACHES ADOPTED FOR PREVENTION OF CRIME

Over a period of time, one has seen the following important approaches being adopted by various countries for the prevention of crime: retribution, deterrence, and rehabilitation/reform/correction.

Retribution

This concept of punishment is based on the philosophy of 'eye for an eye' or 'tooth for a tooth'. The basic focus in this approach is that if one harms the other, then an equivalent harm should be done to them. Through retributive methodology, crime is intended to be prevented with the fear of punishment based on the degree of the crime. The actual enforcing authority for this is the judiciary.

Deterrence

In this approach, the treatment meted out to the criminal is used as an example by which they, and by extension all members of society at large, are dissuaded from committing crimes in the future. By subjecting the prisoners to harsh conditions, authorities hope to convince them to avoid future criminal behaviour and also to exemplify for others the rewards for avoiding such behaviour. This means that the fear of punishment will win over whatever benefit or pleasure the illegal activity might bring. This model goes far beyond the model of 'an eye for an eye' by exacting a more severe punishment than would seem to be indicated by the nature of the crime. Torture has often been used in the past as a deterrent, as has public embarrassment, and in religious communities, excommunication. Executions, particularly gruesome ones such as hanging and beheading, often even for petty offences, are extreme examples of deterrence. This can be enforced by the judiciary. However, due to growing concern towards the rights of criminals (primarily in the form of protection of basic human rights) globally, conventional methods of deterring criminals from crime have come under severe criticism. The latest example being death penalty, on which there is no consensus the world over.

Rehabilitation/Reform/Correction

The basic philosophy in this approach is to reduce criminal activity in society by meaningful reforms in the existing socio-economic system, particularly of those pre-conditions that promote criminal activities. This is done in conjunction with the adoption of a meaningful rehabilitative strategy for criminals so as to prevent recidivism in the long run. A meaningful rehabilitative strategy brings the criminal back into the mainstream of society, mainly through gainful employment. It provides an opportunity to the offender to reform himself/herself and start a new life. In certain countries, the foundation of the rehabilitative strategy is laid in the prison itself where an offender is exposed to various vocational skills during his/her leisure time. This requires concentrated and coordinated efforts by various agencies.

Prevention of crime is very closely linked with the crimogenic factors that increases crime in any society. While investigation of a crime is considered an expert and exclusive domain of the police, prevention of crime cannot be considered as the sole responsibility of only the police, precisely because factors and causes that are responsible for an increase in crime are beyond the formal control of the police.

At the fourth UN Congress on the Prevention of Crime and the Treatment of Offenders held in 1970, these crimogenic factors were identified as urbanization, industrialization, population growth, internal migration, social mobility, and technological change. All these factors are present and responsible for the increasing trend of crime in Delhi. Logically, the police alone cannot control these factors.

It is precisely because of these reasons that the National Police Commission in its second report very clearly argued that:

> The police have a direct or more or less exclusive responsibility in the task of investigating crimes but have a very limited role in regard to prevention of crime for the reason that the various contributory factors leading to crime do not totally and exclusively fall within the domain of police for control and regulation. A coordinated understanding and appreciation of these factors not only by the police but also by several other agencies connected with social defence and welfare would be necessary for effective prevention of crime.[3]

The Vienna Declaration on Crime and Justice: Meeting the challenges of the 21st century, a resolution passed by the UN General Assembly, has very clearly stated that adequate prevention and rehabilitation programmes are fundamental to an effective crime control strategy, and also that such programmes should take into account social and economic factors that may make people more vulnerable and likely to engage in criminal behaviour.[4]

From the above discussion it is clear that prevention of crime and criminal activity in the society is the collective responsibility of different stakeholders in the entire criminal justice system. There are four important players in the prevention strategy of crime: the police, the individual, the community, and the policymakers. The success of any preventive strategy will depend on the meaningful coordination, cooperation, appreciation, and understanding of all the stakeholders. However, their operational participation and initiatives may (and does) vary.

For law enforcing agencies, the prevention of crime occupies a very important role in their day-to-day charter of duties. Maintenance of law and order and prevention of crime are the two cardinal responsibilities of the police anywhere in the world. We are going to discuss the role of the police in prevention of crime in further detail in the discussion below. For a meaningful discussion and understanding of the role of the police in crime prevention, the following issues are very important:

1. There cannot be a fixed strategy for prevention of crime. It is always contextual in nature. Prevention of crime will depend on the nature of crime and the area where the crime is committed. In this sense, preventive strategy will vary from crime to crime and from area to area. In other words, it is time and space specific. It is in a sense also like a hide and seek game or the trial and error method of socialism—as it keeps on changing very frequently. Hough[5] has rightly said that crime prevention is a rather elastic term, which at its broadest encompasses any activity extended to reduce the frequency of events defined as crimes by criminal law.

2. An analysis of crime and the various reasons for its commission will indicate as to which category of crime can be prevented and which category cannot be prevented. The solution for solving or preventing crime also lies very much within the causative factor of crime itself. The 'why' of a crime will indicate the 'how' it can be prevented.

3. Preventive measures could be long term as well as short term in nature. Every preventive strategy will have a particular gestation period. The fruits or results of the preventive strategy will appear only after it has been implemented on the ground. Theoretically speaking, a particular preventive strategy will be effective till the time a new method or pattern of crime does not emerge, which in turn will necessitate the adoption of a different strategy.

4. The prevention of crime and the apprehension of criminals committing the crime are closely linked with each other. In other

words, a meaningful crime prevention strategy also leads to the apprehension of criminals. Therefore, the ultimate objective of a preventive strategy also is the apprehension of criminals. There are lots of examples where preventive policing has led to the red-handed apprehension of criminals by patrol teams. It is often said: prevention is the best method of detection.

5. The success of crime prevention measures is closely linked with the topography, density of population, deployment of policemen in the affected areas, and several other socio-economic factors.

CRIME PREVENTION AND THE ROLE OF POLICE

While talking about the prevention of crime, quite often the police have been accused of not being able to effectively prevent crime from happening. At this point it is very important to address practical issues related to prevention of crime in order to understand the role of the police in a meaningful manner.

1. Can police prevent all types of crime? If not, where can a line be drawn?

2. Should the performance of the police be judged only on the basis of crime committed, or it should be linked with the apprehension of criminals involved in various crimes in the long run?

3. Is crime prevention the sole responsibility of the police, or do citizens also have a role to play?

Before popular preventive strategies adopted by police are taken up, let us briefly examine the above questions one by one.

To meaningfully understand the first question, let us take a concrete example. A resides in a locality with his family. Wife of A develops an illicit relationship with her neighbour. They keep meeting in the absence of A. A's wife conspires with her paramour and kills A, so that she can continue her illicit relationship. After the murder, the paramour and the wife of A run away and go into hiding. The matter is reported to the police. The police take up the investigation and A's wife and the paramour are arrested within 48 hours of the commission of the crime.

In this case, can the police be held accountable for the commission of the crime itself? Theoretically speaking, the answer is no. However, the police can definitely be held responsible for not arresting the accused. This is primarily the job of the police and they cannot absolve themselves of this basic professional responsibility. In other words, although the police cannot be held accountable for not being able to prevent the crime from happening, it can definitely be held accountable for not being able to solve the crime.

Let us take another example. In a posh locality, 50 cars are parked on the road every night. One night, four stereos are stolen from the cars. The matter is reported to the police. Cases are duly registered. After a few days, four more stereos are removed from a different set of cars in the same locality. The matter is reported to the police again. The theft trend continues in that locality for a few more days. Can the police be held accountable for repeated theft in the locality? Theoretically, the answer is partly yes. As a matter of fact, the recurrence of theft in the same locality was due to police apathy. The later thefts could have been prevented had the local police adopted some preventive strategy with the cooperation of the residents after careful study of the pattern of theft. Some related exercises from the professional point of view of the thefts in the area would include the checking of the previous records of criminals arrested for this crime in the past. Has any stereo thief arrested previously in the police station been checked? Is he still in jail or has he been released? These are some logical steps which the police is supposed to take after the commission of any crime as part of their investigation. Apart from taking these steps, the local police should also educate residents regarding installation of some gadgets in their cars to prevent theft.

In the above examples we have seen different levels of participation of the police in dealing with a particular crime committed in an area. This gives rise to the second point: Judging the performance of the police. Objectively speaking, performance of the police should not be judged only on the basis of a crime committed within their jurisdiction. As we have seen in the first example, the particular crime that occurred could not have been prevented by the police at all. However, the police will still remain answerable for the crime, since the basic responsibility of arresting the criminals involved in a crime rests with the police—although as per the Criminal Procedure Code (CPC) in India, even a private individual can arrest any person wanted by the police for a criminal offence. Thus, it is always better to link the performance of the police with the crime as well as the criminals, as they are two sides of the same coin.

At this point, a small discussion about police functioning will not be out of place. The apprehension of a particular criminal is based on a very scientific system of police records. A criminal comes on record only after he has been arrested. As a part of police working, the police prepares a complete dossier of the arrested criminal, mentioning details about his entire life with special focus on his area of operation, expertise in committing a particular crime, methodology used to commit crime, any peculiar features in his operation, and many other details. These details are condensed and a complete dossier of the criminal is prepared, which also includes his photograph. If the same criminal commits a crime more than twice (depending upon the nature of crime) and resides in the home police station, the area police is supposed to create an extensive dossier of the said person. This dossier is opened in the form of a police document called the history sheet.

The basic purpose of the history sheet is to put the criminal and his activities under proper surveillance on a regular basis. Such an exercise is conducted by each police station with respect to criminals residing within their jurisdiction and this deters the criminal from further criminal activities. History sheeters are prime suspects for any crime resembling the nature of their expertise occurring within the jurisdiction of a particular police station. Such micro level data becomes a ready reckoner for the home police station and acts as reference point for other police stations at the macro level.

Now, coming back to the question of prevention of crime and commission of crime, particularly by criminals on record, the police have the primary responsibility in preventing a crime from happening. As a matter of fact, the yardstick to judge the professionalism of any police force should be to relate it with the number of crimes committed by criminals on record. If recorded criminals commit repeated crime in any area, its speaks very poorly about policing of the area by the local police at the micro level, and also reflects poorly on the image of the entire police force at the macro level in the long run. The police cannot have any excuse for the involvement of recorded criminals in crime and their non-apprehension.

At the same time, if the crime is committed by novice criminals, first timers, and the floating population whose details are not available with the police, the reasons behind the increase in crimes committed by such categories of criminals needs to be located beyond the parameters of police functioning and efficiency for the sake of meaningful understanding of the role of the police.

POPULAR CRIME PREVENTION APPROACHES

Several crime prevention approaches are practiced as per local conditions across the world. Few important schemes are discussed below.

Situational Crime Prevention Approach

According to Poyner, situational prevention attempts to prevent crime by changing the situations in which crime occurs.[6] The primary focus of this approach is on the opportunity dimension of an offender. A meaningful situational strategy is designed according to the types of opportunity. Even the Global Report on Crime and Justice has considered the situational crime prevention strategy as perhaps the most innovative mechanism to control crime. It says that 'While beginning in such small projects as designing out crime, this approach has developed into a broadly encompassing set of practical techniques for preventing crime.'[7]

Bennett[8] has identified the following three levels of operation in the situational approach:

    i.   The individual
   ii.   The community
  iii.   The physical environment

Measures Operating at the Individual Level   This level basically refers to the preventive strategy that is initiated by individuals as a part of crime prevention. The following important areas of individual participation can be identified:

1. To Increase Physical Security of Targets: If an analysis of crime has revealed that a particular area is prone to motor vehicle theft and house burglaries, adequate measures are required to be taken for prevention of crime. To prevent such crimes, it is impressed upon the individual/affected residential colony to install iron grills, extra locks, and strengthen perimeter security to make access difficult for the offenders. As a part of preventive strategy of motor vehicle theft and house burglary, this method of crime prevention is very popular. Even in Delhi, Delhi Police has been advising the installation of anti-burglary devices and anti-theft gadgets in cars, through written literature as well as advertisements in the media. Various police stations have organized special camps in affected localities for proper display and demonstrations of these devices. Such devices have proved to be very useful in preventing such crimes.

In one locality, a house was equipped with a burglar alarm system. An attempted theft was foiled as the alarms went off while the offenders were trying to break into the house. After hearing the alarm, they left the house in panic. Shortly afterwards, the same burglars easily burgled another house where no such gazettes were available. Similarly, anti-theft devices, alarms, and other gadgets in cars were very useful in reducing the incident of theft in that area. The usefulness of such systems becomes more important in Delhi, where a substantial number of cars are parked on the roads due to paucity of parking space.

2. Adherence to Some Basic Precautions: Every crime demonstrates the weakness/shortcomings conducive to the commission of a particular crime. Some pro-active and preliminary measures at the individual level does affect the incidence of crime. For example, etching of car registration numbers on the window panes has led to the recovery of stolen vehicles much faster. Similarly, certain precautions like opening the door to a stranger only after establishing his/her identity, verification of domestic help and other household staff has affected the trend of house robberies and thefts committed by this category of people.

Measures to be Adopted at the Community Level

1. Formal Surveillance: This is a kind of preventive strategy which is universally practiced across the globe in the form of patrolling by police forces. According to Mayhew,[9] the effectiveness of formal surveillance is based on the notion that any potential offender will be deterred by the threat of being seen, and that the agencies that perform formal surveillance represent such a threat. As we have seen earlier, every criminal ensures two basic things while committing crime: safe access to the target, and safe escape after committing crime. Formal surveillance by the police acts as a stumbling stock in their whole scheme of things.

The operational implementation of formal surveillance by the police is based on the availability of manpower for a particular area. It will vary from place to place. This system of surveillance as a part of crime prevention measure is also practiced in Delhi.

Every police station has a day and night patrolling roster wherein policemen are deployed for surveillance in different areas according to the vulnerability to crime.

Although surveillance by the police in crime-prone areas has traditionally been a central feature of crime prevention strategy, it has its own operational limitations in preventing crime. Practically speaking, since the area covered by a single policeman as a part of his patrolling duties is very large, crime has taken place in such pockets where there is no adequate police surveillance. It is because of probably this reason that Bright[10] has said that patrolling on foot or vehicles have not been very effective in reducing crime. Bright views are actually based on operational and realistic assessment of police patrolling. The police have come under adverse criticism from citizens whenever crime has occurred in the area despite police presence. Such feelings are not new and they have existed in the subconscious of ordinary citizens for a long time. I would like to cite here a very interesting FIR which was lodged at Kotwali police station way back in 1961. The FIR relates to the theft of a bicycle from a cycle stand at the Delhi Public Library, Chandni Chowk on 3 January 1961. Unlike other FIRs, which were normally recorded in Urdu, this one is a written complaint regarding the theft in English by Raj Kumar Malhotra of Karol Bagh. Malhotra informed that his cycle was stolen from the library cycle stand in the presence of the constable who was on duty. To understand what Malhotra actually felt about the police and its functioning, the last few lines of the FIR are reproduced here:

> The cycle could not be taken away when your Constable was on duty. If the cycle is stolen in front of a Constable, then I don't think what is not possible in their absence. Kindly strict action may be taken against that Constable on duty there.[11]

The text of the FIR reflects the attitude of people towards the police as way as back as 45 years ago when preventing a crime was considered the prime responsibility of the police by citizens. This attitude has not changed much today.

2. Surveillance by Employees: Since it is not possible for any police organization in the world to deploy policemen at each and every doorstep, and formal surveillance by police has its operational limitations, other methods for crime prevention have also come up. Reliance on other methods of surveillance beyond the formal ambit of police work became very necessary in cities that have witnessed rapid urban growth and large-scale migration.

Due to inadequate/occasional coverage by police patrolling, several residents in metropolitan cities have started hiring the services of private guards and security men. In many countries, private security agencies have emerged to take over the functions of some aspects of criminal justice, and this is especially true of policing. While private policing has a long history in industrialized countries, it is also becoming a major growth industry in emerging market economies. Unfortunately, the ratio of private to public police throughout the world is unknown. It is estimated that in the USA there are at least at twice, or maybe even thrice, the number of private policemen as public police, and the gap will continue to widen.[12]

The services of private guards for securing houses have also been adopted by residents on a 24-hour basis. Apart from securing houses and important establishments, private security agencies have also started detective services for private clients upon request. In metros like Delhi and Kolkata, parents have even hired the services of private detectives for mounting surveillance on the activities of their adolescent children. In India, liberalization and globalization has led to the mushrooming of security agencies. This dimension of private policing is increasing day-by-day not only in developed nations, but also in developing nations where multinational corporate companies are extending their tentacles. No doubt, the hiring of such services has reduced the individual's vulnerability to crime at home or at work up to a large extent.

In the light of manpower constraints and preoccupation of the available local police for security, law and order, and other related duties, Delhi Police has always promoted maximum use of private security guards and *chowkidars* in day-to-day policing. The access control of various vital installations in the city is manned by private security guards. The urbanization of the city, economic liberalization, and westernization as well as the growth of a consumerist culture in the city has led to an unprecedented level of increase in the number of business establishments, particularly in the form of shopping malls, multiplexes, and other entertainment arcades. All the shopping malls, cinema halls, multiplexes, and five star hotels in the city have deployed an adequate number of round-the-clock guards for overall security of the premises. Keeping in view the massive participation of security guards in the services sector and its larger implications, not only for the security of the individuals but also of the state as a whole, the Government of India decided to regulate the activities of the security service providers. This led to the enactment of The Private Security Agencies (Regulation) Act in 2005. This Act has provided a broad theoretical framework for the functioning of security agencies in the city. As per the Act, every agency intending to provide security services will have to obtain a prior license from the state government. In pursuance of the Act, Delhi government has issued its own rules and regulations for security agencies.

Environmental Management Approach The basic focus of this approach is to place such measures around a particular locality or colony as can properly regulate access to the complex. As part of access control management, strong walls, gates, and grills are installed around several colonies to deter the easy entry of criminals. This has been adopted by several resident welfare associations (RWAs) in their respective colonies. Various colonies got gates installed to regulate entry to the colonies, with minimum access points primarily with a view to prevent incidences of crime in the area. These efforts did pay dividends in the long run and have had salutary effect on petty thefts. However, securing the colonies through erection of extra gates and grills by the resident welfare associations received a severe jolt recently where some residents of particular colonies went to the High Court and questioned the rationale and arbitrariness of the association in putting up gates and locking access points. While deciding the issue, the High Court made it mandatory for the RWAs to obtain a No Objection Certificate (NOC) from the local police and the land-owning agency before installing and manning (or locking) a gate in their respective colonies. The court also directed that the NOC is to be issued by the police only if there is a consensus regarding installation of such security measures among residents of the colony.

1. Neighbourhood Watch Scheme (NWS): The concept of NWS has emerged out of the philosophy of community policing. Before we discuss some basic ingredients and operational dimensions of NWS, a discussion about community policing will not be out of place. Moreover, this will help us in understanding the gradual evolution of the police into a service-oriented organization.

Historically, we have seen that the police have been considered a repressive organ of the state. During the British period, since the control of police was in the hands of alien rulers, the central focus of policing was to tune itself as per the requirements of the British. Thus, protection and safety of the rulers was more important than the ruled. This fundamental principle of policing and its methodology created a hiatus between the police and the public at large.

After Independence, with changes in the overall socio-economic aspects and emergence of India as a welfare state, the functioning of the police also underwent changes. All the oppressive laws were abolished. Maintenance of law and order and security of citizens assumed significance. This paradigm shift from a repressive organ of an alien state to that of service-oriented organization led to changes in police functioning. The police were not only concerned with controlling the law and order situation, they also had to explain, demonstrate concern and act against increasing road accidents, assault on women, people playing loud music at night, homeless people sleeping on the pavements and streets, stabbing, robberies in moving buses in broad daylight, etc. The police could not be oblivious and indifferent to such day-to-day problems emerging in a fast-changing world. These incidents forced the police to evolve new methodologies in their problem-solving approach. After all, the police had to effectively address its concern towards the larger section of society that is peace loving and law abiding. It is in this backdrop that the concept of community policing becomes important. Community policing is of the people, for the people, and by the people. This is a practice which many advanced countries of the world like the US, the UK, Japan, Mexico, and others have adopted for prevention of crime. The concept of community policing has also emerged out of the fact that prevention of crime is not the sole responsibility of the law enforcing agencies. This participatory approach towards prevention of crime laid the foundation for operation of NWSs in various areas. The operational dimensions of NWS has been summarized in the following paragraph:[13]

> That the residents of a group of houses organize themselves and appoint one or more coordinators depending upon the topography of number of houses. House owners are encouraged to adopt individual as well as collective measures affecting occurrence of crime in their locality. They are also requested to become more vigilant and report suspicious incidence to the police directly or via the coordinator. In this entire exercise the local police of the area plays a very active role till the time the community becomes aware, self sufficient and secure on fundamental principles of individual and community security.

Apart from affecting the trend of crime in a particular area, NWS has proved to be a very effective means for bridging the gap between the police and the residents on the one hand, and amongst residents on the other. This scheme has also been able to break the ethos of anonymity and indifference, typical of urban areas. The success of NWS requires a fundamental attitudinal change in the minds of people. A citizen has to rid oneself of the typical mindset that security of an area and control of crime is the sole responsibility of the police. The introduction of NWS in any particular area does not mean that the police absolve themselves of their basic responsibility to protect citizens and maintain law and order in the society.

Many colonies in different parts of Delhi have adopted NWS. I would like to mention here the success story of a posh colony in south-west district where crime was very high. The area police used to be flooded with perpetual complaints by the residents. At each and every platform, the residents would criticize the indifferent approach and apathy of police towards increasing crime in their colony. All the preventive strategies adopted by the local police with their available resources proved to be ineffective. During my meeting with the RWA of the affected pocket, I explained the usefulness of NWS, and told them that it could be adopted by the residents. As part of this scheme, an extensive survey of the pocket was carried out by the residents with the help of the police, and main access and exit points of the colony were identified. All the unnecessary exits were closed. A systematic door-to-door survey led to the installation of basic safety gadgets in houses, and special camps were organized for verification of domestic help. Centralized garbage collectors and other service providers like plumbers, electricians, milkmen, etc, equipped with photo identity cards were deployed by the RWA. Local police patrolling was integrated with the resource base of the colony. The sincere efforts of the RWA started showing results. As compared to other pockets in the same locality, the overall crime figures for stereo theft, burglaries, and motor vehicle theft came down to zero. I still remember that once a thief tried to steal a car from the pocket but he had to abandon the stolen car inside the pocket itself as he was stopped and questioned at all the exit points by the alert security guards of the colony. In order to motivate residents in other pockets, a documentary was made and shown on the cable TV network for months to serve as a model. In Delhi, there are many more such success stories related to NWS, wherever they have been adopted sincerely by the residents with the help of police.

OTHER COMMUNITY POLICING SCHEMES ADOPTED BY DELHI POLICE

Like NWS, Delhi Police has adopted several schemes for different categories of people on the basis of their vulnerability to crime. Respective districts have introduced these schemes after analysing the vulnerability of concerned groups. Some of the prominent schemes are as follows:

1. Community Liaison Groups: This programme was initiated by the south district police by forming Community Liaison Groups (CLG) in each police station. The average size of the group is 30 members. The members of CLG are selected from different walks of life. It includes principals, lecturers, RWA office bearers, market association office bearers, hawkers, vendors, journalists, etc. Meetings with the CLG are held every month at the police station level.

2. Senior Citizens Scheme: This scheme is actually meant for senior citizens of the city who are staying alone. The respective beat officers interact with the senior citizens of their area and try to solve their problems. Special camps are organized by police stations for verification of domestic helps of senior citizens and installation of basic safety gadgets in the houses. To break urban anonymity and foster healthy relationship among the residents, several districts have involved school students in their interaction with senior citizens as well. 'Sparsh' and 'Naman' are two such schemes launched by south district police for the senior citizens of their area. A comprehensive security audit of the houses of senior citizens is being carried out periodically by the local police. Every district has a senior citizen cell. All the activities of the cell are coordinated with the assistance of active senior citizens. A meeting is also held centrally at the district level under the chairmanship of the district DCP. This is monitored centrally by the Senior Citizens Cell located at the Police Headquarters.

3. Parivartan: The basic focus of this scheme is to prevent violence against women. This was started in north-west district, which registered the highest number of rape cases before the launch of this scheme. A special feature of the scheme is the involvement of policewomen in day-to-day policing, and redressal of grievances and problems of women, particularly those belonging to the lower strata of society. Cases under the category of violence against women, particularly rape cases, have decreased within a year of the introduction of the programme. The International Association of Chief of Police, USA, awarded the Webber Seavey Award 2006 to this programme. The Gender Institute of London School of Economics has also appreciated this programme.

4. Eyes and Ear Scheme: Another important scheme which has proved very effective in prevention and detection of crime is 'Eyes and Ears Scheme'. This was introduced three years back. This scheme aims to reach out to diverse stakeholders in the city, which include such groups as vendors, chowkidars, *patriwalas*, security guards, RWAs members, landlords, and others, and motivate them to collection informations and also seek their cooperation in day-to-day prevention of crime in the city. The local field officers interact with these groups on a regular basis. In the year 2008, 173 cases were solved by Delhi Police with the help of the members of the public. The Annual Review of Crime, 2009 has shown that as many as 310 cases were solved based on inputs provided by the various stakeholders of this scheme. To motivate these people, 357 citizens under various categories were rewarded by police in 2009. Till June 2010, various stakeholders of this scheme have played an instrumental role in solving as many as 353 cases.

5. Bhagidari Scheme: This is the scheme which was launched in 1998 by the Delhi government. The basic philosophy of the scheme is involving people's participation in local governance. This is achieved through the involvement of multiple stakeholders along with the citizens. Local issues related to a particular area are discussed in a

workshop attended by representatives of civic agencies, the Delhi Police, and members of the respective RWAs. The basic objective of the deliberation is to arrive at a solution through discussion. This has facilitated a process of dialogue and solutions between RWAs, market associations, and other public-utility service providers. The scheme has an indirect bearing on many issues, which have a potential for deviance as well as law and order problems. Bhagidari has been able to ignite the innovative spirit of enterprising citizens in fostering a healthy community spirit and a collective approach in solving problems. At the same time, it has also made government agencies and other delivery groups more responsive and accountable to the problems of citizen. This scheme recently got the United Nations Public Service Award.

6. Accessibility to People: Historically speaking, there has been a gap between the police and the citizens. Delhi Police has tried to bridge this gap through several community policing initiatives. It has an institutionalized system for public grievance redressal, which includes hearing of complaints and grievances of citizens by field level officers. Even a JJ cluster citizen can meet the commissioner of police of Delhi in connection with his/her problems and complain against lower functionaries who have not been responsive to their grievances.

VARIOUS HELPLINE SERVICES FOR VARIOUS GROUPS

Apart from these schemes for members of public and general citizens, Delhi Police coordinates and participates in various programmes meant for victims of crime. 'Pratidhi' is one such programme where the needs of crime victims are taken care of by the Delhi Police with the help of NGOs. Similarly, 'Prayas' is a programme run for juveniles. Several helpline numbers are available on the website of Delhi Police for different categories. A separate citizen's charter is also available on the website. Basic safety tips for different target groups are also available on the website. Members of the public can approach senior officers, including the commissioner of police, directly through email, apart from personal meetings. Some of the important helpline numbers started by the Delhi Police over a period of time are given below:

Women	1091
Senior Citizens	1291
Information about Crime	1090
Anti-obscene Calls	27894455 & 1096
	email: acp-sit-dl@nic.in
Anti-stalking Cell	27894455 & 1096
	email: acp-sit-dl@nic.in
Anti-threat (by recovery agents)	26184455
	email: acp-aec-dl@nic.in
Traffic	23010101 & 1095
Missing Persons	23241210 & 1094
PCR	100

DEPLOYMENT OF POLICE AND CRIME RATE

There is a logical relationship between increase in population, increase in crime, and deployment of police strength. The year-wise total crime and IPC crime per lakh population in Delhi, along with the total available strength of the police force for the period 1970 to 2007 can be seen in Appendix 10.1. The table clearly demonstrates that with an increase in population there is a subsequent increase in IPC crime, as well as total crime every year. More specifically, with minor fluctuations every year, there is an increase in total crime per lakh population. Moreover, the table also demonstrates that there is no proportionate increase in the strength of the police force with the increase in population and crime.

Increase in crime and prevention of crime is closely linked with the deployment of policemen in a particular area. Increasing crime rate in the area alongside an increase in population has always been an area of concern for field police officers and policymakers alike. Ideally, this calls for a proportionate increase in the strength of the police force. Perusal of correspondence files regarding increasing the strength of Delhi Police during 1933 reveals that while arguing for the creation of a separate traffic unit for Delhi Police, the then SSP mentioned that since the traffic is being manned by watch and ward staff of the police stations, it has affected the crime trend of the police stations as regular beat patrolling is not possible. Expressing concern at the increasing crime rate in the area, the then SSP writes:

> Beats everywhere are left unpatrolled every night for lack of men in the jurisdictions of Kotwali, Kashmere Gate, and Sadar Bazar police stations. 11, 10 and 9 beats respectively are always left unpatrolled and unprotected. It is an admitted fact that adequate protection has not been afforded to citizens of Delhi for many years. I continually receive applications from residents of important areas such as Press Quarters in the Faiz Bazar Police Station for regular police patrols and have to reply that I regret men are not available.

The SSP quoted the following statistics (shown in Table 10.1 below) of (crimes which are preventable by police patrols) reported at Old and New Delhi headquartered police stations:[14]

TABLE **10.1**   Thefts and Burglaries Reported at Old and New Delhi Headquartered Police Stations (1926–32)

Year	Crime
1926	1032
1927	1070
1928	1002
1929	1292
1930	1222
1931	1330
1932	1656

TABLE **10.2** Population of Old and New Delhi (1921 and 1931)

Population	Old Delhi	New Delhi
1921	2,48,259	31,456
1931	3,47,922	64,984

To substantiate his argument, the officer also mentioned the following figures shown in Table 10.2 of population for 1921 and 1931 in old and New Delhi.

The officer argues that despite an increase in population and crime in old and New Delhi, the number of watch and ward staff has remained practically the same. The total number of head constables and foot constables during 1924 and 1933 for both headquarter police stations was 43 head constables, 431 foot constables, and 36 head constables and 441 foot constables, respectively. It is in tune with the logical relationship of prevention of crime and increase in the number of policemen that the officer argues elsewhere in the proposals of 1933 that: '[T]he more men are available, the more beats can be created and consequently the greater security can be offered to the property of citizens of Delhi.'

However, just as the crime incidence in an area is a deceptive pointer to the crime situation, the absolute strength of police personnel is also not a true indicator of the magnitude of crime and its combating machinery, as well as performance of the other assigned tasks by the police.[15] The number of policemen per hundred square kilometres and also per thousand population is considered to be important indicators in planning their deployment. The distribution of policemen per lakh population in the states and union territories may be seen in Appendix 10.2. In the map it is clear that there are seven states/union territories which have a deployment of more than 500 policemen per lakh population—with Mizoram being the highest with 768 policemen per lakh population. As far as Delhi is concerned, there are 348 police men per lakh population.

It is important to mention here that although the area covered by policemen may be constant, the density of population is expected to increase with the passage of time. The UTs of Delhi and Chandigarh have recorded significantly higher density values at 3805.3 and 3564 policemen per 100 sq km, respectively. It is significant to note that the national average was 44.4 in 2006. According to the NCRB, the number of policemen available per lakh population varied on an average between 122–33 during the decade 1996–2009, with 133 per lakh population during 2009.[16] Density of police personal during 2009 may be seen in Appendix 10.3.

It is generally believed that countries with higher proportions of police personnel in the system also have high rates of police per lakh population. Singapore has the second highest rate (1074.68 per lakh population) closely following the Russian Federation (1224.58), while Mexico (4.6) has the lowest police per lakh population, followed by Madagascar (21.31). The median for developing countries was 283 police per lakh population compared to 346 for developed countries.[17] The ratio of policemen per thousand population in different countries of the world can be seen in Appendix 10.4.

Keeping in view the crime rate and population growth of the city, as well as the vastness of area covered by a police station in Delhi, every district in Delhi requires additional police stations to ease the burdens of the existing police station. After the assassination of Indira Gandhi in 1984, the Bureau of Police Research and Development, Government of India, constituted a committee under the chairmanship of Srivastava to reorganize the structure of Delhi Police and suggest measures for further re-strengthening of the force. The committee recommended the following norms for creation of a police station:[18]

1. The population in the jurisdiction of a police station should not exceed 75,000.

2. The incidence of crime that a police station should be expected to deal with in a year should not be more than 500.

3. To ensure proper organization and supervision of beats and keeping the policing requirements within manageable limits, the jurisdiction of a police station even in the semi-urban or rural areas in the union territory of Delhi should not be more than 20 sq km. In the densely populated areas, the area would have to be much less and the location of a police station would be governed by consideration of population density.

In the light of the above guidelines and recommendation, the number of police stations in Delhi has been increasing over a period of time. This will logically facilitate better policing by enabling the coverage of less area by more policemen. Despite logical problems involved in relating crime statistics with the presence of police in a particular area the world over, it has been argued that low crime rate has something to do with the number of police on the ground keeping the crime rate down. Such an argument is supported by countries like Singapore. Singapore has a very high rate of policing (1075 per lakh) and its crime rates for both murder (1.71) and theft (919.56) are very low.[19]

Crime is a by-product of various social, psychological, sociological, and economic factors. It needs to be analysed in its complexities. A meaningful preventive strategy will have to take into account all these factors and adopt adequate pro-active and reactive measures.

11

CONCLUSION

In a democratic society, the police have emerged as an important service delivery organization. Like any other service delivery institution, the performance of the police is always judged and evaluated on how it has been able to deliver its services to the people in its day-to-day functioning. Emphasizing the service dimension of the police in a democracy, Dr Manmohan Singh, the Prime Minister of India observed:[1]

> Today police forces have to serve the interests of the people, not rulers. In a democratic framework, as we are in today, there is a need to have in the police forces a managerial philosophy, a value system and an ethos in tune with the times. I had emphasized the need to ensure that police forces at all levels change from a feudal force to a democratic service. The spirit of public service of respect for the rights of individuals, of being just and humane in our actions must permeate the entire police force.

As a formal organization with multiple roles and responsibilities, the police is accountable to many stakeholders in society, in the process of the delivery of its services. The prevention and detection of crime and the overall maintenance of law and order in society constitute the core dimension of police responsibility. This can also be considered as the exclusive responsibility of the police. The evaluation and performance of any police agency across the world is done on the basis of how it has been able to contain the menace of increasing crime, and maintain general law and order in the city.

An evaluation of the overall performance of the Delhi Police regarding its basic responsibility towards the prevention and detection of crime, and the maintenance of law and order, is now called for. As far as crime is concerned, the city has been registering numerically more and more cases every year. However, if we evaluate the increase in crime against the yardstick of crime per lakh of population—a yardstick generally followed worldwide for an analysis of crime figures—one finds fluctuating trends over the years. The overall diversity of Delhi also gets reflected in the variation of crime figures.

A police station-wise analysis of crime reflects a very distinctive pattern in incidence of crime in Delhi. Let us take the latest crime figures for Delhi, for the year 2010 up to June. The police station-wise breakup of total Indian Penal Code (IPC) crimes shows that 12,810 (50 per cent) of these cases were reported from 56 police stations. Out of these 56 police stations, 47 are located outside the Ring Road. Eighty-five (50 per cent) police stations recorded 68 per cent of all cases. Table 11.1 clearly reflects the percentage increase of crime in different police stations in Delhi.

Out of 155 territorial police stations, 79 police stations (51 per cent) registered an increase, and 76 police stations (49 per cent) registered a decline, or remained at par with the previous year's trend. This is evident in Table 11.2.

The analysis of police station-wise crime reflects that only selected police stations—mostly those situated outside the Ring Road and

TABLE 11.1 Crime Patterns in Delhi 2010 (up to June)

Sl No	Magnitude	Number of Police Stations
1	Increase over 10 per cent	68
2	Increase between 5 to 10 per cent	7
3	Increase up to 5 per cent	10
4	At Par	1
5	Decline	83

TABLE 11.2   Crime Patterns Compared 2010 (up to June)

	Outside Ring Road Including Trans Yamuna	Trans Yamuna	Inside Ring Road
Total Police Stations	109	30	46
Police Stations with Increase	67	18	12
Police Stations with decline/at Par	42	12	34

the trans Yamuna area—have registered an increase in the number of cases when compared to police stations in other areas. The increasing trend in these police stations is due to the crimogenic factors prevailing in the area. It is this part of Delhi which has seen the maximum population growth, the maximum presence of floating population over the years, along with an increased pace of urbanization. Over and above these factors, these areas are also close to (and exposed to) the activities of the criminals of neighbouring NCR towns.

General crime in Delhi, viewed in the perspective of per lakh of population for comparison of crime, reveals a fluctuating trend over the years. This is evident through the bar chart of crime for the last ten years in Appendices 11.1 and 11.2.[2]

While analysing crime, it is also important to mention that, apart from other crimes, motor vehicle theft is a very important area of concern. It accounts for 27 per cent of all cases registered in Delhi. It will not be out of place to mention that, till 1963, there was no motor vehicle theft in Delhi. It is only 1964 onwards that Delhi started getting cases of motor vehicle thefts. No doubt this was also because of the lesser number of vehicles in those years as compared to the present day. The acute shortage of parking space and the normal practice of parking vehicles on roadsides, coupled with the apathy and indifference of vehicle owners towards installing anti-auto theft equipment are major factors responsible for the increasing trends in this crime. We have also seen that this crime has seen the involvement of several interstate gangs. Vehicles stolen from Delhi have been found disposed of in UP, Bihar, West Bengal, Jammu and Kashmir, the north-eastern states, Nepal, and Bangladesh.

As we have seen, the increase in crime is a result of various factors which are beyond the control of the police. Despite the fact that the city has seen numerous gangs specializing in different forms of crime, the local police have been able to address this problem professionally and neutralize their activities in a short span of time. The year 2008 saw an increasing numbers of incidents perpetrated by the infamous 'Biker Gang' which used to kill its victims during robbery. Several cases happened in broad daylight all over Delhi. The city was termed as having become lawless by the media, and the analyses of the incidents continued for days. The Delhi Police rose to the occasion and was able to eliminate all the members of the gang in a very short span of time.

Since there were several such cases, a sense of insecurity was created in the minds of the people of Delhi. Effective policing steps which were gradually undertaken restored the confidence of the people in a short span of time. This has been a very consistent trend regarding the professional performance of the Delhi Police. From 1998 onwards, the city witnessed several sensational cases of kidnapping for ransom in the backdrop of increasing activities of international syndicates. The Delhi Police was able to rescue the victims in all cases *without* paying any ransom amount in all the cases that were reported to the police. Except for a few cases over the years, the overall performance of the organization has been very good. The Delhi Police has not allowed any organized criminal gang, which could create terror across the city, to come up. It speaks volumes about the basic policing done by the force.

There are some important measures that have been undertaken by the Delhi Police which have helped fight the menace of crime in the city.

THE GENERAL EXPANSION OF THE FORCE

Crime and criminal activities in any place gets effectively influenced by the visibility of force on the streets. This visibility is logically linked with the availability of human resources in a police station. Mobile and static visibility enacts psychological pressure on the minds of criminals and law breakers. The Delhi Police has grown in numbers over a period of time. The expansion of the force has three distinctive dimensions which have been in tune with both the urbanization of the city and the new challenges of policing. First, more manpower has been made available to police stations across the city for the prevention and detection of crime. Second, more police stations have been created in areas which have come up gradually with the urbanization of the city. More and more police stations were created in upcoming townships in the city. This was achieved through the reorganization and bifurcation of police station boundaries on the basis of the statistical analysis of the incidence of crime in the area. The basic philosophy behind this increase has been to establish a manageable balance between the area population and police station.

The third distinctive characteristic of the expansion was the creation of specialized units of policing, in tune with the newer forms of crime emerging as a result of urbanization and modernization. The creation of the economic offences wing, cyber crime, and other units need to be seen in this context.

EFFECTIVE PRESSURE ON THE RECORDED CRIMINALS AND BUDDING GANGS

The urbanization of the city has produced new categories of criminals. An analysis of crime over the years has shown an increasing involvement of first timers and budding criminals in various crimes, and a reduction in the participation of recorded *dus numberis* and 'history sheeters' in criminal incidents. This trend is in tune with the national trend. According to data released by Crime in India (28,49,205) during 2009, there were as many as 91 per cent new offenders, 6.3 per cent were convicted once in the past, whereas only 1.8 per cent were convicted twice and merely 0.9 per cent were convicted three times or more.[2] The local police have been able to prevent the involvement of recorded criminals in crime through effective surveillance of their activities and through intelligence inputs.

Community Policing

The Delhi Police cannot take the entire credit for preventing the menace of crime. Alert and vigilant citizens of the mega city also share the credit for this. In a fast urbanizing and growing city anywhere in the world, no police organization on its own can succeed in fighting the menace of crime. It has to take the people into confidence in day-to-day policing. The need for community policing was realized by the Delhi Police long ago. Through constant interaction, the area police have been able to involve the residents in the overall prevention and detection of crime. Area-specific community policing schemes have been introduced by the police and, gradually, the citizens of Delhi are coming to realize that the police does need their cooperation and assistance in the prevention dimension of policing.

No doubt, the basic responsibility for controlling crime in any area lies with the local police. It is the one area in which the police have to take proactive and reactive measures in preventing a crime from occurring. However, the prevention of crime cannot be considered the exclusive domain of the police. It is here that a distinction between general prevention and specific prevention becomes important. General preventive measures are adopted by law enforcing agencies to project a sense of security in citizens, as well as instil deterrence in criminals on the basis of the deployment of available static and mobile resources. Since the area covered is vast, such general preventive measures have their own operational limitations in preventing crime. As a result, specific crime prevention measures are required to be undertaken to prevent specific crimes in particular areas on the basis of a systematic analysis. As a part of the strategy for specific crime prevention, law enforcing agencies adopt some measures, while other proactive initiatives and measures are adopted by the citizens of the area.

It is cooperation, coordination, and the blending of private and public resources which ultimately prevent crime. In fact, while analysing the pattern of crime across the globe, the active participation of people in crime prevention has also been recognized by the UN. Informing the public about practical crime prevention measures (that are proven effective) was a very important issue which was taken up at the United Nations Ninth Congress on the Prevention of Crime and the Treatment of the Offenders, held in Cairo in 1995, as well as the Fourth World Conference on Women, held in Beijing in 1995.

Community policing schemes like Nagrik Suraksha Samiti has proved to be a very effective platform for establishing communal harmony in several areas of Delhi that have a mixed population. Over the years, the Delhi Police has emerged as a role model in areas of community policing for other police organizations in the country. The MHA, Government of India, has recently issued an advisory to all the states regarding the prevention, registration, investigation, and prevention of crime in July 2010. The Delhi Police can take pride in the fact that most of the directions issued in the circular have been an integral part of its day-to-day policing for a long period. The Eyes and Ears Scheme introduced a few years ago in Delhi (which figures in the said circular) has been able to motivate peripheral stakeholders in sharing useful information related to policing. The timely input by one such stakeholder which averted a major bomb blast in Connaught Place in the year 2008 is a good example of the success of this scheme.

MANAGEMENT OF TRAFFIC CONGESTION AND REGULATION

In a city like Delhi, where 6.5 million vehicles were registered in the beginning of 2010, and where road experts believe that approximately 1000 vehicles are added every day on the road, the management of traffic and regulation is not an easy job. Delhi Traffic Police has been trying to control ever-increasing traffic congestion and discipline on the road through the Three Es: enforcement, engineering, and education. The coordination and blending of the three has ensured that the city's traffic keeps moving.

1. Enforcement: The focus of enforcement is essentially to ensure that the basic rules of the road are respected by road users. An effective enforcement of rules by the traffic police is able to prevent fatalities and ensure the smooth movement of vehicles on the road. Every year, lakhs of people are prosecuted for different traffic violations. However, despite these prosecutions, the overall attitude of the average motorist in Delhi, in terms of conformity with the rules, is not very healthy.

2. Engineering: It is a very important aspect of traffic regulation in the city. The thrust in engineering is to introduce structural measures to ease the pressure and congestion on the road. The construction of flyovers, the closing of unnecessary 'cuts', the creation of the central verge, the provision of speed breakers, the insistence on one way traffic on some roads, etc., constitute important dimensions of traffic engineering. These measures are adopted and introduced on the basis of a systematic analysis of traffic incidents in different areas by the traffic police, in coordination with other civic agencies. Delhi today is a city of flyovers. These flyovers and other traffic engineering measures have been able to ease pressure on the road in several areas. A good example is today's journey to Civil Lines via the Ring Road. Delhites who used to travel to Civil Lines via the Ring Road a year back, enjoy a different feeling today, travelling on the signal-

free road on the Geeta Colony side, parallel to the Ring Road to go to Delhi University or Civil Lines. Traffic engineering has played an important role in achieving this comfort level.

Traffic engineering is likely to get more techno friendly with the introduction of Intelligent Traffic System (ITS). Under this system, an urban traffic control system enabling real-time traffic management, video surveillance, variable message signs at important locations for the guidance of motorists and general public, and red speed check cameras will be set up in due course of time. For online monitoring of the traffic situation, high resolution digital Internet protocol (IP) cameras are going to be set up, which will be remotely controlled to capture the flow of traffic and abnormal incidents.

3. Education: The education of road users is a very important part of traffic regulation. Levi Strauss, a famous French anthropologist, said that signals and other signs on the road are considered the language of the road. A road user must understand this language while driving a car. The Traffic Police conducts educative programmes in this regard in day-to-day policing to educate Delhi's road users. Regular messages on FM Radio also play an important role in educating citizens. In order to make young school children more responsible and informed drivers on the road, regular interactions are held in schools. School children are also taken to various traffic parks in the city to learn through practical demonstration. In the year 2010, Delhi Traffic Police constituted a Road Safety Club in the city. Several schools have joined the club as members and have taken active participation in various road safety activities in the city.

Manpower crunch is a very serious issue in the effective enforcement and regulation of traffic in the city. This constraint has been taken care of through the introduction of more than 600 traffic patrol motorcycles with dedicated beats all across the city. This scheme is also called 'Chase, Check and Challan' against those indulging in traffic violations, particularly over speeding, lane jumping, red light jumping, riding without helmet, triple riding, etc. These mobile traffic cops are able to regulate important and heavy intersections from the traffic point of view on a regular basis. The traffic police in Delhi started a Facebook page in the month of June 2010 to seek the assistance of the citizens of Delhi in the identification and prosecution of dangerous drivers. This techno-friendly initiative by the Delhi Police received a very positive response from the residents of Delhi. Very soon, the Facebook page was full of video clips and digital photographs of rule violators on the road, uploaded by from various 'digital' informants. Approximately 43,000 citizens are connected with the traffic police through Facebook. On the basis of the inputs received, the traffic police have prosecuted several people. Keeping in tune with the tradition of innovative schemes of community policing, the Delhi Police is the first police organization in the country to start this. Although many police departments in the USA have Facebook pages which are used to educate drivers and inform them about changing rules and by-laws, the use of Facebook by the Delhi Traffic Police is surely a unique initiative.

The Maintenance of Law and Order in the City

As pointed out earlier, Delhi attracts many crowds in the form of political rallies and public meetings from various parts of the country. In most cases, the issues raised in the protest rallies and public meetings are local in nature. They have nothing to do with the problems of Delhi. Since the seat of power is located in Delhi, the focus of the organizers is to project their strength before the ruling establishment. This is major challenge for the Delhi Police in day-to-day policing. It requires very mature, professional handling and planning so that the rallies take place even as the city gets going without any major problems. The Delhi Police has acquired a very high level of professional competence in handling such major law and order arrangements.

There are three important aspects of this expertise. Prior negotiation with the organizers is the first step. The local police gets in touch with the organizers of the rally as soon as information is received. This meeting takes place at the level of the SHO and the area ACP. During this meeting, the local police come to know of the actual number of participants and the route likely to be used by them to reach the meeting venue. In the first interaction itself, the organizers and the local police enter into a basic understanding on how the meeting will continue, up to what extent the protestors will be allowed to gather, and which route they will follow. The second stage is the assessment of the manpower and logistics required for handling the crowd and its proper mobilization. The third stage is the placement of logistics—like barricades—a day before the function at the designated place. Finally, on the final day, arrangements as per the plan are executed.

Normally, the force is placed at important places three hours before the arrival of the people. All the manpower deployed on duty is headed by a responsible officer, not below the level of an inspector. Every man deployed on duty is sensitized to the precautions to be undertaken while handling the crowd, and to all issues of human rights. Barring a few exceptions, the Delhi Police has been able to discharge this duty very effectively without any major problem. This stands proved by the successful completion of the 2010 Commonwealth Games. The Delhi Police received much praise and accolade for all arrangements which ensured a safe and secure Commonwealth Games 2010. The extensive arrangements for the Commonwealth Games 2010 was one of the largest law and order and security exercise undertaken by the Delhi Police since its formation.

The urbanization and growth of population in Delhi has been posing several challenges before the police in its day-to-day policing. The Delhi Police has been trying to cope with these emerging problems through changes in the style of working, as well as towards immediate concerns relating to other issues of policing. The basic philosophy behind policing has always been to instil a sense of security and confidence in the minds of the ordinary citizens of Delhi, despite several constraints in its day-to-day working.

Crime is bound to increase in the city, with several factors being responsible for it. It is not crime per se that is important. A meaningful analysis of crime is one which also tries to understand the 'Why?' factor behind it. The real test of any professional police force is how prompt its response is to a particular crime. The citizens of Delhi can take pride in the fact that Delhi Police has not allowed any particular gang or organized crime syndicate to create terror in the city. Even if any particular type of crime has grown and generated feelings of insecurity in the minds of citizens through media hype, Delhi Police has risen to the occasion and restored public confidence by quickly responding to the situation and apprehending the culprits. This is very much evident from the detection rate of the force in working out sensational cases. The overall detection rate of heinous offences till 31 October 2010 is 87 per cent. The Delhi Police has always shown extra zeal, commitment, and professional competence in solving cases which affect the general security of an ordinary citizen in the city.

A good example can be seen in the case of the Bunty Gang which committed seven meaningless murders within a span of 7 days in 2009 and created panic and fear in the minds of ordinary citizens. The situation was so bad that a leading newspaper in Delhi carried the headline: 'Lawless Delhi'. The gang was neutralized within a very short span of time by a dedicated team of officers of the Delhi Police. The professionalism and dedication of the force in working out sensational cases also stands proven with the recent apprehension of offenders in a sexual assault case involving a victim from the north-east which took place in December 2010. The case was solved within one week.

With twenty-three years of field experience, and the handling of very important cases, I can say that the professional commitment of field officers in working out heinous cases in Delhi has put the force on a very high pedestal, making it a reference point for other police forces in the country. Over the years, the force has evolved as a role model for other police forces in the country in various areas of professional policing.

Despite media bashing on specific cases, Delhi still continues to be the safest city as far as security and safety are concerned. The Liveability Index Report 2010 recently published its conclusions after the mapping of 37 cities in India by the Confederation of Indian Industry (CII) and the Institute of Competitiveness. More than 300 indicators were used to assess the overall liveability conditions of important cities in India on a ten-year timeline series. The report concluded:

> On safety, contrary to negative press against Delhi, it turns out to be the safest; followed by Bhopal, Bangaluru, Mumbai, Chennai, Hyderabad and Pune in sequence. Jammu (33rd), Srinagar (34th), Dehradun (35th), Gurgaon (36th) and Noida (37th) have the worst record. Delhi could be a simple victim of devils like Gurgaon and Noida bearing proximity.[3]

Similar views were expressed by the union home minister of India while commenting on the crime scenario in Delhi. He observed:[4]

> ... the universally accepted measure of the incidents of crime is number of crime per 100,000 populations. The total number of crimes recorded in Delhi in 1999 was 58.701 per cent in subsequent years it has declined marginally. In 2009, the total number was 50,251 and in 2010 it was 51292. Crime per 100,000 has shown significant decline. The population of Delhi has increased from 134.18 lakh in 1999 to 182.31 lakh in 2010. Taking all IPC crimes together, the ratio has declined from 437.48 per 100,000 (1999) to 281.34 (2010).

Policing Delhi today is full of challenges, and every new challenge is an acid test for the police. The day-to-day preoccupations of an average policeman in Delhi, loaded with several miscellaneous responsibilities at the same time, keeps him away from normal crime prevention duties, and also from being concerned about the many aspects of basic policing. The basic focus of day-to-day policing is to generate a sense of security in the minds of the common citizen and win his trust. The force needs to introspect and analyse as to why, despite sincere efforts in preventing and detecting crime in a million plus city, it often lacks the support and trust of the citizens of Delhi. This is a very important concern. Unlike other places, the working of an average policeman in Delhi is always under microscopic scrutiny by various agencies, including the print and visual media. The expectation of an average citizen in Delhi from the police is very high. Everyone expects quick response and redressal of their grievances. Thus, winning the trust and confidence of the people of Delhi in day-to-day policing is crucial. This can be achieved through the development of an empathetic and helpful approach by police officers, particularly at the level of addressing the problems of people who visit the police station. The initial response of the police officer in the police station towards the problem of a citizen plays a very important role in the image building of the force. It is at this stage that the behaviour, courtesy, proper action, and guidance of the first responder is critical and crucial. A police officer should always remember that normally citizens come to police station with a problem and expect that they will get a patient hearing. This is what a citizen expects from the police across the world. Years ago, the motto of the police as a service organization was conceptualized by very first metropolitan commissioners, Charles Rovan and Richard Mayne, when they stated:[5]

> Every member of the police force must remember his duty is to protect and help members of the public, no less than to apprehend the guilty persons. Consequently, whilst prompt to prevent crime and arrest criminals, he must look upon himself as the servant and guardian of the general public and treat all law abiding citizens, irrespective of their position, with unfailing patience, courtesy and good humour.

The Delhi Police need to be more responsive to the needs of the people, particularly the underprivileged, weaker sections of society, and other vulnerable sections like women and children, so that it comes close to the vision of the police which the father of our nation, Mahatma Gandhi thought of. He wrote:

... the police of my conception will however be of a different pattern from the present day force. Its ranks will be composed of believers in non violence. They will be servants, not masters of the people. The people will instinctively render them every help, and through mutual cooperation, they will easily deal with ever decreasing disturbances.[6]

NOTES

INTRODUCTION

1. Delhi Police Museum (1950).
2. Manmohan Singh, 2010, 'Inaugural speech', Annual Conference of Director Generals of Police, 26 August.
3. National Police Commission, 1981, *Seventh Report of National Police Commission*, Chapter on 'Urban Policing', para 48.4.
4. Second Administrative Reforms Commission (2005), *Fifth Report on Public Order*, p. 66.

CHAPTER 1

1. Hearn Gordon, 1906, *Seven Cities of Delhi*, Calcutta: W. Thacker, p. 1.
2. Ibid., p. 73.
3. Ibid., p. 103.
4. Ibid., p. 104.
5. Lucy Peck, 2005, *Delhi—A Thousand Years of Building*, New Delhi: Lotus Collection, p. 59.
6. Hearn Gordon, *Seven Cities*, p. 77.
7. Ibid., p. 118.
8. Ibid., p. 119.
9. Lucy Peck, *Delhi*, p. 77.
10. A.K. Jain, 2000, *The Cities of Delhi*, Delhi: Management Publishing Company, p. 61.

11. Ibid., p. 69.
12. A. Bernier, 1968, *Travels in the Mughal Empire, 1656–1668*, Delhi: S. Chand & Co., p. 241.
13. Narayani Gupta, 1981, *Delhi Between Two Empires*, New Delhi: Oxford University Press, p. 2.
14. Ibid.
15. H.K. Naqvi, 1968, *Urban Centres and Industries in Upper India*, Delhi, p. 87.
16. In Percival Griffiths, 1971, *To Guard My People: History of Indian Police*, London: Benn, p. 14.
17. Narayani Gupta, *Delhi*, p. 13.
18. Ibid., p. 27.
19. Ranjana Sengupta, 2007, *Delhi Metropolitan: The Making of an Unlikely City*, New Delhi: Penguin Books, p. 31.
20. Ibid., p. 28.
21. A.K. Jain, *Cities of Delhi*, p. 22.
22. Ranjana Sengupta, *Delhi Metropolitan*, p. 34.
23. A.K. Jain, *Cities of Delhi*, p. 97.
24. Ibid.
25. Jagmohan, 1985, *Challenge of Cities*, New Delhi: Government of India Publications Division, p. 184.
26. Patwant Singh, 1989, *Delhi—The Deepening Urban Crisis*, Delhi: Sterling Publishers, p. 17.
27. Jagmohan, 1978, *Island of Truth*, New Delhi: Allied Publishers, p. 177.
28. Government of India, 1912, *The Gazette of India, Extraordinary* (October), p. 6.
29. Ibid.
30. Ibid.
31. Ibid.
32. A. Bopegamage, 1957, *Delhi: Study in Urban Sociology*, Bombay: University of Bombay, p. 32.
33. Ibid.

CHAPTER 2

1. V.K.R.V. Rao and P.V. Desai, 1965, *Greater Delhi: A Study in Urbanization (1840–1957)*, Bombay: Asia Publishing House, p. 36.
2. Ibid.
3. Government of Delhi, 1976, *Gazetteer of India: Delhi*, Gazetteer Unit, Delhi Administration, p. 121.

4. Romi Khosla (ed.), 2005, *The Idea of Delhi*, Mumbai: Marg Publishers, p. 69.
5. Ibid.
6. Government of India, 1961, *Census of India, 1961*, p. 104.
7. Ibid.
8. Richard D. Lambert, 1962, 'Some Impact of Urban Society upon Village Life in India's Urban Future', in Roy Turner (ed.), *India's Urban Future*, Berkeley: University of California Press, p. 136.
9. Government of Delhi, 2006, *Delhi Human Development Report 2006*, New Delhi: Oxford University Press.
10. Isabelle Biogiotti, 2007, *Emerging Cities: Keys to Understanding and Acting*, Paris: AFD, p. 38.
11. Amitabh Kundu, 2007, 'Migration and urbanization in India in the context of poverty alleviation', available at www.networkideas. org/ideasact/Jun07/Beijing...07/Amitabh_Kundu.ppt (accessed on 2007).
12. Home Department, Government of India, 1933, Correspondence Files, p. 5.
13. Government of Delhi, 1976, *Gazetteer of India: Delhi*, Delhi: Gazetteer Unit, p. 665.
14. Ministry of Home Affairs, Government of India, 2010, *Annual Report 2010*, p. 82.

CHAPTER 3

1. Srivasatva Committee Report (1985), p. 5.
2. Khosla Commission Report, (1966–8), p. 16.
3. In Jagmohan, 1978, *Island of Truth*, New Delhi: Allied Publishers, p. 171.
4. Louis Wirth, 1964, 'Urbanism as a Way of Life', in *On Cities and Social Life, Louis Wirth: Selected Papers*, Chicago: University of Chicago Press, p. xx.
5. R.K. Mukherjee, 1965, *The Sociologist and Social Change in India*, New Delhi: Prentice-Hall of India, p. 24.
6. Ranjana Sengupta, 2007, *Delhi Metropolitan: The Making of an Unlikely City*, New Delhi: Penguin, p. 178.
7. Ibid., p. 179.
8. Ibid., p. 69.
9. Yogendra Singh, 1973, *Modernization of Indian Tradition*, Delhi: Thomson Press, p. 108.

10. R. Ramachandran, 1989, *Urbanization and Urban Systems*, New Delhi: Oxford University Press, p. 92.
11. Srivastava Committee Report (1985), p. 7.
12. Ibid., p. 8.

CHAPTER 4

1. Charts related to General (1912–1994) crime figures may be seen in Appendix 4.1a.
2. District-wise crime figures along with their profile as per the 2001 census may be seen in Appendix 4.2a.

CHAPTER 5

1. *Daily Telegraph*, 14 August 1999.
2. Isabelle Biogiotti, 2007, *Emerging Cities: Keys to Understanding and Acting*, Paris: AFD, p. 38.
3. Jagmohan, 1985, *Challenge of Cities*, New Delhi: Government of India, Publications Division, p. 7.
4. Government of India, 1961,*Census of India 1961*, p. 69.
5. Jagmohan, *Challenge*, p. 7.
6. Personal Interview.
7. Fernand Braudel, 1992, *Civilization and Capitalism, 15th–18th Century*, vol. I, p. 474 in *State, Pluralism, and the Indian Historical Tradition* by Satish Chandra, 2008, p. 75.
8. William Foot Whyte.
9. Amitabh Kundu, 'Migration and urbanization in India in the context of poverty alleviation', available at www.networkideas.org/ideasact/Jun07/Beijing...07/Amitabh_Kundu.ppt (accessed on 2007).
10. Appendix 5.1.
11. 'Out in Open and Cold', *Times of India*, 3 January 2011.
12. Government of Delhi, 2008, *Economic Survey Report, 2007–08*, p. 160.
13. Veronique Dupont, Emma Tarlo, and Denis Vidal (eds), 2000, *Delhi: Urban Space and Human Destinies*, New Delhi: Manohar, p. 31.
14. Manmohan Singh, 2010, 'Address to IPS Probationers' (24 December).
15. National Police Commission, Government of India, 1981, *Seventh Report of National Police Commission*, Chapter 48, para 48.4.

CHAPTER 6

1. Second Administrative Reforms Commission, 2005, *Fifth Report on Public Order*, para 2.2.3 (Terrorism), p. 11.
2. *India Today*, September 2008, p. 36.
3. Ministry of Home Affairs, 2010, *Report Card of Ministry of Home Affairs* (December).
4. English, 2009, p. 3.
5. Ibid., p. 4.
6. Julio Ribero, p. 548.
7. *Global Risks 2011* (6th edition)
8. Available at www.satporg.org
9. Available at www.rediff.com
10. Manmohan Singh, 2010, 'Address to IPS probationers' (24 December).
11. Raza Maroof (ed.), 2009, *Confronting Terrorism*, New Delhi: Penguin-Viking, pp. 80–97.
12. Delhi Police, 1998, *Annual Review*.
13. P. Chidambaram, 2009, 'IB Centenary Endowment Lecture'.
14. Second Administrative Reforms Commission, 2005, *Fifth Report on Public Order*.
15. Kofi Annan, 'A Global Strategy to Fight Terrorism', *The Hindu*, 12 March 2005.

CHAPTER 7

1. Available at www.crime.org/links_inter.html (accessed on 2008).
2. See graph in Appendix 7.3b.
3. A detailed study appeared in O.P. Mishra, 2004, 'A World Within—A Sociological Study of Sex Workers in G.B. Road, Delhi', *Indian Police Journal* (March), BPR&D.
4. Beauvoir, Simone De, 1972, *Second Sex*, Harmondsworth: Penguin Books.
5. Azim Sherwani, 1998, *Girl Child in Crisis*, Delhi: Institute of Social Sciences, p. 63.
6. See Appendix 7.4.
7. *Outlook*, 23 June 2008, p. 41.

CHAPTER 8

1. Media Release of Australian Institute of Criminology (AIC) dated 11 February 1998, 'Crime Control Technology—Help or Hindrance' as stated by Dr Adam Graycar, Director, AIC.
2. P. Chidambaram, 2009, 'IB Centenary Endowment Lecture' (23 December).
3. Ministry of Home Affairs, Government of India, 2010, *Annual Report*, p. 49.
4. Ibid., p. 148.

CHPATER 9

1. R.K. Merton, 1968, *Social Theory and Social Structure*, Glencoe: Free Press.
2. Taken from Woody Guthrie's album 'Pretty Boy Floyd'.
3. Discussion on the Pardhi community is based on M. Kennedy's *History of Criminal Classes in India* (1985) and a booklet called 'A note on criminals belonging to Pardhi community' (1992) prepared by Neeraj Kumar, the then DCP south.
4. O.P. Mishra, 2003, 'Courier Bag Robbers', *Indian Police Journal* (October), BPR&D.

CHAPTER 10

1. Ministry of Home Affairs, Government of India, 2007, *Report of the Committee on Draft National Policy on Criminal Justice* (July).
2. UNODC, 1994, *Global Report on Crime and Justice*, p. 191.
3. National Police Commission, Government of India, 1979, *Second Report of National Police Commission*. p. 13.
4. UN Resolution, (55/99) (2001), p. 2.
5. M. Hough and Mayhew Clarke (eds), 1980, *Designing Out Crime*, London: HMSO, p. 1.
6. B. Poyner, 1983, *Design against Crime: Beyond Defensible Space*, London: Butterworths, p. 5.
7. UNODC, *Global Report*, p. 200.

8. T. Bennett, 1986, 'Situational Crime Prevention from the Offenders' Perspective', in K. Heal and G. Laycock (eds), *Situational Crime Prevention: From Theory into Practice*, London: HMSO, p. 42.
9. M. Hough and Mayhew Clarke, *Designing*, p. 119.
10. J.A. Bright, 1969, 'The Beat Patrol Experiment', London: Home Office Police Research and Development Branch.
11. FIR No. 120, dated 3 January 1961, U/S 379 IPC, PS Kotwali.
12. UNODC, *Global Report*, p. 126
13. Michael Doherty (ed.), 2000, *The Criminology*, London: Old Bailey Press, p. 130.
14. Home Department, Delhi, Correspondence Files between 1912–1935 (Regarding Expansion of Police Force).
15. National Crime Records Bureau, Ministry of Home Affairs, Government of India, 2006, *Crime in India*, p. 169.
16. NCRB, *Crime*, p. 169.
17. UNODC, *Global Report*, p. 124
18. *Srivastava Committee Report*, 1985, p. 14.
19. UNODC, *Global Report*, p. 127.

CHAPTER 11

1. Manmohan Singh, 2009, 'Address to DGs/IGs State/UT' (6 October).
2. National Crime Records Bureau, Ministry of Home Affairs, Government of India, 2009, *Crime in India*, p. 139.
3. Liveability Index Report, 2010, p. 15.
4. Ministry of Home Affairs, Report Card for December.
5. Second Administrative Reforms Commission, 2005, *Fifth Report on Public Order*, Section 4. 8.1, p. 70.
6. R.K. Prabhu and U.R. Rao (eds), 1967, *The Mind of Mahatma Gandhi*, Ahmedabad: Navjeevan Publishing House, p. 158.

APPENDICES

2.1 Distribution of Population

Territory	T/R/U	Population		Urban Population	
		Persons	Males	Females	Per cent
India	T	1,027,015,247	531,277,078	495,738,169	27.8
	R	7,41,660,293	381,141,184	360,519,109	
	U	285,354,954	150,135,894	135,219,060	
State/Union Territory					
J&K	T	10,069,917	5,300,574	4,769,343	24.9
	R	7,564,608	3,925,846	3,638,762	
	U	2,505,309	1,374,728	1,130,581	
Himachal Pradesh	T	6,077,248	3,085,256	2,991,992	9.8
	R	5,482,367	2,754,251	2,728,116	
	U	594,881	331,005	263,876	
Punjab	T	24,289,296	12,963,362	11,325,934	34.0
	R	16,043,730	8,500,647	7,543,083	
	U	8,245,566	4,462,715	3,782,851	
Chandigarh	T	900,914	508,224	392,690	89.8
	R	92,118	56,837	35,281	
	U	808,796	451,387	357,409	
Uttarakhand	T	8,479,562	4,316,401	4,163,161	25.6
	R	6,309,317	3,143,380	3,165,937	
	U	2,170,245	1,173,021	997,224	

(contd...)

2.1 *(contd...)*

Haryana	T	21,082,989	11,327,658	9,755,331	29.0
	R	14,968,850	8,017,622	6,951,228	
	U	6,114,139	3,310,036	2,804,103	
Delhi	T	13,782,976	7,570,890	6,212,086	93.0
	R	963,215	533,219	429,996	
	U	12,819,761	7,037,671	5,782,090	
Rajasthan	T	56,473,122	29,381,657	27,091,465	23.4
	R	43,267,678	22,394,479	20,873,199	
	U	13,205,444	6,987,178	6,218,266	
Uttar Pradesh	T	166,052,859	87,466,301	78,586,558	20.8
	R	131,540,230	69,096,765	62,443,465	
	U	34,512,629	18,369,536	16,143,093	
Bihar	T	82,878,796	43,153,964	39,724,832	10.5
	R	74,199,596	38,510,686	35,688,910	
	U	8,679,200	4,643,278	4,035,922	
Sikkim	T	540,493	288,217	252,276	11.1
	R	480,488	255,386	225,102	
	U	60,005	32,831	27,174	
Andhra Pradesh	T	1,091,117	573,951	517,166	20.4
	R	868,429	453,560	414,869	
	U	222,688	120,391	102,297	
Nagaland	T	1,988,636	1,041,686	946,950	17.7
	R	1,635,815	846,651	789,164	
	U	352,821	195,035	157,786	
Manipur	T	2,388,634	1,207,338	1,181,296	23.9
	R	1,818,224	923,428	894,796	
	U	570,410	283,910	286,500	
Mizoram	T	891,058	459,783	431,275	49.5
	R	450,018	233,718	216,300	
	U	441,040	226,065	214,975	
Tripura	T	3,191,168	1,636,138	1,555,030	17.0
	R	2,648,074	1,359,288	1,288,786	
	U	543,094	276,850	266,244	
Meghalaya	T	2,306,069	1,167,840	1,138,229	19.6
	R	1,853,457	939,803	913,654	
	U	542,612	228,037	224,575	
Assam	T	26,638,407	13,787,799	12,850,608	12.7
	R	23,248,994	11,983,157	11,265,837	

(contd...)

2.1 *(contd...)*

	U	3,389,413	1,804,642	1,584,771	
West Bengal	T	80,221,171	41,487,694	38,733,466	28.0
	R	57,734,690	29,606,028	28,128,662	
	U	22,486,481	11,881,666	10,604,815	
Jharkhand	T	26,909,428	13,861,277	13,048,151	22.3
	R	20,922,731	10,660,430	10,262,301	
	U	5,986,697	3,200,847	2,785,850	
Orissa	T	36,706,920	18,612,340	18,094,580	15.0
	R	31,210,602	15,711,853	15,498,749	
	U	5,496,318	2,900,487	2,595,831	
Chhattisgarh	T	20,795,956	10,452,426	10,343,530	20.1
	R	16,620,627	8,290,983	8,329,644	
	U	4,175,329	2,161,443	2,013,886	
Madhya Pradesh	T	60,385,118	31,456,873	28,928,245	26.7
	R	44,282,528	22,975,256	21,307,272	
	U	16,102,590	8,481,617	7,620,973	
Gujarat	T	50,596,992	26,344,053	24,252,939	37.4
	R	31,697,615	16,289,423	15,408,192	
	U	18,899,377	10,054,630	8,844,747	
Daman and Diu	T	158,059	92,478	65,581	36.3
	R	100,740	63,576	37,164	
	U	57,319	28,902	28,417	
Dadra and Nagar Haveli	T	220,451	121,731	98,720	22.9
	R	169,995	91,887	78,108	
	U	50,456	29,844	20,612	
Maharashtra	T	96,752,247	50,334,270	46,417,977	42.4
	R	55,732,513	28,443,238	27,289,275	
	U	41,019,734	21,891,032	19,128,702	
Andhra Pradesh	T	75,727,541	38,286,811	37,440,730	27.1
	R	55,223,944	27,852,179	27,371,765	
	U	20,503,597	10,434,632	10,068,965	
Karnataka	T	52,733,958	26,856,343	25,877,615	34.0
	R	34,814,100	17,618,593	17,195,507	
	U	17,919,858	9,237,750	8,682,108	
Goa	T	1,343,998	685,617	658,381	49.8
	R	675,129	339,626	335,503	
	U	668,869	345,991	322,878	

(contd...)

2.1 *(contd...)*

Lakshadweep	T	60,595	31,118	29,477	44.5
	R	33,647	17,196	16,451	
	U	26,948	13,922	13,026	
Kerala	T	31,838,619	15,468,664	16,369,955	26.0
	R	23,571,484	11,450,785	12,120,699	
	U	8,267,135	4,017,879	4,249,256	
Tamilnadu	T	62,110,839	31,268,654	30,842,185	43.9
	R	34,869,286	17,508,985	17,360,301	
	U	27,241,553	13,759,669	13,481,884	
Pondicherry	T	973,829	486,705	487,124	66.6
	R	325,596	163,586	162,010	
	U	648,233	323,119	325,114	
Andaman & Nicohar Islands	T	356,265	192,985	163,280	32.7
	R	239,858	128,837	111,021	
	U	116,407	64,148	52,259	

Source: Census of India 2001.

4.1 General Chart of Crime showing Period from 1912–95

4.1a Crime in Delhi 1912 to 1950

Crime Heads	1912	1920	1930	1940	1950
Dacoity	4	1	25	8	8
Murder	6	15	22	29	60
Att. to Murder	2	2	8	13	53
Robbery	8	8	34	35	73
Riot	10	10	21	30	91
Rape	–	–	–	–	–
Arson	–	1	6	2	30
Total	1440	1551	2276	3261	8563

Source: Research Cell, Crime Branch.

4.1b Crime in Delhi 1963 to 1972

Crime Heads	1963	1964	1965	1966	1967	1968	1969	1970	1971	1972
Dacoity	–	2	10	3	8	6	2	29	14	27
Murder	69	59	76	73	65	86	94	123	113	133
Att. to Murder	54	45	84	66	65	71	90	121	159	165
Robbery	52	73	50	54	41	35	44	363	329	379
Riot	86	89	72	102	95	78	93	201	240	447
Rape	29	26	41	38	35	37	34	38	48	37
Arson	–	–	–	–	–	–	–	–	–	–
Total	4691	5012	5878	5352	4789	5480	5584	6003	6073	6191

Source: Research Cell, Crime Branch.

4.1c Crime in Delhi 1973 to 1982

Crime Heads	1973	1974	1975	1976	1977	1978	1979	1980	1981	1982
Dacoity	24	30	18	5	19	70	61	31	19	22
Murder	153	173	165	120	183	182	190	184	198	237
Att. to Murder	240	273	194	108	205	269	328	263	261	234
Robbery	418	343	256	142	355	667	621	295	186	155
Riot	454	282	147	38	147	303	394	180	164	163
Rape	47	57	41	42	46	57	53	47	62	67
Arson	–	–	–	–	–	–	–	–	–	–
Total	34174	33825	28571	23106	35856	43408	44083	37585	30646	27162

Source: Research Cell, Crime Branch.

4.1d Crime in Delhi 1983 to 1995

Crime Heads	1983	1984	1985	1986	1987	1988	1989	1990	1991	1992	1993	1994	1995
Dacoity	15	29	26	21	23	7	13	17	33	35	27	19	36
Murder	245	317	312	276	311	295	342	390	496	521	487	492	520
Att. to Murder	230	271	257	306	276	244	359	386	501	535	472	479	577
Robbery	211	235	256	203	197	203	214	226	284	294	326	377	555
Riot	173	452	126	179	173	113	151	300	329	325	219	172	210
Rape	83	118	78	89	103	121	152	177	214	276	306	309	372
Arson	–	–	–	87	93	83	60	103	119	82	87	72	79
Total IPC	27360	30773	30412	29828	25846	28013	30523	31848	34876	36302	36579	38223	47686

Source: Research Cell, Crime Branch.

4.2   Basic Data Sheet of Census: District-wise
4.2a   District South *(09), Delhi (07)

Population

Persons	2,267,023	Number of households	466,444
Males	1,260,025	Household size (per household)	5
Females	1,006,998		
Growth (1991–2001)	50.27	Sex ratio (females per 1000 males)	799
Rural	160,761	Sex ratio (0–6 years)	887
Urban	2,106,262		
Scheduled Caste population	354,258	Scheduled Tribe population	–
Percentage to total population	15.63	Percentage to total population	–

Literacy and Educational Level

Literates		*Education level attained*	
Persons	1,583,540	Total	1,583,540
Males	955,438	Without level	15,744
Females	628,102	Below primary	250,170
Literacy rate		Primary	313,497
Persons	81.96	Middle	242,046
Males	88.26	Matric/Higher Secondary/Diploma	436,353
Females	73.94	Graduate and above	325,459

Workers

		Age groups	
Total workers	778,558	0–4 years	229,058
Main workers	739,173	5–14 years	500,588
Marginal workers	39,385	15–59 years	1,421,999
Non-workers	1,488,465	60 years and above (Incl. A.N.S.)	115,378

Scheduled Castes (Largest three)

		Scheduled Tribes (Largest three)
1. Chamar etc.	122,203	No Scheduled Tribes in this area
2. Chuhra (Balmiki)	97,323	
3. Koli	30,885	

Religions (Largest three)

		Amenities and infrastructural facilities	
1. Hindus	1,824,645	Total inhabited villages	16
2. Muslims	314,015	Amenities available in villages	
3. Sikhs	75,102		No. of villages
		Drinking water facilities	16

(contd...)

4.2a *(contd...)*

Important Towns (Largest three)				
	Population	Safe drinking water		16
		Electricity (Power Supply)		16
1. DMC(U) Part	714,784	Electricity (Domestic)		1
2. DMC(U) Part	556,756	Electricity (Agriculture)		1
3. DMC(U) Part	379,138	Primary Schools		12
		Middle Schools		10
		Secondary/Sr Secondary Schools		14
		College		1
		Medical Facility		7
House Type		Primary Health Centre		2
Type of house (% of households occupying)		Primary Health Sub-Centre		–
		Post, telegraph and telephone facility		15
Permanent	92.1	Bus Services		16
Semi-permanent	4.7	Paved approach road		16
Temporary	3.2	Mud approach road		2

Source: Census of India 2001.

4.2b District South West *(08), Delhi (07)

Population

Persons	1,755,041	Number of households	384,511
Males	983,615	Household size (per household)	5
Females	771,428		
Growth (1991– 2001)	61.29	Sex ratio (females per 1000 males)	784
Rural	225,454	Sex ratio (0–6 years)	845
Urban	1,529,587		
Scheduled Caste population	258,835	Scheduled Tribe population	–
Percentage to total population	14.75	Percentage to total population	–

Literacy and Educational Level

Literates		*Education level attained*	
Persons	1,258,033	Total	1,258,033
Males	761,917	Without level	10,007

(contd...)

4.2b   *(contd...)*

Females	496,116	Below primary	184,787
Literacy rate		Primary	237,497
Persons	83.61	Middle	201,308
Males	89.86	Matric/Higher Secondary/Diploma	396,897
Females	75.55	Graduate and above	227,609

Workers		**Age groups**	
Total workers	602,546	0–4 years	171,609
Main workers	569,836	5–14 years	380,759
Marginal workers	32,710	15–59 years	1,122,699
Non-workers	1,152,495	60 years and above (Incl. A.N.S.)	79,974

Scheduled Castes (Largest three)		**Scheduled Tribes (Largest three)**
1. Chamar etc.	89,506	No Scheduled Tribes in this area
2. Chuhra (Balmiki)	66,947	
3. Julaha (Weaver)	15,868	

Religions (Largest three)

Amenities and infrastructural facilities

1. Hindus	1,612,169	Total inhabited villages	51
2. Muslims	76,429	Amenities available in villages	
3. Sikhs	29,470		No. of villages

Important Towns (Largest three)

	Population		No. of villages
		Drinking water facilities	51
		Safe drinking water	47
		Electricity (Power Supply)	51
1. DMC(U) Part	695,488	Electricity (Domestic)	11
2. DMC(U) Part	334,821	Electricity (Agriculture)	11
3. DMC(U) Part	168,990	Primary Schools	49
		Middle Schools	30
		Secondary/Sr Secondary Schools	50
		College	1
		Medical Facility	26
		Primary Health Centre	2

House Type

		Primary Health Sub-Centre	2
Type of house (% of households occupying)		Post, telegraph and telephone facility	49
Permanent	91.7	Bus Services	51
Semi-permanent	5.3	Paved approach road	51
Temporary	2.9	Mud approach road	3

Source: Census of India 2001.

4.2c District West *(07), Delhi (07)

Population

Persons	2,128,908	Number of households	432,782
Males	1,163,084	Household size (per household)	5
Females	965,824		
Growth (1991–2001)	47.81	Sex ratio (females per 1000 males)	830
Rural	86,974	Sex ratio (0–6 years)	859
Urban	2,042,114		
Scheduled Caste population	317,683	Scheduled Tribe population	–
Percentage to total population	14.92	Percentage to total population	–

Literacy and Educational Level

Literates

Education level attained

Persons	1,533,738	Total	1,533,738
Males	884,861	Without level	13,948
Females	648,877	Below primary	220,759
Literacy rate		Primary	289,230
Persons	83.39	Middle	222,665
Males	87.85	Matric/Higher Secondary/Diploma	463,594
Females	77.99	Graduate and above	323,357

Workers

Age groups

Total workers	720,915	0–4 years	198,333
Main workers	686,517	5–14 years	448,086
Marginal workers	34,398	15–59 years	1,340,763
Non-workers	1,407,993	60 years and above (Incl. A.N.S.)	141,726

Scheduled Castes (Largest three)

Scheduled Tribes (Largest three)

1. Chamar etc.	113,072	No Scheduled Tribes in this area
2. Chuhra (Balmiki)	58,455	
3. Koli	33,376	

Religions (Largest three)

Amenities and infrastructural facilities

1. Hindus	1,745,810	Total inhabited villages	9
2. Muslims	107,079	Amenities available in villages	
3. Sikhs	247,312		No. of villages
		Drinking water facilities	9

(contd...)

4.2c   *(contd...)*

Important Towns		Safe drinking water	9
(Largest three)		Electricity (Power Supply)	9
	Population	Electricity (Domestic)	1
1. DMC(U) Part	968,505	Electricity (Agriculture)	1
2. DMC(U) Part	469,963	Primary Schools	9
3. DMC(U) Part	312,034	Middle Schools	7
		Secondary/Sr Secondary Schools	11
		College	–
		Medical Facility	5
		Primary Health Centre	–
House Type		Primary Health Sub-Centre	–
Type of house (% of households occupying)		Post, telegraph and telephone facility	9
Permanent	92	Bus Services	9
Semi-permanent	4.9	Paved approach road	9
Temporary	3.1	Mud approach road	1

Source: Census of India 2001.

4.2d   District North *(02), Delhi (07)

Population

Persons	781,525	Number of households	148,927
Males	427,882	Household size (per household)	5
Females	353,643		
Growth (1991–2001)	13.30	Sex ratio (females per 1000 males)	826
Rural	46,585	Sex ratio (0–6 years)	885
Urban	734,940		
Scheduled Caste population	134,623	Scheduled Tribe population	–
Percentage to total population	17.23	Percentage to total population	–

Literacy and Educational Level

Literates		*Education level attained*	
Persons	540,192	Total	540,192
Males	314,103	Without level	5,647

(contd...)

4.2d   *(contd...)*

Females	226,089	Below primary	84,263
Literacy rate		Primary	116,492
Persons	80.10	Middle	90,266
Males	84.64	Matric/Higher Secondary/Diploma	155,998
Females	74.54	Graduate and above	87,355
Workers		**Age groups**	
Total workers	256,596	0–4 years	72,979
Main workers	244,890	5–14 years	171,219
Marginal workers	11,706	15–59 years	492,289
Non-workers	524,929	60 years and above (Incl. A.N.S.)	45,038

Scheduled Castes (Largest three)   **Scheduled Tribes (Largest three)**

1. Chamar etc.	36,892	No Scheduled Tribes in this area
2. Chuhra (Balmiki)	24,936	
3. Koli	16,817	

Religions (Largest three)   **Amenities and infrastructural facilities**

1. Hindus	609,493	Total inhabited villages	5
2. Muslims	126,093	Amenities available in villages	
3. Sikhs	20,819		No. of villages
		Drinking water facilities	5
Important Towns		Safe drinking water	4
(Largest three)		Electricity (Power Supply)	4
	Population	Electricity (Domestic)	2
1. DMC(U) Part	397,256	Electricity (Agriculture)	1
2. DMC(U) Part	132,947	Primary Schools	3
3. DMC(U) Part	122,102	Middle Schools	3
		Secondary/Sr Secondary Schools	2
		College	–
		Medical Facility	3
		Primary Health Centre	–
House Type		Primary Health Sub-Centre	–
Type of house (% of households occupying)		Post, telegraph and telephone facility	4
Permanent	89.1	Bus Services	5
Semi-permanent	4.5	Paved approach road	4
Temporary	6.3	Mud approach road	1

Source: Census of India 2001.

4.2e   District North West *(01), Delhi (07)

Population

Persons	2,860,869	Number of households	561,945
Males	1,571,869	Household size (per household)	5
Females	1,289,180		
Growth (1991–2001)	60.12	Sex ratio (females per 1000 males)	820
Rural	263,363	Sex ratio (0–6 years)	856
Urban	2,595,506		
Scheduled Caste population	553,162	Scheduled Tribe population	–
Percentage to total population	19.34	Percentage to total population	–

Literacy and Educational Level

Literates		*Education level attained*	
Persons	1,957,902	Total	1,957,902
Males	1,161,047	Without level	16,320
Females	796,855	Below primary	336,760
Literacy rate		Primary	414,858
Persons	80.57	Middle	309,552
Males	86.67	Matric/Higher Secondary/Diploma	550,540
Females	73.08	Graduate and above	329,431

Workers

		Age groups	
Total workers	919,439	0–4 years	294,204
Main workers	872,412	5–14 years	669,176
Marginal workers	47,297	15–59 years	1,751,640
Non-workers	1,941,430	60 years and above (Incl. A.N.S.)	145,849

Scheduled Castes (Largest three)   **Scheduled Tribes (Largest three)**

1. Chamar etc.	203,869	No Scheduled Tribes in this area
2. Chuᴸra (Balmiki)	117,968	
3. Koli	45,617	

Religions (Largest three)   **Amenities and infrastructural facilities**

1. Hindus	2,540,491	Total inhabited villages	62
2. Muslims	173,409	Amenities available in villages	
3. Sikhs	91,723		No. of villages
		Drinking water facilities	62

(contd...)

4.2e *(contd...)*

Important Towns			Safe drinking water	62
(Largest three)			Electricity (Power Supply)	62
		Population	Electricity (Domestic)	11
1. DMC(U) Part		1,279,582	Electricity (Agriculture)	9
2. DMC(U) Part		404,787	Primary Schools	57
3. DMC(U) Part		174,142	Middle Schools	31
			Secondary/Sr Secondary Schools	46
			College	–
			Medical Facility	44
			Primary Health Centre	2
House Type			Primary Health Sub-Centre	1
Type of house (% of households occupying)			Post, telegraph and telephone facility	60
Permanent		91.1	Bus Services	62
Semi-permanent		5.8	Paved approach road	61
Temporary		3.1	Mud approach road	9

Source: Census of India 2001.

4.2f District Central *(06), Delhi (07)

Population

Persons	646,385	Number of households	120,616
Males	350,831	Household size (per household)	5
Females	295,554		
Growth (1991–2001)	(1.91)	Sex ratio (females per 1000 males)	842
Rural	–	Sex ratio (0–6 years)	902
Urban	646,385		
Scheduled Caste population	150,815	Scheduled Tribe population	–
Percentage to total population	23.33	Percentage to total population	–

Literacy and Educational Level

Literates		*Education level attained*	
Persons	450,989	Total	450,989
Males	255,253	Without level	9,341

(contd...)

4.2f   *(contd...)*

Females	195,736	Below primary	65,525
Literacy rate		Primary	101,683
Persons	79.69	Middle	75,263
Males	82.73	Matric/Higher Secondary/Diploma	119,540
Females	76.05	Graduate and above	79,593

Workers		**Age groups**	
Total workers	233,851	0–4 years	54,916
Main workers	213,324	5–14 years	133,996
Marginal workers	10,527	15–59 years	415,837
Non-workers	422,534	60 years and above (Incl. A.N.S.)	41,636

Scheduled Castes (Largest three)		**Scheduled Tribes (Largest three)**
1. Chamar etc.	66,663	No Scheduled Tribes in this area
2. Chuhra (Balmiki)	20,324	
3. Khatik	13,797	

Religions (Largest three)		**Amenities and infrastructural facilities**
1. Hindus	423,592	Total inhabited villages
2. Muslims	193,137	Amenities available in villages
3. Sikhs	17,126	No. of villages
		Drinking water facilities
Important Towns		Safe drinking water
(Largest three)		Electricity (Power Supply)
	Population	Electricity (Domestic)
1. DMC(U) Part	307,191	Electricity (Agriculture)
2. DMC(U) Part	195,556	Primary Schools
3. DMC(U) Part	140,248	Middle Schools
		Secondary/Sr Secondary Schools
		College
		Medical Facility
		Primary Health Centre
		Primary Health Sub-Centre
House Type		Post, telegraph and telephone
Type of house (% of households occupying)		facility
Permanent	87.2	Bus Services
Semi-permanent	5.4	Paved approach road
Temporary	7.4	Mud approach road

Source: Census of India 2001.

4.2g District New Delhi *(04), Delhi (07)

Population

Persons	179,112	Number of households	39,633
Males	99,956	Household size (per household)	5
Females	79,156		
Growth (1991–2001)	2.47	Sex ratio (females per 1000 males)	792
Rural	–	Sex ratio (0–6 years)	897
Urban	179,112		
Scheduled Caste population	39,803	Scheduled Tribe population	–
Percentage to total population	22.22	Percentage to total population	–

Literacy and Educational Level

Literates		*Education level attained*	
Persons	131,196	Total	131,196
Males	78,540	Without level	1,655
Females	52,656	Below primary	17,489
Literacy rate		Primary	24,105
Persons	83.24	Middle	21,377
Males	88.62	Matric/Higher Secondary/Diploma	36,440
Females	76.33	Graduate and above	30,013

Workers

		Age groups	
Total workers	67,594	0–4 years	14,382
Main workers	64,425	5–14 years	36,626
Marginal workers	3,169	15–59 years	120,349
Non-workers	111,518	60 years and above (Incl. A.N.S.)	7,755

Scheduled Castes (Largest three)   Scheduled Tribes (Largest three)

1. Chamar etc.	20,846	No Scheduled Tribes in this area
2. Chuhra (Balmiki)	6,407	
3. Khatik	4,659	

Religions (Largest three)   Amenities and infrastructural facilities

1. Hindus	155,594	Total inhabited villages
2. Muslims	11,416	Amenities available in villages
3. Sikhs	6,263	No. of villages
		Drinking water facilities

(contd...)

4.2g *(contd...)*

Important Towns (Largest three)	Population	
1. DMC(U) Part	74,994	Safe drinking water
2. DMC(U) Part	59,132	Electricity (Power Supply)
3. DMC(U) Part	31,067	Electricity (Domestic)

		Safe drinking water
		Electricity (Power Supply)
		Electricity (Domestic)
		Electricity (Agriculture)
		Primary Schools
		Middle Schools
		Secondary/Sr Secondary Schools
		College
		Medical Facility
		Primary Health Centre
House Type		Primary Health Sub-Centre
Type of house (% of households occupying)		Post, telegraph and telephone facility
Permanent	82.1	Bus Services
Semi-permanent	7.2	Paved approach road
Temporary	10.7	Mud approach road

Source: Census of India 2001.

4.2h   District East *(04), Delhi (07)

Population

Persons	1,463,583	Number of households	287,638
Males	794,074	Household size (per household)	5
Females	669,509		
Growth (1991–2001)	41.61	Sex ratio (females per 1000 males)	843
Rural	18,223	Sex ratio (0–6 years)	865
Urban	1,445,360		
Scheduled Caste population	238,984	Scheduled Tribe population	–
Percentage to total population	16.33	Percentage to total population	–

Literacy and Educational Level

Literates		Education level attained	
Persons	1,068,139	Total	1,068,139
Males	613,061	Without level	9,826

(contd...)

4.2h *(contd...)*

Females	455,078	Below primary	152,458
Literacy rate		Primary	199,177
Persons	84.91	Middle	157,781
Males	89.65	Matric/Higher Secondary/Diploma	310,647
Females	79.26	Graduate and above	238,014

Workers		**Age groups**	
Total workers	475,310	0–4 years	141,176
Main workers	456,216	5–14 years	315,156
Marginal workers	19,094	15–59 years	918,414
Non-workers	988,273	60 years and above (Incl. A.N.S.)	88,837

Scheduled Castes (Largest three)		**Scheduled Tribes (Largest three)**	
1. Chamar etc.	104,915	No Scheduled Tribes in this area	
2. Chuhra (Balmiki)	60,288		
3. Khatik	13,088		

Religions (Largest three)		**Amenities and infrastructural facilities**	
1. Hindus	1,213,295	Total inhabited villages	3
2. Muslims	140,335	Amenities available in villages	
3. Sikhs	51,157		No. of villages
		Drinking water facilities	3
Important Towns		Safe drinking water	3
(Largest three)		Electricity (Power Supply)	3
	Population	Electricity (Domestic)	–
1. DMC(U) Part	541,277	Electricity (Agriculture)	–
2. DMC(U) Part	262,275	Primary Schools	1
3. DMC(U) Part	210,055	Middle Schools	–
		Secondary/Sr Secondary Schools	–
		College	–
		Medical Facility	–
		Primary Health Centre	–
		Primary Health Sub-Centre	–
House Type		Post, telegraph and telephone facility	2
Type of house (% of households occupying)			
Permanent	93.2	Bus Services	3
Semi-permanent	3.4	Paved approach road	3
Temporary	3.4	Mud approach road	–

Source: Census of India 2001.

4.2i   District North East *(03), Delhi (07)

Population

Persons	1,768,061	Number of households	310,887
Males	956,078	Household size (per household)	6
Females	811,983		
Growth (1991–2001)	62.52	Sex ratio (females per 1000 males)	849
Rural	141,547	Sex ratio (0–6 years)	875
Urban	1,626,514		
Scheduled Caste population	295,092	Scheduled Tribe population	–
Percentage to total population	16.69	Percentage to total population	–

Literacy and Educational Level

Literates		Education level attained	
Persons	1,141,035	Total	1,141,035
Males	676,627	Without level	13,821
Females	464,408	Below primary	227,702
Literacy rate		Primary	270,927
Persons	77.53	Middle	211,702
Males	84.78	Matric/Higher Secondary/Diploma	300,605
Females	68.94	Graduate and above	121,084

Workers

Workers		Age groups	
Total workers	500,425	0–4 years	201,204
Main workers	470,993	5–14 years	459,472
Marginal workers	29,432	15–59 years	1,032,752
Non-workers	1,267,636	60 years and above (Incl. A.N.S.)	74,633

Scheduled Castes (Largest three)   Scheduled Tribes (Largest three)

Scheduled Castes (Largest three)		Scheduled Tribes (Largest three)
1. Chamar etc.	149,967	No Scheduled Tribes in this area
2. Koli	39,439	
3. Chuhra (Balmiki)	33,134	

Religions (Largest three)   Amenities and infrastructural facilities

Religions (Largest three)		Amenities and infrastructural facilities	
1. Hindus	1,232,960	Total inhabited villages	12
2. Muslims	481,607	Amenities available in villages	
3. Sikhs	22,322		No. of villages
		Drinking water facilities	12

(contd...)

4.2i *(contd...)*

Important Towns				
(Largest three)		Safe drinking water		12
		Electricity (Power Supply)		7
	Population	Electricity (Domestic)		5
1. DMC(U) Part	426,549	Electricity (Agriculture)		2
2. DMC(U) Part	353,401	Primary Schools		7
3. DMC(U) Part	217,397	Middle Schools		4
		Secondary/Sr Secondary Schools		4
		College		–
		Medical Facility		4
		Primary Health Centre		–
House Type		Primary Health Sub-Centre		–
Type of house (% of households occupying)		Post, telegraph and telephone facility		8
Permanent	94.6	Bus Services		12
Semi-permanent	3.5	Paved approach road		9
Temporary	1.9	Mud approach road		3

Source: Census of India 2001.

4.3 District-wise Crime 1991 to 2006

District	Head	1991	1992	1993	1994	1995	1996	1997	1998	1999	2000	2001	2002	2003	2004	2005	2006
North	Total IPC	3055	3517	4118	3820	4952	6484	5903	4671	4459	4081	3998	3681	3391	3418	3306	3016
	Total Act	1371	1118	936	870	1315	1496	1503	1128	1124	1127	1340	1923	2193	2641	2747	2717
North-West	Total IPC	3762	3854	3910	4747	6764	7930	8558	9635	9826	9589	10001	9191	8782	9840	11019	11146
	Total Act	1100	1821	2076	2306	2829	2966	2176	1680	2368	2496	2852	3288	3769	4394	4789	5993
Central	Total IPC	2754	2691	2767	3305	3808	4853	4697	4795	3847	3652	3750	3578	2998	3335	3529	3706
	Total Act	2275	2336	2385	2183	2053	2019	1951	1639	1197	1252	1407	1745	2187	2580	2978	3109
New-Delhi	Total IPC	2973	3065	2655	2582	2642	3839	4307	4158	3124	2826	2660	2406	2177	2651	2295	2288
	Total Act	365	233	285	247	294	289	248	115	174	221	263	318	353	373	373	391
East	Total IPC	2536	2755	2859	2700	2890	3397	3867	4224	4460	4740	4443	3881	4331	5528	5453	5573
	Total Act	1075	899	1116	1270	1268	1259	1064	330	448	742	898	1407	2043	2486	2714	2621
North-East	Total IPC	2700	2675	2536	2666	3296	5120	4956	5345	4515	3956	3449	2975	3332	3896	4849	5389
	Total Act	1056	1245	1495	1758	1528	1222	908	369	589	660	1009	1659	2031	2425	2428	2726
South	Total IPC	5817	6595	6587	6772	9603	12250	12748	13444	11149	11147	10745	9306	8440	9672	10529	10854
	Total Act	1240	1230	848	631	992	1241	1492	932	541	594	771	814	1285	1564	1618	2252
South-West	Total IPC	3768	3906	3689	3828	4918	5542	5969	5898	5804	5749	5390	4814	5179	5932	5762	6584
	Total Act	618	621	535	534	563	631	935	451	594	771	814	1285	1564	1618	1440	2252
West	Total IPC	5814	5454	5813	6085	7116	8782	8220	9617	8377	7690	7148	7077	7343	7217	7368	7368
	Total Act	2652	2284	2260	2465	2815	3061	3260	1874	3283	2970	3277	3710	4290	4210	4180	4637

Source: Research Cell, Crime Branch.

5.1 NCT Delhi—Percentage of Slum Population to Total Population
(Wards of DMC)

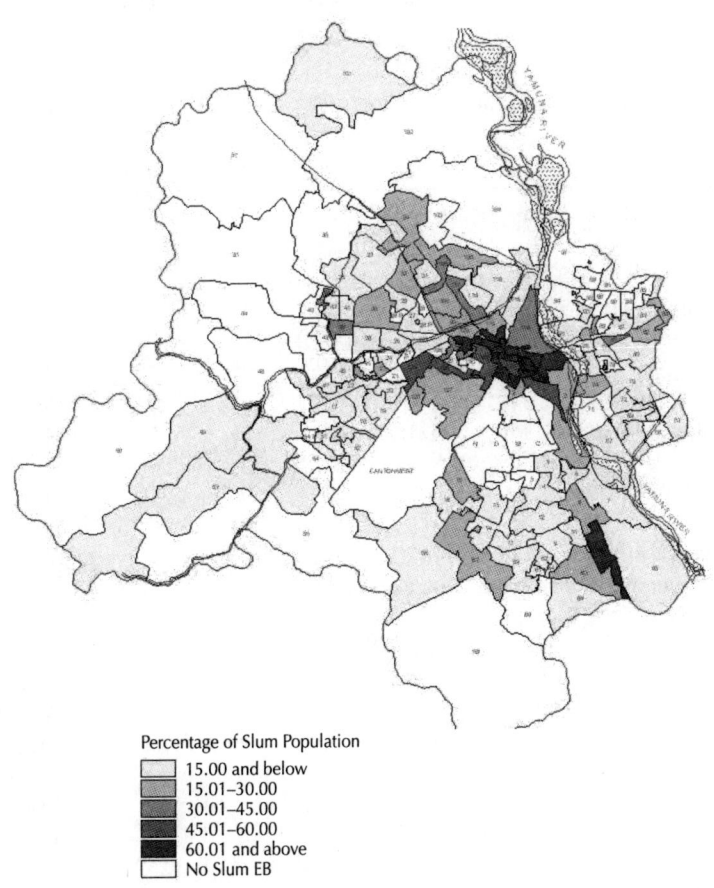

Percentage of Slum Population

- 15.00 and below
- 15.01–30.00
- 30.01–45.00
- 45.01–60.00
- 60.01 and above
- No Slum EB

7.1 Crime against Women

Crime	2003	2004	2005	2006	2007
Dowry Prohibition Act	14	11	9	15	6
Dowry Death	130	126	114	137	138
Molestation of Death	489	601	762	718	868
406 IPC (Related to Dowry)	7	12	6	11	6
Rape	490	551	658	623	598
Kidnapping/Abduction of Women	797	881	1106	1066	1167
498-A IPC (Cruelty by husband or in-laws)	1211	1254	1324	1728	1787
Eve Teasing	1599	2132	1714	556	414

Source: Research Cell, Crime Branch.

7.2 Analysis of Rape Cases (up to 30-4-08)

		2003	2004	2005	2006	2007	2008
1.	Cases regsistered	490	551	658	623	598	168
2.	Cases worked out	456	521	644	592	572	144
		(93.06%)	(94.56%)	(97.87%)	95.02%)	(95.65%)	
3.	Not Worked Out Cases	34	30	14	31	26	24
4.	Persons Arrested	624	737	856	778	731	173
5.	Relationship of the accused with the victim						
i)	Relatives	50	39	57	56	63	14
	a) Father	11	14	14	6	14	1
		(0.61%)	(2.54%)	(2.12%)	(1.96%)	(2.34%)	(0.60%)
	b) Step Father	3	6	5	5	4	0
		(0.61%)	(1.08%)	(0.75%)	(0.80%)	(0.67%)	(0.00%)
	c) Grand Father	2	–	–	1	0	1
		(0.40%)			(0.17%)		(0.69%)
	d) Brother	–	–	1	1	3	0
				(0.15%)	(0.16%)	(0.50%)	(0.00%)
	e) Ex-Husband	3	2	1	3	2	1
		(0.61%)	(0.36%)	(0.15%)	(0.48%)	(2.01%)	(0.60%)
	f) Uncle	8	2	12	12	10	4
		(1.63%)	(0.36%)	(1.82%)	(1.93%)	(1.67%)	(2.38%)

(contd...)

7.2 *(contd...)*

	g) Cousin	4	3	7	5	6	0
		(0.81%)	(0.54%)	(1.06%)	(0.80%)	(1.00%)	(0.00%)
	h) Brother-in-law	18	7	11	20	13	7
		(3.67%)	(1.27%)	(1.67%)	(3.21%)	(2.17%)	(4.17%)
	i) Father-in-law	1	4	6	3	1	0
		(0.20%)	(0.72%)	(0.91%)	(0.48%)	(0.17%)	(0.00%)
	j) Step Son	–	1	–	0	0	0
			(0.18%)				(0.00%)
ii)	Neighbour	216	249	350	331	351	101
		(44.08%)	(45.19%)	(53.19%)	(53.13%)	(58.07%)	(6012%)
iii)	Friend/Lover/ Relative Friend	71	112	123	115	98	17
		(14.48%)	(20.32%)	(16.69%)	(18.45%)	(16.12%)	(10.12%)
iv)	Servant	7	2	3	2	0	2
		(1.42%)	(0.36%)	(0.45%)	(0.33%)		(1.19%)
v)	Landlord	12	22	21	18	15	10
		(2.44%)	(3.99%)	(3.19%)	(2.89%)	(2.51%)	(5.95%)
vi)	Tenant	18	8	21	17	20	3
		(3.67%)	(1.45%)	(3.19%)	(2.73%)	(3.34%)	(1.79%)
vii)	Employed/Co- Worker	7	8	20	27	18	11
		(1.42%)	(1.45%)	(3.03%)	(4.33%)	(3.01%)	(6.55%)
viii)	Instructor/Tutor/ Principal	4	4	7	1	1	2
		(0.81%)	(0.72%)	(1.06%)	(0.16%)	(0.17%)	(1.19%)
ix)	Doctor	3	2	1	1	0	0
		(0.61%)	(0.36%)	(0.15%)	(0.16%)		(0.00%)
x)	Police/Army Personnel	2	4	3	2	0	1
		(0.40%)	(0.72%)	(0.45%)	(0.32%)		(0.60%)
xi)	Priest/Tantrik	1	5	2	5	4	1
		(0.20%)	(0.90%)	(0.30%)	(0.80%)	(0.67%)	(0.60%)
xii)	Other Known Persons	65	72	33	37	18	5
		(13.26%)	(13.06%)	(5.01)	(5.94%)	(3.01%)	(2.98%)
xiii)	Total Known Persons	456	527	641	612	588	167
		(93.06%)	(95.64%)	(97.42%)	(98.23%)	(98.33%)	(99.40%)
xiv)	Not Known Persons	34	24	17	11	10	1
		(6.94%)	(4.36%)	(2.58%)	(1.77%)	(1.67%)	(0.60%)
6.	No. of Accused Involved						
	i) Single	429	487	589	552	532	154
		(68.75%)	(66.07%)	(69.37%)	(88.60%)	(88.96%)	(91.67%)
	ii) Double	35	43	34	39	34	6
		%.60%)	(5.83%)	(4%)	(6.26%)	(5.69%)	(3.57%)

(contd...)

7.2 *(contd...)*

iii) Multiple	26	21	35	32	32	8
	(4.16%)	(2.84%)	(4.2%)	(5.14%)	(5.35%)	(4.76%)
7. Elopement	91	92	139	107	109	18
	(18.57%)	(16.69%)	(21.12%)	(17.71%)	(18.23%)	(10.71%)
8. Age Group of Accused						
i) Upto 18 Years	39	72	70	68	44	14
	(6.25%)	(9.76%)	(8.17%)	(8.74%)	(6.02%)	(8.09%)
ii) 18 to 25 Years	375	463	495	452	407	115
	(60.09%)	(62.82%)	(57.82%)	(58.10%)	(55.68%)	(66.47%)
iii) 25 to 35 Years	151	158	218	196	230	32
	(24.19%)	(21.43%)	(25.46%)	(25.19%)	(31.46%)	(18.50%)
iv) 35 to 50 Years	51	38	65	53	42	10
	(8.17%)	(5.15%)	(7.59%)	(6.81%)	(5.75%)	(5.78%)
v) Above 50 Years	8	6	8	9	8	2
	(1.28%)	(0.81%)	(0.93%)	(1.16%)	(1.09%)	(1.16%)
Total	**624**	**737**	**856**	**778**	**731**	**173**
9. Educational Standards of Accused						
Illiterate	186	243	179	178	147	31
	(29.80%)	(32.97%)	(20.91%)	(22.88%)	(20.11%)	(17.92%)
School Dropout	200	298	376	326	349	86
	(32.05%)	(40.43%)	(43.92%)	(41.90%)	(47.74%)	(49.71%)
Upto 10th	162	149	225	186	171	44
	(25.96%)	(20.12%)	(26.28%)	(23.91%)	(23.30%)	(25.43%)
Upto 12th	60	36	51	71	48	6
	(9.61%)	(4.88%)	(5.95%)	(9.13%)	(6.57%)	(3.47%)
Graduate	12	8	17	15	14	4
	(1.92%)	(1.08%)	(1.98%)	(1.93%)	(1.92%)	(2.31%)
Professional	4	3	8	2	2	2
	(0.64%)	(0.40%)	(0.93%)	(0.26%)	(0.27%)	(1.16%)
Total	**624**	**737**	**856**	**778**	**731**	**173**
10. Social Status of Accused						
i) Upper	2	2	6	8	5	1
	(0.32%)	(0.27%)	(0.70%)	(1.03%)	(0.68%)	(0.58%)
ii) Middle	124	182	193	148	143	37
	(19.87%)	(24.69%)	(22.54%)	(9.02%)	(19.56%)	(78.03%)
iii) Poor	498	553	657	622	583	137
	(79.80%)	(75.03%)	(76.75%)	(79.95%)	(79.75%)	(78.03%)
Total	**624**	**737**	**856**	**778**	**731**	**173**

(contd...)

7.2 *(contd...)*

11.	Educational Standards of Victim					
	Illiterate	212	190	228	328	299	83
		(43.00%)	(34.23%)	(34.23%)	(52.39%)	(49.66%)	(53.28%)
	School Dropout	134	162	217	214	224	58
		(27.18%)	(29.18%)	(32.58%)	(34.18%)	(37.20%)	(35.03%)
	Upto 10th	112	161	157	69	69	21
		(22.71%)	(29.00%)	(23.57%)	(11.02%)	(11.46%)	(8.02%)
	Upto 12th	23	40	56	12	6	5
		(4.66%)	(7.20%)	(8.40%)	(1.91%)	(1.99%)	(3.64%)
	Graduate	12	2	8	3	3	–
		(2.43%)	(0.36%)	(1.20%)	(0.47%)	(0.49%)	
	Professional	–	–	–	–	1	–
						(0.16%)	
	Total	**493**	**555**	**666**	**626**	**602**	**168**
12.	Age Group of Victim						
	Upto 2 Years	1	4	5	3	4	0
		(0.20%)	(0.72%)	(0.75%)	(0.48%)	(0.67%)	(0.00%)
	2 to 7 Years	41	45	52	38	56	14
		(8.32%)	(8.11%)	(7.81%)	(6.10%)	(9.36%)	(8.33%)
	7 to 12 Years	45	47	56	44	49	15
		(9.13%)	(8.47%)	(8.41%)	(7.06%)	(8.19%)	(8.93%)
	12 to 16 Years	208	240	303	272	214	63
		(42.20%)	(43.24%)	(45.50%)	(43.66%)	(35.79%)	(37.50%)
	16 to 18 Years	78	77	92	91	126	24
		(15.41%)	(13.87%)	(13.81%)	(14.61%)	(21.07%)	(14.29%)
	18 to 25 Years	74	84	102	115	108	28
		(15.01%)	(15.13%)	(15.31%)	(18.46%)	(18.06%)	(16.67%)
	Above 25 Years	48	58	56	63	45	24
		(9.73%)	(10.45%)	(8.41%)	(10.11%)	(7.53%)	(14.29%)
	Total	**493**	**555**	**666**	**626**	**602**	**168**
13.	Social Status of Victim						
	Upper	312	307	351	394	474	124
		(63.29%)	(53.32%)	(52.70%)	(63.24%)	(79.26%)	(73.81%)
	Middle	178	246	302	230	126	43
		(36.10%)	(44.32%)	(45.34%)	(36.92%)	(21.07%)	(25.60%)
	Poor	3	2	13	2	2	1
		(0.61%)	(0.36%)	(1.95%)	(0.32%)	(0.33%)	(0.60%)
	Total	**493**	**555**	**666**	**626**	**602**	**168**

Source: Research Cell, Crime Branch.

7.3a Ten-year Chart of Rape Cases (per lakh)

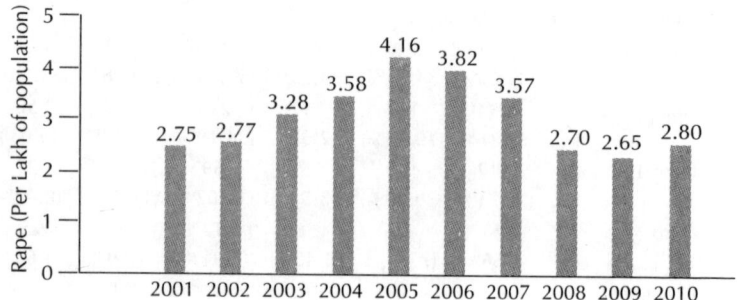

Source: Annual Review, 2010.

7.3b Rape per Lakh of Population—Major Cities of the World

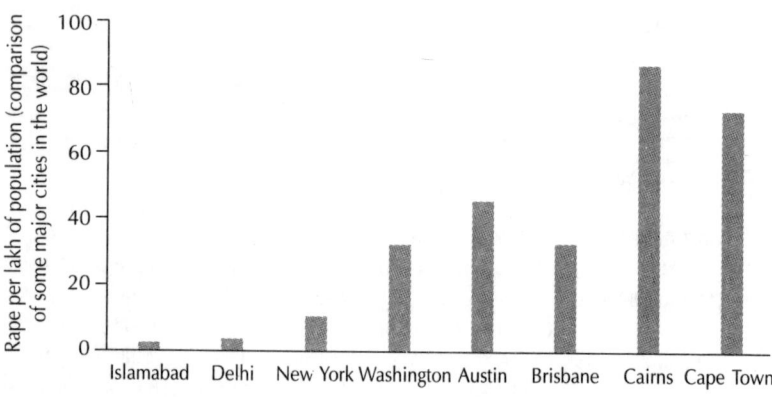

Source: Annual Review, 2010.

7.3c Comaprison of Rate of Incidence of Rape Cases in Major Cities in the World

City	Country	Rate	Year of Observation
Islamabad	Pakistan	2.1	2008
Delhi	India	3.6	2007
New York	USA	10.6	2007
Washington	USA	32.6	2007
Austin	USA (Black Dominated)	45.8	2007
Brisbane	Australia	33.0	2007
Cairns	Australia	87.0	2007
Cape Town	South Africa	73.0	2007
Delhi	India	2.8	2010

Source: Annual Review, 2010.

7.4   Trafficking Map Showing Source Areas

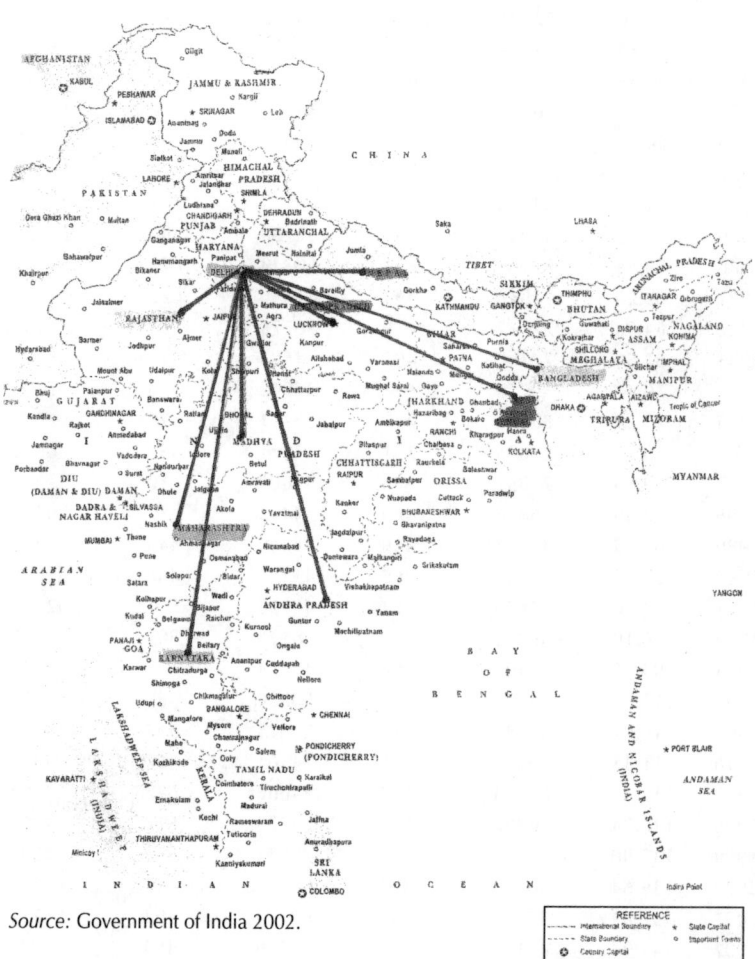

Source: Government of India 2002.

10.1   Year-wise Total Crime and IPC Crime Per Lakh of Population in Delhi

Year	Population in Lakhs	IPC Crime	IPC Crime per Lac of Population	Total Crime	Total Crime per Lac of Population	Total Force
1970	39.26	31269	797	37272	949	16926
1971	40.66	29235	719	35311	868	17180
1972	43.90	32391	738	38582	878	18064
1973	47.14	34174	725	40528	859	18617
1974	50.38	33825	671	41071	8J5	18657
1975	53.61	26571	496	34195	637	19797
1976	54.50	23106	424	30859	566	20928
1977	55.01	35856	652	42323	769	21301
1978	55.55	43408	781	54134	974	21879
1979	57.49	44083	767	57150	994	22852
1980	59.54	37585	631	50323	845	23423
1981	62.20	30646	493	41850	672	25166
1982	64.96	27162	419	36779	566	30981
1983	67.59	27360	405	34593	511	31354
1984	70.40	30773	457	37942	538	31408
1985	73.29	30411	415	38211	521	31753
1986	76.28	29828	391	37521	491	36672
1987	79.35	25832	326	32600	410	37984
1988	82.50	28017	340	34443	417	40450
1989	85.75	30524	356	38249	446	52212
1990	89.10	31848	357	41245	462	52202
1991	93.70	34876	372	46950	501	52450
1992	96.10	36302	377	48316	502	52679
1993	99.76	36597	366	48774	488	52532
1994	113.53	38223	369	50706	489	53213
1995	110.61	47686	431	61613	557	53314
1996	111.35	59871	538	74364	667	53324
1997	115.46	60883	527	74666	647	54403
1998	120.34	64882	539	73775	614	54498
1999	135.00	58701	435	70074	519	57582
2000	139.64	56249	402	68075	487	58674
2001	137.83	54384	394	68133	494	58712
2002	144.94	49137	339	67409	465	58877
2003	149.00	47404	318	69314	465	59077
2004	154.00	53623	348	78759	511	59077
2005	157.43	56065	356	82638	525	59077
2006	162.00	57963	357	88335	545	58972
2007	167.00	56065	336	77059	461	69645

Source: Research Cell, Crime Branch.

10.2   Policemen per lakh Population during 2009
(All-India 133)

Source: Crime in India (NCRB), 2009.

10.3   Density of Police Personnel during 2009
(All-India 49.2)

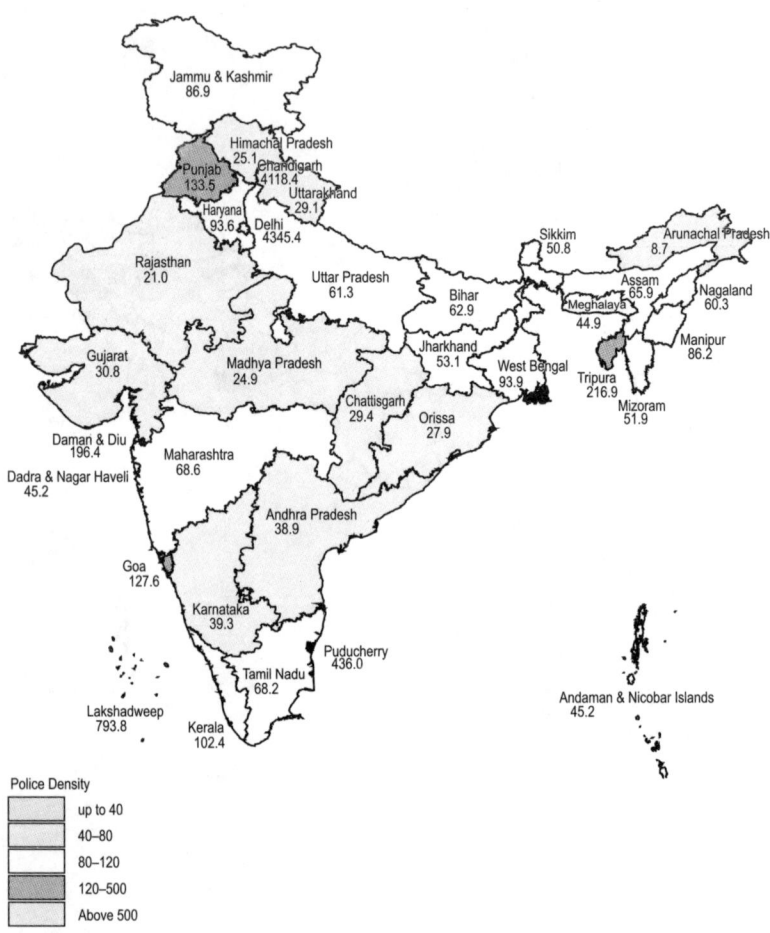

Police Density

	up to 40
	40–80
	80–120
	120–500
	Above 500

Source: Crime in India (NCRB), 2009.

Note: Density of police personnel means number of policemen per 100 sq. km of area.

10.4 Police (per capita) (most recent) by Country

(per 1000 people)

Rank	Country	Amount
1	Montserrat	7.81501
4	Italy	5.55565
5	Hong Kong	4.79374
32	Australia	2.09293
33	France	2.049
34	United Kingdom	2.04871
35	Switzerland	1.92448
40	Japan	1.81103
42	Canada	1.70767
47	India	0.956207

Source: Seventh United Nations Survey of Crime Trends and Operations of Criminal Justice Systems.

11.1 Last Ten Years of Crime

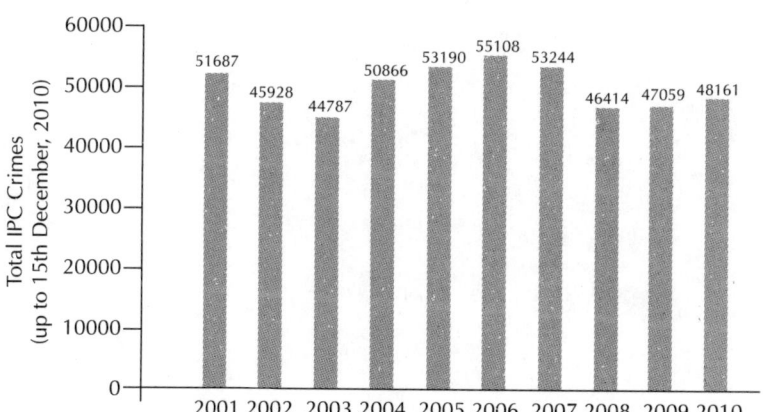

Source: *Annual Review*, 2010.

11.2   Last Ten Years of Crime

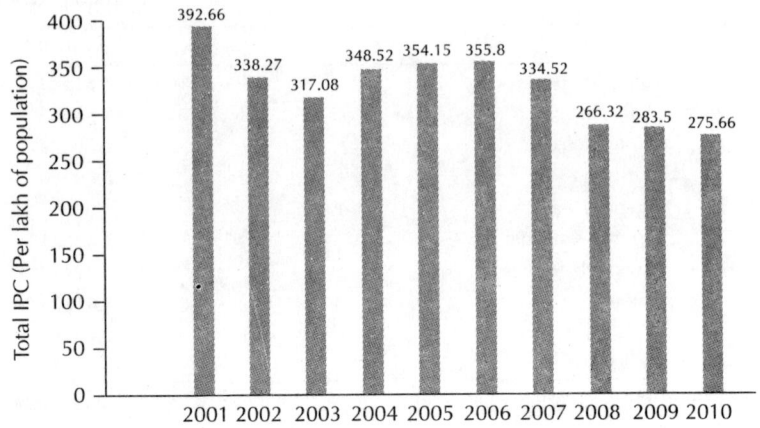

Source: *Annual Review*, 2010.

BIBLIOGRAPHY

PRIMARY SOURCES AND REPORTS

Annual Reports, Ministry of Home Affairs, Government of India (2009 and 2010).

Evaluation Study of DMA Towns in NCR, Town and Country Planning Organization, Government of India.

First Information Reports (FIRs), Nehru Memorial Museum Library.

George Peterson, Patricia Clarke Anncz (eds), 2007, *Financing Cities*, The World Bank.

Gazetteer Unit, Delhi Administration, 1976, *Gazetteer of India: Delhi*.

Government of Delhi, 2006, *Delhi Human Development Report 2006*.

Government of Delhi, *Economic Survey Reports* (various years).

Government of India, 1912, *The Gazette of India, Extraordinary* (October).

Home Department, Delhi, *Correspondence Files between 1912–1935* (Regarding Expansion of Police Force). Delhi Police, *Annual Review* (various years) [for crime figures].

Ministry of Home Affairs, 2007, *Report of the Committee on Draft National Policy on Criminal Justice* (July).

Ministry of Home Affairs, Government of India, *Report of the Delhi Police Commission* (by Justice G.D. Khosla), 1966–8 (Vols I and II),

National Capital Region Planning Board, 1999, *Delhi—1999: A Fact Sheet*.

National Crime Records Bureau, Ministry of Home Affairs, Government of India, 2006, *Crime in India*.

National Crime Records Bureau, Ministry of Home Affairs, Government of India, 2009, *Crime in India*.

National Police Commission, Government of India, 1979, *Second Report of National Police Commission*.

National Police Commission, Government of India, 1981, *Seventh Report of National Police Commission*, Chapter 48: Urban Policing.

OECD, India, 2007, *Economic Surveys*.

Office of Registrar General of India, Census Records (various years).

Reports of Government of India and Delhi Government.

Second Administrative Reforms Commission, 2005, *Fifth Report on Public Order*.

Social Development Report, 2008, New Delhi: OUP.

Srivastava Committee Report, 2005.

U N, 1995; 2005; 2006, *Study of World Urbanization Prospects*.

UNODC, 1994, *Global Report on Crime and Justice*.

UNDP, *Human Development Report* (2006, 2007–08).

The World Bank, *World Development Indicators: 2007*.

BOOKS

Alexander, P.J. (ed.), 2002, *Policing India in the New Millennium*, New Delhi: Allied Publishers.

Bernier, A., 1968, *Travels in the Mughal Empire, 1656–1668*, Delhi: S Chand & Co.

Beauvoir, Simone De, 1972, *Second Sex*, Harmondsworth: Penguin.

Basu, Kaushik, 2007, *The Oxford Companion to Economics in India*, New Delhi: Oxford University Press.

Bennett, T., 1986, 'Situational Crime Prevention from the Offenders Perspective', in K. Heal and G. Laycock (eds), *Situational Crime Prevention: From Theory into Practice*, London: HMSO.

Bopegamage, A., 1957, *Delhi: Study in Urban Sociology*, Bombay: University of Bombay.

Breese, Gerald (ed.), 1969, *The City in Newly Developing Countries: Readings on Urbanism and Urbanization*, Englewood Cliffs, NJ: Prentice-Hall.

Biogiotti, Isabelle, 2007, *Emerging Cities: Keys to Understanding and Acting*, Paris: AFD.

Bright, J.A., 1969, 'The Beat Patrol Experiment', London: Home Office Police Research and Development Branch.

Cox, Edmund, 1911, *Police and Crime in India*, London: Stanley Paul & Company.

Doherty, Michael (ed.), 2000, *The Criminology*, London: Old Bailey Press.

Dupont, Veronique, Emma Tarlo and Denis Vidal (eds), 2000, *Delhi: Urban Space and Human Destinies*, New Delhi: Manohar.

Edwards, S.M.,1924, *Crime in India*, Oxford: Oxford University Press.

English, Richard, 2009, *Terrorism: How to Respond*, Oxford: Oxford University Press.

Gupta, Narayani, 1981, *Delhi Between Two Empires*, Delhi: Oxford University Press.

Griffiths, Percival, 1971, *To Guard My People: History of Indian Police*, London: Benn.

Gordon, Hearn, 1906, *Seven Cities of Delhi*, Calcutta: W. Thacker.

Hough, M. and Mayhew Clarke (eds), 1980, *Designing Out Crime*, London: HMSO.

Jagmohan, 1978, *Island of Truth*, New Delhi: Allied Publishers.

————, 1985, *Challenge of Cities*, New Delhi: Government of India, Publications Division.

Jain, A.K., 2000, *The Cities of Delhi*, Delhi: Management Publishing Company.

Khosla, Romi (ed.), 2005, *The Idea of Delhi*, Mumbai: Marg Publishers.

Kennedy, M., 1985, *The Criminal Classes of India*, Delhi: Mittal Publications

Lambert, Richard D., 1962, 'Some Impact of Urban Society upon Village Life in India's Urban Future', in Roy Turner (ed.), *India's Urban Future*, Berkeley: University of California Press.

Majumdar, P.S. and Ila Majumdar, 1978, *Rural Migration in Urban Settings*, Delhi: Hindustan Publishing Corp.

Merton, R.K., 1968, *Social Theory and Social Structure*, Glencoe: Free Press.

Mukherjee, R.K., 1965, *The Sociologist and Social Change in India*, New Delhi: Prentice-Hall of India.

Mitra, Ashok, 1970, *Delhi—Capital City*, New Delhi: Thomson Press.

Naqvi, H.K., 1968, *Urban Centres and Industries in Upper India*, Delhi.

Peck, Lucy, 2005, *Delhi—A Thousand Years of Building*, New Delhi: Lotus Collection.

Poyner, B., 1983, *Design against Crime: Beyond Defensible Space*, London: Butterworths.

Prabhu, R.K. and U.R. Rao (eds), 1967, *The Mind of Mahatma Gandhi*, Ahmedabad: Navjeevan Publishing House.

Rao, V.K.R.V. and P.V. Desai, 1965, *Greater Delhi: A Study in Urbanization (1840–1957)*, Bombay: Asia Publishing House.

Ramachandran, R., 1989, *Urbanization and Urban Systems*, New Delhi: Oxford University Press.

Rajagopal, P.R., 1987, *Social Change and Violence*, New Delhi: Uppal Publishing House.

———, 1988, *Violence and Response*, New Delhi: Uppal Publishing House.

Raza, Maroof (ed.), 2009, *Confronting Terrorism*, New Delhi: Penguin-Viking.

Sengupta, Ranjana, 2007, *Delhi Metropolitan: The Making of an Unlikely City*, New Delhi: Penguin.

Sherwani, Azim, 1998, *Girl Child in Crisis*, Delhi: Institute of Social Sciences.

Siva Ramakrishnan, K.C., 1978, *The Indian Urban Scene*, Shimla: IIAS.

Singh, Khushwant, 1983, *Delhi—A Portrait*, Delhi: Oxford University Press.

Singh, Patwant, 1989, *Delhi—The Deepening Urban Crisis*, Delhi: Sterling Publishers.

Singh, Yogendra, 1973, *Modernization of Indian Tradition*, Delhi: Thomson Press.

Wirth, Louis, 1964, 'Urbanism as a way of life in on cities and social life', *Louis Wirth: Selected Papers*, Chicago: University of Chicago Press.

ARTICLES

Chattoraj, B N, 1998, 'Urban Crimes and the Criminal Justice System', National Seminar on Safer Cities.

Chidambaram, P., 2009, 'IB Centenary Endowment Lecture' (23 December).

Daily Telegraph, 14 August 1999.

The Hindu, 12 March 2005.

Kumar, Neeraj, 1992, 'A note on criminals belonging to Pardhi community', prepared as DCP, south district.

Kundu, Amitabh, nd, 'Migration and urbanization in India in the context of poverty alleviation', www.networkideas.org/ideasact/Jun07/Beijing...07/Amitabh_Kundu.ppt

Leslie, B., 1912, 'Delhi: The Metropolis of India', *Journal of Royal Society of Arts*.

Ministry of Home Affairs, 2010, *Report Card of Ministry of Home Affairs* (December).

Mishra, O.P., 2003, 'Courier Bag Robbers', *Indian Police Journal* (October), BPR&D.

———, 2004, 'A World Within—A sociological Study of Sex Workers in G B Road, Delhi', *Indian Police Journal* (March), BPR&D.

———, 2010, 'Prevention of Crime: Need for Public Private Partnership', Delhi Police Day Souvenir.

Outlook, 23 June 2008, p. 41.

Singh, Manmohan, 2009, 'Address to DGs/IGs State/UT' (6 October).

———, 2010a, 'Inaugural speech', Annual Conference of Director Generals of Police, 26 August.

———, 2010b, 'Address to IPS probationers' (24 December).

Times of India, 3 January 2011.